# Praise for
## *Philosophy in Word and Name*

"This singular book is plurivocal in a challenging and intellectually invigorating way. It allows the voices of myth, philosophy, and theology to sound together and indeed to sing in a kind of companioning togetherness. Philosophy is returned to a practice closer to its older and nobler vocation, while myth and theology are oriented in fitting eschatological and apocalyptic directions. William Hackett is engaged with a constellation of themes and thinkers in a manner that is intellectually passionate and existentially engaged. The writing is informed and illuminating in an insightful way that makes porous the normal academic boundaries between mythology, philosophy, theology, and indeed politics. Warmly recommended."—WILLIAM DESMOND, Villanova University

"In a multi-faceted series of studies in diverse styles, William Hackett opens to us a vista on the state of Christian thought today. Here is our contemporary Kierkegaard: probing old ideas, launching new ones, prodding us to be ever more vigilant, not only in our thinking about religion but in our practice of it."—KEVIN HART, University of Virginia

"Rarely does a genuinely groundbreaking book come along. Even more rare is a book that accomplishes this in the realm of philosophy and religion. Well, with no exaggeration, this is that book: an intellectual and mystical masterpiece that makes believable a truly universal speculative thinking about ultimate meaning in our own day. Dealing death-blows to the dualisms and reductions haunting our contemporary horizon, Hackett immerses himself in the fundamental sources of human reflection (myth, wisdom, apocalypse), which in his hands light up the splendor of existence in a strikingly fresh way, exposing myriad new openings. Above all, a work anchored in prayer and profound faith in Jesus Christ."—CONOR SWEENEY, author of *Abiding the Long Defeat*

"With *Philosophy in Word and Name: Myth, Wisdom, Apocalypse* we can sense a new voice appearing on the stage. This remarkable first

book of William Hackett sounds forth with newness, confidence, and truth, and is sure to establish him as one of the most original and energetic voices of contemporary Catholic thought. A must read."
—AARON RICHES, Benedictine College

"Re-enacting Daniel's prophetic reading of the three words to the Babylonian king, William Hackett applies three key divine words to all our modern intellectual kingdoms: *myth*, *wisdom*, and *apocalypse*. Through these words, Hackett explains the reason and revelation of Christ and the Christian tradition, attaching crucial names and texts to each word for commentary, corroboration, and confirmation. Yet, unlike in Daniel, this philosophical prophecy against today's all-too-human kingdoms of so-called knowledge culminates, not in a powerful political overcoming, but in prayerful obedience to divine truth, an apocalypse masterfully and poetically sketched out in these pages."
—FR. BONAVENTURE CHAPMAN, OP, Dominican House of Studies, Washington DC

"We need words. We need names. We can turn these into keys. We need keys, plural, if we would unlock certain gates when one key is not enough. Along the way we need the help of texts, classical and not yet classical: from Holy Writ and Plato to Milbank and Marion. With toil and some good fortune, we shall learn how to use well the words we need—myth, wisdom, apocalypse. But this means that some all too clear words—philosophy, revelation, others—will prove unclear and needful of a phenomenological clarification. Now, phenomenology is no key, but is a way of finding keys and using them. American phenomenology, as illustrated by Chris Hackett, is both careful and ambitious. Hackett has read deeply and broadly and has something to say only he can say. Read his book."—JEAN-YVES LACOSTE, Clare Hall, Cambridge

"Myth, wisdom and apocalypse are no mere words for William Chris Hackett: they are keys for crossing into the history of salvation. Invoking the names and ideas of contemporary philosophy—from John Milbank to Jean-Luc Marion—but passing also through Thomas Aquinas, Schelling, and many others, he leads us on a vast journey rich with reflections on 'revelation at the end of time' as the possibility for present humanity to accelerate what it cannot ignore."—EMMANUEL FALQUE, Institut catholique de Paris

# Philosophy in Word and Name

*Myth, Wisdom, Apocalypse*

WILLIAM C. HACKETT

# Philosophy in Word and Name

*Myth, Wisdom, Apocalypse*

First published in the USA
by Angelico Press 2020
© William C. Hackett 2020

For information, address:
Angelico Press
169 Monitor St.
Brooklyn, NY 11222

angelicopress.com
info@angelicopress.com


ISBN 978 1 62138 503 5 pb
ISBN 978 1 62138 504 2 cloth
ISBN 978 1 62138 505 9 ebook

Cover image: Hilma af Klint,
Altarpiece No. 1, Group X, 1915
Cover design: Michael Schrauzer

*To My Parents*

[In the Bible] even the incomprehensibility of God is given anthropomorphic expression. . . . Thus Yahweh is never clearly and completely portrayed; there are only partial descriptions of him. Along with these anthropomorphisms, we find a portrayal of God as inaccessible and transcendent. Its climax is the prohibition of images in the decalogue, which is a radical restriction of all attempts to give material expression to the knowledge of God, except in word and name.[1]

1. Werner Post, "Anthropomorphism II. Biblical," *Encyclopedia of Theology: A Concise* Sacramentum Mundi, ed. Karl Rahner (London: Burns and Oats, 1975), 14.

# CONTENTS

# Preface

P SEUDO-DIONYSIUS the Areopagite argued that the true theologian is God, and that humans are only "theologians" by extension. Theology is a matter of divine authority: only God
properly speaks about himself. And only the authors of holy writ,
prophets and apostles, properly speak about God because God
speaks through them. Perhaps the rest of us can be theologians, if we
end up saying something true in our exegetical meditation on the
Word of God, but only as a gift from above. The tradition of "right
use" (*orthé chrēsis*) of the late Neoplatonism of Iamblichus and Porphyry, of which the Areopagite was a founder, understood *theologia*
to be a hymn in praise to the divine, of which the highest mode is
*sigé*, silence, and which corresponded to some kind of indescribable
union with the divinity that is identically the secret center both of
the truest self and of the tri-level cosmos that human being recapitulates in its own way. Yet it is a union hidden from both the farthest
reaches of our intellect and of our deepest affective interiority.

The Areopagite's contemporary disciple, Jean-Luc Marion, once
suffered widespread calumny and disbelief (among concerned
European intelligentsia) when he said, in print, that the bishop
(when he presides over the Eucharist) is the "only true theologian."
He stated a truism. He was theologically correct: in their unenviable
role of shepherds of the community of the baptized the bishops
bear an authority regarding faith and morals as well as some kind of
minimal promise pertaining to the guidance in the task—they will
not f--k the *entire* thing up (I paraphrase Joseph Ratzinger here).[1]

---

1. The Holy Spirit does not "entirely abandon us. . . . Probably the only assur-
ance he offers is that the thing cannot be totally ruined." From a 1997 interview on
Bavarian television quoted by John J. Allen, Jr. "A Quick Course in Conclave 101,"
*National Catholic Reporter*, February 15, 2013. http://ncronline.org/blogs/all-things-
catholic/quick-course-conclave-101.

And when in the context of the liturgy the bishop (rightly) interprets the Word of God, he is perhaps coming as close to pure theology in the Christian sense as is possible for post-apostolic Christianity. Theology is an academic discipline, but it is one only as a derivative, as Thomas Aquinas states from the beginning of his introductory text on the subject. To him—to Thomas Aquinas himself, for whom theology involves a share in the divine self-knowing!—what matters first is the *lived practice* of "the highest wisdom" that blends theoretical and practical kinds of knowledge into a single activity. Its source is God, who fills human efforts of understanding and of love with divine power of comprehension—not in the sense, he says, of grasping exhaustively, which is absurd, but as, simply, a truly being in the presence of the realities that it, wisdom, seeks.

Wisdom, then, in the most important sense is theological, involving an entrance into the infinite and qualitative *diastēma* between Creator and creature where we are held before God as the nothing that is; it is based on an *eschatological* conviction that is incomprehensible. And yet the soul feels its necessity most deeply: *ho theós ta panta en pasin*, "God *all in all*." It *is* eternity—which already secretly pervades time—accessed through a divine unlocking of the "place" of unravelling paradox where an always-greater confrontation with the Living One before us only more acutely unfolds out of a corresponding ever-deepening interiority within us. The question of the highest human wisdom is classically coordinated by reference to its divine source, is one with its divine goal. This double reference and the names by which it has ultimately revealed itself are taken as a given (and sometimes taken for granted) in the Christian tradition. What is not constant is the manner or mode of explication of this wisdom—even, or especially, among its most venerable authors. Yet for all of these thinkers not only is Holy Scripture the source but it is also the paradigm for what the literary activity of Christian intelligence should be. The words on the page are a consequence and an effecting of a theological thinking. This (or something like it) was what the Areopagite meant when he also said that you would never comprehend "our way of philosophy" without knowing Holy Scripture. At the far end now of the "conflict of the faculties" (among

2

Preface

many other things) in the West, and with the heightened awareness
of the labyrinthine catholic depths of the living traditions of human
civilization the world over, the Christian thinker, finding new, surprising springs of life in the "drowning desert" of modern life, is
again, today, more and more like some disciple from ages past,
shaken to the core by Easter morning, who, with every step he takes,
opens out onto a new adventure in which the full range of possibilities his life (he now sees) has always demanded from the world is
brought into play. He finds himself startled, at times, by the awareness of a fire burning just beneath the surface of his being, and at
other times, by another fire sweeping slowly, through the ages of
humanity, over the surface of the earth. He may even try to write a
book that captures something of it.

W.C.H.

# Three Keys

FIRST KEY—*Mythos*
He is the image of the invisible God,
the firstborn of all creation.
For in him were created all things in heaven and on earth,
the visible and invisible,
whether thrones or dominions or principalities or powers;
all things were created through him and for him.
He is before all things,
and in him all things hold together.
He is the head of the body, the church.
He is the beginning, the firstborn from the dead,
that in all things he himself might be preeminent.
For in him all the fullness was pleased to dwell,
and through him to reconcile all things for him,
making peace by the blood of his cross
through him, whether those on earth or those in heaven.[1]


SECOND KEY—*Sophia*
We can hardly guess at what is on earth,
and what is at hand we find with labor;
but who has traced out what is in the heavens?
Who has learned your counsel,
unless you have given wisdom
and sent your holy spirit from on high?
And thus the paths of those on earth were set right,
and people were taught what pleases you,
and were saved by wisdom.[2]

1. The Epistle to the Colossians 1:15–20.
2. Wisdom of Solomon 9:16–18.

THIRD KEY—*Apocalypsis*
Blessed be the name of the God from age to age,
for wisdom and power are his.
He changes times and seasons,
    deposes kings and sets up kings;
he gives wisdom to the wise
and knowledge to those who have understanding.
He reveals deep and hidden things;
he knows what is in the darkness,
and light dwells with him.
To you, O God of my ancestors,
I give thanks and praise,
for you have given me wisdom and power,
and have now revealed to me what we asked of you,
for you have revealed to us what the king wants to know.[3]

3. Daniel 2:20–23.

# First Words

IN ITS ENDLESS and endlessly provisional exercise in the time that remains, Christian self-understanding labors at a single task: to exegete its primary words, "Christ is risen!" This work is elaborated against the background of the paradoxical identification of intellectual internalization, "orthodoxy," and ecstatic encounter, "*orthé chrēsis*," investigated elsewhere.[1] And it makes use of three keys. Three keys, therefore, to Christianity's *philosophy of the word*, a Philosophy in Word and Name: myth, wisdom, apocalypse. These keys open a door that otherwise, on my reckoning, remains locked. This door is inscribed with three words: *Word of God*. What modern philosophers and theologians term "revelation" is what passes through the door. The ancients did not really have a concept in the same sense, and that is fine: intellectual progress can be made, although, perhaps, not without a concomitant veiling-over (*kaluptein*) as well. If a wisdom *unveiled* (*apo-kaluptein*) "from above" is the key that unlocks ourselves, this divine wisdom first speaks the primary human language of *myth*, which, when decanted through traditions of human pondering and brought to a certain maturity, is called *wisdom*—the love of which is an important, I would say crucial, human enterprise in its pursuit of the absolute conditions that make humanity what it is, and which, traditional wisdom says, is found in God.

God is the source and goal of such wisdom: that is, human wisdom is one with divine wisdom. And such is the difficulty. It is impossible. And, therefore, in the last analysis, it can only be given by God if it is to be realized by humanity. This divine wisdom speaks the language of myth, first, and primarily; *human* wisdom decants this divine speech, not in order to isolate the essential, timeless

---

1. A start at this is made in *Eclipse of World* (in preparation).

kernel from the primitive, historical husk, but rather to live this wisdom for itself, to pursue and to love it, to enter more fully into the encounter with the God who is, and who speaks, who *unveils* the truth of what matters most, but what otherwise remains hidden from us.

Just stated, then, is the thesis of the present exercise of Christian intelligence. It only wants to meditate on, from a few angles, the keys that unlock, for intelligence, the door of "revelation." And it begins and ends with the recognition that these keys themselves are given by God—though only given, only ever given, through the permanent, restless labor of humanity to understand itself. To unlock the door, one must also walk through it, and this walking through is itself found nowhere but in the practice of *religion*. If I try here in this second book to isolate three further conceptual centers basic to the Christian intellectual work, it is not because by conceptualization I reach and own and command the thing itself. Rather, conceptualization is a *means* to a higher degree of immersion in the real things about which one speaks and thinks, that one tastes and sees in religion, and understands through mythic intelligence. What matters to lovers is their embrace; their poetry, thoughts, and their longing are only ways of anticipation of the real thing.

Philosophy, reflection on what is given humanity to think as most important, enduring, necessary, or absolute in the way that *one human life* has received it—distilling it into conceptual centerings, elaborating it in theoretical sketches, arguments, engagements with other proposals, etc.—is a site of receptivity and transformation of which God himself may make "right use" in order to *make known* his word, that is, the "perfect expression" of his deepest self.[2] The value of this site is found in and judged by its concrete grasp of the ultimately ungraspable nodes of dense intelligibility that promise to show us what we are. These ungraspable things are the things that matter most, and wisdom's first task, as far as a Philosophy of the Word is concerned, is to remind us of these things, to lead us

---

2. *En eschata*, "in the last days," God has spoken to us through his son, *charakter tes hypostasteos autou*—"[the] perfect expression of his substance": Heb 1:3.

some way into their wilderness, where we must engage them, *on their terms.* Christianity believes that what this becomes—a combat with an unknown assailant, in the dark, in an unfamiliar place—is an encounter with God. Only time, and the angel of my death, when I stand before him, with drawn sword and fire for words, will tell me—I may hope—if such a wild belief is right. Until that time when all will be unveiled for what it is, there is the work of preparation, of understanding, of descent into the nights of longing for the truth of things, these human and divine things.

The contours of the first key can be sketched perhaps the most succinctly. My task is not a philosophy of mythology, though myth is ever-present in the domain of Christian belief and practice, including its reasoning (discernment of its necessary contours—second key, contours that are *finally*, and therefore firstly, eschatological—third key). Yet precisely as primordial and permanent, as the context for theoretical reflection, myth is difficult to grasp, though perhaps simple to express in some of its essentials. On the other end, apocalypse parallels myth, inasmuch as the Beginning and End frame our conceptual-theoretical undertakings, offering to them, through narrative and image and metaphorical understanding, primary conditions for their enactment, which is always reciprocally critical *and* justificatory of these given forms that exceed them, which, for Christianity (affirmed the Areopagite) bear divine privilege *precisely* as given.

The work undertaken in the present book is only to elaborate briefly on three keys or words of a Philosophy of the Word initiated in another book to which it is a companion.[3] I do so through preliminary—always only preliminary—elaboration on the key words, which are each followed by a set of investigations on the theme. If the former work of a Philosophy of the Word was (for the author at least) a set of spiritual exercises, the present work is only a sketchbook with some studies. There is no complete picture, but what I

---

3. *Eclipse of World*, noted above.

offer is an attempt to name what is essential and to draw around it some investigations that open paths of inquiry and close off others. This sketchbook of three keys to a Philosophy in Word and Name anticipates a subsequent work on further words that here become only more and more problematic and call for explication.[4]

---

4. The reader will have to await *Essay on the Apophatics of the Sensible* (forthcoming, University of Notre Dame Press) and *Orthodoxy in Eschatological Perspective* (in preparation) in order to bring to some completion the thought that begins here.

# Leading Sketch:
# An Initial Classification

T HE WORD OF GOD is a decisive intervention into human affairs; it is not first the conveyance of timeless information. It is a *call*: "follow me." The disciple follows; he is drawn, attracted. He is gripped and falls in love. His life is from now on a life of fidelity—or not—to the One who calls him.

The world of human affairs is rich, yet one may venture a simple distinction that orders it, reveals its basic rhythm, and makes it intelligible: that between *work* and *rest*. Like that of other animals, the human world is one of survival first, and when that is taken care of, when dangers are at bay, humans establish a field of rest in which they may contemplate their world as such. But this contemplation, this wondering about the totality, is contextualized by definitive or normative occasions of meaning, such as death, birth, coming of age, marriage, cooking, eating, sleeping, waking up, hunting (and story-telling), warfare, getting sick, getting well, building, destroying, memorializing, sacrificing, worshiping, etc. It is in this context, the human context, that a first frame of intelligibility, a presupposition, is found: the divine.

God speaks with human words in the world of human affairs. The first word of human contemplation on its affairs in their totality is *myth*, the primary coordination of human intelligence in the world by the poles of Origin and End. The human world spins on the axis that connects these two poles. Myth is tied to *ritual*: prescribed action and repetition are the first words of memory, and memory gives us a capacity, a background, a horizon of expectations through which we may look forward, as a *human* community, in order to encounter the new, to receive it, to pass through it. Ritual pervades the field of rest. Its source is, however, the field of work, of survival: song and music communicate the meaningfulness of what is occurring in the field of work, beyond its obvious material sustenance. Bodies keep time together in dance and there feel and incarnate the one human community as it becomes transparent to the sacred, which is life itself and the source of life. In this collective kinaesthetic rhythm, what is being sustained? Does it reveal the rhythm, the unity of the entire human pattern of work and rest, of survival and play? The *human* world—the world of the beings that can contemplate the world as a whole, the beings who *have a world*, whose interest transcends the sphere of survival, whose capacities and thirsts stand in surplus when the work of survival—is (provisionally) completed. This world, the world of rest, even claims its own primacy: it is the site where the *source* of sustenance is encountered.

Nature or *cosmic religion* emerges from the background of tribal society, at the ("Neolithic") agricultural revolution, 5500 years ago in the Middle East, and with roots as far as 12000 years ago according to evidence of the first plant and animal domestication.[1] The first city and first farms are found around the Mediterranean, but, like writing, both cities and farming were independently created at the basis of other civilizations many times over, such as in China, the Andes (Inca Civilization, minus writing), and Central America (Olmec Civilization).[2] Agriculture solidified and intensified human society's new dependence on the regular rhythms of nature for its sedentary sustenance, on the rain, the sun, the earth, the rivers and lakes, natural rhythms that become incarnate at the heart of its

1. The background is apparently far deeper into prehistory than previously conceived: Paleolithic cave art (twelve to thirty-eight thousand years old, at famous sites in Turkey, Spain, France, and Germany) is now interpreted as a sophisticated method of astrological date-keeping based on the precession of the equinoxes through the representation of a primitive zodiac, and evinces even (as difficult as it is to believe) a common tradition spread over tens of thousands of years. See Martin B. Sweatman and Alistair Coombs, "Decoding European Palaeolithic Cave Art: Extremely Ancient Knowledge of Precession of Equinoxes," *Athens Journal of History* 5.1, 1–30.

2. See Graeme Barker, *The Agricultural Revolution in Prehistory: Why did Foragers become Farmers?* (Oxford/New York: Oxford University Press, 2009).

mythic existence in ritual—whereas in pre-agrarian tribal society human beings continue to discern their place in the middle of the cosmic milieu and to enact their crucial role of touching the sacred heart of reality and enacting moments of union in their own bodily existence transformed through identification with mythic reality in order to secure pathways for a divine passage in the world, and the renewal thereby of the cosmic order. Yet the central difference with the tribal order is found in the cosmic order itself and in human participation in it: no longer a simple act of identification through ritual and renewal of the human totality, now the gap between mythic beings and humanity is widened, and the "system of communication" between them is concretized and intensified in order to span this gap, becoming what we recognize as sacrifice in the ritual order, and differentiated hierarchy in the political order.[3] It is in this context of planting and harvest, moon, sun, rain, and the securing of human sustenance in a cosmos where humanity keeps the agricultural and social order in tune with the gods through enacting and making the world newly present to the founding, trans-historical realities from which the order came, that the *Call of God* breaks out.

*Revealed religion*, which tells its story starting from the figure of Abraham to that of John the Baptist, transposes the cosmic religion of the agricultural sacred into one of a *passage of God* through the world, a passage that cuts a *straight path* through—and symbolically beyond—the cycles of death and new life, of burying the seed and reaping its fruit, of harmonization through sacred repetition of the founding realities. This passage of God is anticipated in the ritual event, but here becomes historical; it becomes *exodus*, a passageway *through* the cycles of birth and death that rule humanity in its cosmic existence. The agrarian festivals of planting and harvest become transfigured through the *memory* of God's passage, of God's call; and the human exodus is enacted from one world, ruled by "principalities and powers," to another, to come, *ruled by God*. This completion or ratification of the divine rule through an exodus of a people is prefigured in the creation proem by the seventh day of

---

3. See Henri Hubert and Marcel Mauss, *Sacrifice: Its Nature and Function*, trans. W. D. Halls, rev. edition (Chicago: University of Chicago Press, 1981).

creation, the Day of Enthronement, and signified as the final destiny forged into the creation from the beginning by the One who spoke it into existence. In the context of the creation proem, and the parallel liturgies of the First Temple, this rule of God is mediated by angelic beings, into which the privileged human gatekeepers of the temple-garden are ritually transformed, being transfigured into or identified with their angelic counterparts in the heavenly realms.[4] If the "primordial misdirection" according to biblical religion is a *result* of human action and located at the very root of our being, it touches on our divine-like or angelic role to "guard and keep" the earth, symbolized as a temple-garden, to maintain and deepen its refreshing, fruitful, and peaceful character, in short, to accomplish the divine will for the creation.[5] The call of Abraham, the election of Israel, her vocation as bearer of the divine Law, is understood as the divine means to enact this rule and to correct, ultimately, this primordial misdirection that cuts through human being itself and plagues our labors.

The third phase in this progressive unfolding of the divine Word is that of a final unveiling, *eschatological religion*. Here the exodus, the tabernacling passage of the God who calls, becomes (so to speak) unqualified; the universal purpose inherent within the election of Abraham is programmatically carried out: the human world in its entirety, and the whole sacred cosmos, the creation, is called out of the *dark cave* where (divine-)humanity lay clothed in death, and into the light of an eighth day, wherein the sun never sets, wherein the cycle of death is broken, liberated from its "bondage to decay" and ushered into the unfading glory of the "sons of God."[6] Here the economy of the "fundamental elements of the world," of angelic mediation of the divine rule, is definitively replaced by another economy, a human one, with the resurrected Christ at the

4. I point here in a general direction indicated by the thought of Margaret Barker, especially in *The Hidden Tradition of the Kingdom of God* (London: SPCK, 2007), though without accepting all of her conclusions.

5. Gen 2:15. Compare the use of these terms in the Book of Numbers to describe the priestly ministry in the tabernacle: Num 3:7–8, 8:26, 18:5–6.

6. Rom 8:21.

head.[7] This new economy is eschatological and proleptic; the other economy remains permanently eclipsed but in place as long as the world lasts. Christian existence in history, the (very appropriately called) "delay of the Parousia," is a result of this continuation of the former economy with, alongside, the new—which for Christianity's permanently paradigmatic theologian (St. Paul) is tied to the grace of the Creator in the face of the Beloved People's non-acceptance of the Lordship of the Crucified Christ and its implications.[8]

This threefold classification just sketched is one internal to the Christian account, self-understood as an heir to the promises of Abraham, in possession of the secret destiny of the world in the resurrection of Christ, and somehow participant in that destiny in an advance manner through entrance into the community of the baptized, which symbolizes a passing from the reign of mediatory principalities and powers (the gods of the nations), to the (definitive) reign of God. In the passage from "cosmic" or agrarian religion to the "revealed" religion, a massive constriction takes place: this constriction is symbolized by the singularity of the call of Abraham, by the inheritance of a land, a temple, a national monarchy, and a law. Abraham and his chosen progeny are given the promises of divine presence at the heart of the community and of a divine way of life (the law). Yet the constriction of the call, the illumination of Abraham, Isaac, Jacob, and the twelve patriarchs does not damn the world to darkness; the election of the People Israel is not an end in itself: Abraham's blessing is, from the beginning, for the sake of "all the peoples of the earth."[9] On the Christian understanding, this promise is fulfilled, or rather, being fulfilled, through Christ, whose death brings the angelic economy (and the law itself) to its appointed end (or "fulfillment") and whose resurrection transposes that administration of the divine rule to a human regent, which discloses the final purpose of the Creator (and which extends the

7. Gal 4:3; Col 2:8, 20.
8. Rom 9–11.
9. Gen 12:3, 22:18.

15

exclusive covenant relation to all of humanity in a new, eschatological community ruled by a transfigured law: "the law of the Spirit of life").[10] Christianity will always be first a "sect" of Judaism, a particular interpretation of the Jewish traditions, but with remarkable success at incorporating Gentile cultures into its interpretation, which latter quickly became its central *modus operandi*. This has caused difficulties from the beginning with the Rabbinic schools. And yet every interpretation of Judaism, including Christianity, was fundamentally transformed by the destruction of the Second Temple, the prognostication of which, in the Gospel portraits, was a central feature of the teaching of Jesus of Nazareth. Since the death of the apostolic generation, the central leadership of the Christian sect has not been Jewish, although the New Testament is written by Jews (or their post-Pagan Gentile associates) who consider themselves to be bringing the truth of God for the world out of the heart of Israel. Above all, Christianity is a Jewish messianic movement become worldwide religion; its messianism is essential to its character. In this way it understands itself to be essentially Jewish. Now, as distinct from Judaism, therefore, Christianity needs the Jew, the People of the Law, in order to be itself. It must recognize God in this people, in order to claim God within itself.[11]

The community of the baptized stretches from one end of the world to the other, but does the voice of God echo in other cultures and civilizations far from the stories of Israel, with their own stories, traditions, and pathways through the enigma of existence that are so clearly ancient, venerable, and full of spiritual riches? I can only say yes. In doing so I would not be minimizing or relativizing the election of Israel and the salvific universalism of the death and resurrection of Christ, in union with whom the Gentile is grafted onto the Jewish Body of God and made a child of the Covenant. The drama of salvation is played out on the pathway of sanctification. This pathway bridges the infinite and qualitative difference between

10. Rom 8:2. Or see The Epistle of St. James: "the perfect law, the law of liberty" (1:25).

11. See Paula Frederikson, *Augustine and the Jews: A Christian Defense of Jews and Judaism* (New Haven: Yale University Press, 2010).

Creator and creature; only God can bridge this gap. Human action apart from or over against God (this is possible, relatively speaking) fails. This gap opens wide from within the interior depths of every human being. If the great religions of the world partake of this interiority and express it in their practices and chart it in their scriptures, they also share this interiority with the revealed religion and its eschatological intensification. The "protreptic (forward-leading) inner orientation" enacted in Christian religious experience is nothing but the experience of humanity brought into the encounter with God on the fully human plane.[12] Human spirituality shares an anthropological form, which I call inwardness or interiority. This inwardness reaches into the supernatural precondition of our consciousness, and of all of nature, and surpasses knowledge into an Unknowing; Christianity is simply the active collecting of the paradigms, symbols, narratives, rituals, and practices of humanity's diverse traditions of interiority, in order to bring them into the passage of Christ's passover, from within the heart of Israel, "for the life of the world."[13] Without "dialogue" there is no Christianity at all, since Christianity *is* "right use" as an eschatological existence from out of the region that stands before, next-to, facing the *eschaton*.

12. This phrase comes from Jacques-Albert Cuttat, *The Spiritual Dialogue of East and West*, 20.
    13. Jn 6:51.

17

# I
# MYTH

THE GOAL OF PHILOSOPHY is universality, the truth of things in itself, but this truth is only touched at the very limits of the reaches of reason, at the beginning and at the end, and hence through the particularities of myth. This recognition, basic, even defining, for philosophy in my view, leads to the further recognition that not only the beginning and the end—the origin from which are all things and the purpose for which are all things—are encountered only *through* the veils of myth, but thus *so also is the middle itself*. That is: reason, by making the essential recognition, awakens to its own mythologicality, its total debt to the mythic encounter with the Absolute, an encounter that possesses an intelligible density exceeding reason and that, in fact, founds it. And it is this recognition that dignifies reason, making it capable, as if for the first time, of the very matters themselves—the insoluble problems of human life—that are the perennial topics of philosophy.

For the sake of its further illumination, I want to acknowledge a corollary classification, from the evolutionary approach to religion, but which overlaps somewhat with that of the phases of biblical religion I have portrayed in the leading sketch.[1]

Worship in the sense I give it—formal act of reverence for deity or deities constituting sacrifice, the enactment of a sacred meal in which the deity is host and offering—is indeed a product of the "Neolithic revolution": in what one could call "tribal society," ritual and myth involved—as always—the transcendence through linguistic and kinaesthetic "objectification" of the radical limitations placed on human existence in its native, embodied, temporal condition through symbolization. But tribal myth-ritual (let us just say

1. My debt to Robert Bellah for what follows is plain, as well as to Eric Voegelin, his great forebear. For some major elements of the typology that follows see in particular Bellah's early programmatic essay "Religious Evolution" (*American Sociological Review* 29.3 [1964], 358–74) and also "God and King" (*The Robert Bellah Reader*, ed. Robert Bellah and Steven M. Tipton [Durham: Duke University Press, 2006], 357–89), as well as, of course, *Religion in Human Evolution*.

"religion"), by contrast to that of later "archaic societies" (emerging at the tail end of the Neolithic era, in the "Bronze Age," marked by the development of writing systems, for example cuneiform in Mesopotamia and hieroglyphs in Egypt) is marked by, first, the "proximity" of the world of myth to the world of experience and its "fluidity," where parts are exchanged and representation is flexible. The world of myth, *in illo tempore,* is not far away. Secondly, ritual in this context is an event of *identification* with the ancestors or localized deities—not worship, formalized adoration through the awe of distance wherein the encounter is highly (not minimally) layered. This layering and complexification seems to grow in relation to the greatness and transcendence of the deity, which corresponds to an analogous process in city political administration. In the tribal realm, ritual is the site where humans *become one* with the myth and its world. There are no, or minimal, mediations; hierarchies securing the communication between the divinities and human participants are not required, but come at a later stage. There is one world, the world of myth, and human myth-telling involves the wager that this world is framed and underpinned by that which the myth signifies, whereas ritual enacts this wager, justifying it.

*Archaic society* is the site where divinities are aggrandized, and to various degrees unified, to the point, at least once, of a proto-monotheism (as in the elevation of Aten, the sun disk, to the status of sole God by Akhenaten in the eighteenth dynasty of Egypt—but which died with him c. 1336 BC). But more often the unification can be discerned in the so-called "Henotheism" wherein various gods become aspects, powers, faces, or subsidiaries of a hidden, hyper-transcendent "Most High God." As is well attested, *co-emergent* with this tendency toward unification of the pantheon in archaic religion is the rise of the phenomenon of *kingship.* The former—as can clearly be seen in the case of Aten—is a means of securing state power in the hands of a sole ruler. Archaic society can nearly be defined by this correlation, and, it has been argued, for the rise of the idea of the One God, and exclusive worship. Exclusive worship of the king's God corresponds to exclusive respect for the king's rule. There is more: the proximity and fluidity of the relation of humans to the ancestors-deities of tribal religions becomes focused on a single human lord, the high God's representative on earth (common in Mesopotamia) and in Egypt in particular the high God's "Son." Here the proximity and fluidity become unqualified identification—similarly later in Octavian Augustus's conscription of the title *Divi filius* at the apotheosis-death of his great-uncle, Julius Caesar.[2] In Israel, God's identification as the only true king, not only implies an "axial" criticism of archaic socio-religious order but (among other things) corresponds to her unique monotheism.

Another feature that emerges in this context is the beginnings of a differentiation between myth and critical reflection (through the establishment of "craft literacy," learned circles of professional scribes), or, more generally, "narrative understanding" and "theoretical understanding."[3] The birth of theoretical reflection, the grasp of the human totality via various degrees of abstract conceptualization ("names" writ large, generalized) and theory formation, occurs through *interrogation* of myth, the tracing of its limitations and the discernment of the transcendence of the major elements within it (God, evil, goodness, justice, "meaning") as *problems* myth may only accentuate but is itself *incapable* of providing satisfactory answers to human intelligence. This felt dissatisfaction with myth and its corresponding political forms seems to occur always under the goad of the tremors and earthquakes of human experience, such as, especially, political upheaval. The point I want to retain here is that *lógos* is tied to myth, intrinsically. Whether *lógos* remembers this womb and matrix, this permanent condition, is another question altogether.[4]

I will call this emergence of theoretical culture within the milieux of myth, wisdom-tradition, or, following the ancients, more simply, *wisdom*. One may even call it proto-philosophy, but the "love of

2. Though let us respect Eric Voegelin's insight that tempers and circumscribes this notion of identification, at least for Egypt and *mutatis mutandis*, for first-century Rome: see *Order and History*, vol. 1: *Israel and Revelation, Collected Works*, vol. 14, ed. Maurice P. Hogan (Columbia: University of Missouri Press, 2001), 91–155.

3. To use Bellah's typology in *Religion and Human Evolution*.

4. Bellah of course observes that the avowed separation of *lógos* and myth, and the latter's eradication by the former, is a feature of the "modern" era, the post-Latin West from the sixteenth century, that is, from the rise of modern science, wherein theoretical symbolization is taken, uniquely, as self-sufficient.

wisdom" properly speaking only emerges in the "Axial" age, and as (perhaps its crucial feature) *lógos* itself becomes a way of life: a life that loves wisdom, pursues it, but does not claim to possess it (as in Pythagoras, evidently; and subsequently, Socrates): critical but recognizing the divinity of the myths. This is self-consciously by contrast to the ancient Sages, that is, wise men (wonderworkers, poets, prophets, and great statesmen—more often than not a mixture of some or all of these). The Sages of archaic societies, veiled in the mists of the past, were above all great rulers: often accomplished in the art of warcraft, they solidified and unified society. They received their gift of wisdom from above, from a divine source. Yet the "*love of* wisdom" was born out of the failures of these societies through the vicissitudes of history—famine or drought leads to starvation, mass migration, abandonment and failure of cities, even civilizations, just as prosperity leads to cultural decay and the immoderate interest of foreign powers: all of this and much more leads to critical reflection on the proximity and fluidity of a ruling social order and its claims to eternal order, and of the *sufficiency* (I do not say *validity*) of the basic myths and ritual order that undergird them.

Myth and Word: if the Word of revelation speaks the language of Myth, it is not the disclosure of information that may be manipulated for mundane, human ends. It is a decisive intervention, a call, as I have said, into the story of humanity that alters that story, reorienting it. Myth has always been a "response" to the divine presence; but the ritual encounter in the transformation of Myth by the Call of the Presence that has always pervaded ritual is itself transformed: it is an act of obedience in Response to the Call that precedes understanding, but serves as its source. The Ritual act becomes a journeying together on the pilgrimage of an unfolding disclosure. The Call of the God who pervades all human religious experience in the various forms that reach, collectively, into the unifying singularity of the Origin and End, founds the Response that forms human religious experience and provides the implicit content of its cultural forms, primarily religion and then everything that depends on it (philosophy, art, and science). All religious experience that advances towards and breaks out towards the ultimate Unity of God partakes of this Call that pervades all. The cultural forms of human life are therefore patterns of response to the one divine Word. One may not judge the value or veracity of their response, but one may, and in fact must, judge their fruit. If it is good—if it partakes of the divine goodness that one knows, if it anticipates the divine goodness within which one has placed all one's earthly hopes—then one may be allowed to recognize the goodness of the form, its symbols, narratives, and concepts. This is very difficult work and would require, on the Christian account, prayer and the impartation of a divine gift. This is far beyond me; I only want to suggest that others may be able to take it up. Yet this Word was made flesh within the history of the People Israel, under the form of her myths, as its single *telos*.[5] In the incarnation, then, the Call and Response take on an identification that is—of course—unprovable and even illegitimate according to the standards of judgment provided by the present form of the world. But nevertheless it is this identification that is the essence of Christianity's all-determining fidelity to the significance for all humanity of the Empty Tomb. It takes the form, within the cosmic order of history, of a divine promise that has broken in from beyond its limiting strictures and the response of human entrustment to the promise that recognizes its universal validity.

The Key of Myth is discovered in the recognition of its permanence, the necessity and presence of a pre-theoretical narrative order that accounts for the human situation in its most profound and problematic dimensions. It is the constant, living milieu of any intellectual effort that wants to reach into these, its fundamental, and again, permanent questions.

5. The singularity of this *telos* ought to be uncompromising, but let us agree to accept that perhaps the most uncompromising Christian of all, Paul of Tarsus, understood that the significance of Israel which does not recognize the Lordship of Jesus does not diminish with his resurrection from the dead, but is actually strangely foundational for the present extension of the covenant to the nations.

# STUDY 1

WORD: Political Theology

NAME: Antoine Arjakovsky

STYLE: Annotation

MATTER: Comments on Arjakovsky, *Russie-Ukraine: De la guerre à la paix?* (2014)

IN A RECENT BOOK,[1] Antoine Arjakovsky examines the basic features of the Russian-Ukrainian war. This is the first book to examine the state of affairs between Ukraine and Russia since the events of November 2013. It is written by a theologian deeply involved in Latin-Greek ecumenical engagements, a spiritual heir to the "Sophiological" school of Florensky and Bulgakov.[2] Arjakovsky observes that contemporary political science has failed and will continue to fail to understand world events to the degree that it does not possess and apply what he calls the "theologico-political key." This key is essential to understanding human collectivities, what they do and why, especially nation-states, the major actors in the unfolding of global history at the present time. This key is, simply, the centrality of myth and the theological (I do not use the term "religious," which is partially helpful but also misleading) to political action. We examine here only the first part of the second chapter of this book, "La clef theologico-politique," concerned with defining "mythological thought" and constructing the "elements of

---

1. *Russie-Ukraine: De la guerre à la paix?* (Paris: Parole et Silence, 2014). See also a set of articles I translated for the Australian *ABC Religion and Ethics* website edited by Scott Stevens.

2. Antoine Arjakovsky, *Essaie sur le père Serge Bulgakov: Philosophe et théologien chrétien* (Paris: Parole et Silence, 2006).

a methodology" by which one can interpret the events.[3] The entirety of this elaboration restricts itself to these opening few pages of this chapter, unless otherwise specified. The remainder of the chapter, to which I can only recommend the reader, describes the basic, motivating myths that explain Ukrainian and Russian self-understandings.

The military conflict between Russia and Ukraine, according to Arjakovsky, is determined by the conflict of their respective myths, which articulate the same religious, ethnic, and cultural symbols in divergent ways, and claim the same sacral geographical territory for different ends. Both ends are determined by mythic visions that define them respectively as peoples and as nations. What is myth? And how is it understood? Why is it so important? Let us begin modestly and therefore answer the last question first: Arjakovsky says that it is "dangerous to ignore the resources of mythology and political theology," for without these it is impossible to understand the principal events of the last decades—from the fall of communism to the crisis of liberal capitalism, from (let us add) the American invasion of Iraq and its unfathomable consequences (only now fully coming to light, with, for example, the religious cleansing of growing regions of the Middle East, the wider and wider cultural and political organization of militant Islam not seen for 500 years) to the Arab Spring (and its uncertainties). Arjakovsky frames his presentation by way of proposing an alternative to Samuel Huntington's once highly influential thesis of a "clash of civilizations."[4] Arjakovsky observes that Huntington is right to see the centrality of a religion-culture-society matrix in political events, which must be factored into any proposal about international politics. They agree, says Arjakovsky, regarding the importance of modern religious renewal vis-à-vis the fall of communism in Russia or Ukraine (and we can add of course Poland, among other nations). But beyond

---

3. Ch. 2:27–56, §1: 31–35.

4. Samuel Huntington, *The Clash of Civilizations and the Remaking of World Order* (NY: Simon and Shuster, 1996)—which used to be required reading of the US State Department before 9/11.

Huntington one must come to terms with the full "presence and power" of the mythological. To do this it must be distinguished, essentially, from logical rationality if only that we may then be able to see properly the radical and necessary relation between them.

Because of this latter necessity, the rationalist thinking that dominates political science, making it blind to the most fundamental factors behind international events and increasingly impotent to understand them—and even, most importantly, *dangerous* in its influence on the actions of Western powers—tends, says Arjakovsky, to understand myth in two misguided ways: first, it wants to "assimilate *mythos* to *logos*," that is, to understand myth wholly from within the domain of a separated rationality, to see myth as only a confused, primitive science or as a preparatory context that gives birth to the miracle of an autonomous reason. This kind of correlation leads to the total delegitimization of myth: "mythology is then understood as the fabulous or allegorical thinking of antiquity with no link whatsoever with reality." A false path, albeit a commonplace in Western civilization. The second misguided manner of understanding *lógos* and *mûthos* is "to negate them both" as a consequence of the recognition of the necessary mythic context and character of reason. Here, says Arjakovsky in a deeply acerbic tone, "one speaks of 'ideologies' . . . forms of thought that are outmoded for us, who live in the era of the complete awakening of civilizations." Both manners of approach that form the misunderstanding of myth are deleterious inasmuch as they lead us to misunderstand ourselves in our humanity. The first way reduces myth to an image of itself as proto-*lógos*; the second way complementarily sees mythic consciousness, so *clearly* present in the past, as a contamination of reason, and consequently forgets its own (all the more) ideological character that is more dangerous still because it does not understand its mythic ground and, hence, its essential limits. It would not be too far off to call this way a will-to-power unmasked to itself. Both paint over the primacy and necessity of myth for reason, even the most reduced or "purified" kind of rationality that marks Western "modernity."

Before getting to the nature of this primacy and necessity of the mythical, Arjakovsky draws an analogy that allows us to see the character of the difference between *mûthos* and *lógos*, for it is essential that myth be allowed to stand on its own two legs, to present the coherence and dense intelligibility that mark it from end to end: *mûthos* differs from *lógos* "a little like" memory should be distinguished from history: "On the one hand there is a personal narrative, founded on an authentic and dynamizing experience, but which does not enjoy universal recognition. On the other hand, one has an authorized narrative, founded on verified proofs, but which no longer has available through itself immediate compelling force." Memory is essential, but it is not history; it forms the foundation of history, for there is no history without memory as the vast, collective landscape through which history (partially abstract and ideal) can be proposed. Memory, individual or collective and cultural, forms persons; memory only claims universality when it appeals to the historicity of events; this appeal separates the event from the person, giving the event a distinct absoluteness that can be examined and requires ceaseless interpretation (one could almost say "re-memorization") to be accepted. History is memory examining itself and put in question, proposed and no longer immediate, objectivized. After Christianity (in fact), with its claim of a founding *historicity* that is all-determining (the resurrection of the crucified man, historical, but in excess of history, an excess reached through memory of a community of faith—hence the Gospels), memory and history are distinguished in a unique manner that has determined the world, creating the possibility of the conception of a history acknowledged as independent of memory.

Arjakovsky proceeds in the next paragraph to a rapid and condensed positive description of myth: "Theologico-political analysis consists precisely in making visible the mythical or symbolical, the non-rational, not immediately communicable dimension of our reasonings and our actions, offering it frameworks for its expression, a [greater] self-understanding, and allowing it to be led back in a more clarified and coherent way to its ultimate object." Here we see a number of basic features of myth: (1) It is non-rational. This does not mean "irrational" but rather "hyper-rational"—in excess of the determining rationality of modern existence, conceptual objectivity, for which (to express it in a Cartesian way) the clearest

29

and most distinct idea is the greatest possible grasp of the reality in question. Myth (as Vico and then Schelling understood) cannot be understood in these terms. This distinguishing of the appropriate "autonomy" of mythic consciousness was the main burden of Arjakovsky's previous comments. (2) It is not immediately communicable. Myth, as the articulation of the unity of the world, as a meaningful "place" where the community of which I am a part lives meaningfully, is felt (so to speak), known antepredicatively by being the means through which I grasp the world before *it* (myth) is comprehended. That comprehension of myth itself can only happen at a second remove from it, at a remove that holds it in question and could neutralize it. Whence the beginning of theoretical intelligence. Myth is a shared heritage, a cultural and lived background, a lifeworld that is received as already given, awoken to as already inside the shape of one's life and thought. If the spell of myth is broken (whether by rationality or by the surgence of a competing myth) then so is the rationality on which it depends. Therefore (3) it is a hidden and basic feature of our reasonings and actions. And this because (4) it is "of its nature to gravitate towards an ultimate object." Myth proposes an ultimate and final framework of value, a basic orientation in the world at the root of every decision in history and conceptualization. The "clarity and coherence" in theologico-political analysis that Arjakovsky recommends seeks to give to mythic consciousness a better understanding of itself precisely as that rich elementary key in its own right that makes possible the humanity of man (especially in the political-social-religious-cultural matrix through which humanity reaches itself) inasmuch as it itself is the tending of humanity towards an ultimate objective, an absolute goal that (according to the logic of the framework of value that it gives) forms the gravity of any social-political-cultural-religious entity.

Myth is the presence of the final gravity of humanity in history. In this way myth is basic to politics—and analogically to every human cultural endeavor (not to lose sight of our intention with this explication). Citing Roland Barthes and Guy Lanque, Arjakovsky exposes this mythic root of the political: if for Barthes political rhetoric is "the mythification of relations of power within the social order," then for Lanque myth, or rather the political process of "mythification," far from being a "falsification of reality," is the "elaboration of a narrative text that attempts to give [reality] new meaning" by "defining a ritual field" and providing "a new cognitive map" to experience.[5]

This orientating discussion allows Arjakovsky to present the two basic mythic-narratives in play in the Russian-Ukrainian conflict. First, there is the myth of the lost grandeur of Holy Russia, destined, as the bearer of a "third" (and final) Rome, to succeed decaying Western civilization on the world-stage and to accomplish what it did not for the common good of humanity. A litmus test of the decadence and accelerating death of Western civilization, on this score, is its loss of a defining myth that articulates its historical and spiritual significance. At any rate, Russia's goal, notes Arjakovsky, is to regather under one head the Russian-speaking lands in order to create a "vast Euroasian empire" that will be able to "propose a counter-model to Western civilization, secularized and entering into a phase of accelerated decay."

The Ukrainian myth motivates a desire for escape from the corrupt hegemony of the Kremlin and incorporation into the free society of Western Europe, and is based on the universality of values, especially the dignity of human beings, that forge the conditions for the basic features of modern liberal society, values themselves irreplaceably built on the religious vision of Judeo-Christianity. The basic biculturality of Ukraine, composed of Russian and Ukrainian speakers, of Orthodox and Catholic cultures, is traced back to the long history of a Ukrainian transcendence of the basic division of Christendom, a defining feature of world Christianity since 1054: Ukrainian Christianity existed in double-communion with the Eastern Orthodox and Western Catholic forms of Christianity for hundreds of years following the formal split, a transcendence that was only brought to an end owing to the play of wider European

---

5. See Barthes, *Mythologies* (1957) and Lanque's preface to Dominique de Juriew, *Mythes politiques et identités en Ukraine post-soviétique* (Paris: Harmattan, 2003).

politics on Ukrainian soil in the 17ᵗʰ century. This capacity for transcendence of the "clash of civilizations" basic to the genius of Ukrainian culture is traced back to its founding myth (which is basic to
its conflict with Russia: the latter sees this origin as its own possession, and rightfully enfolded into the heart of Russian, Euroasian
civilization). Kiev is indeed the cradle of Russian culture, but in its
own right is the center of "Ukrainian" mixed culture, which mediates between Western and Eastern realms by participating in both at
once and can become, through this Ukrainian genius, exemplary
for each, injecting the Judeo-Christian spirituality back into the
heart of European culture and thus rejuvenating its values as well as
mediating democracy and freedom into Russian culture, precisely
as the authentic expression of Judeo-Christianity on which Russia
depends. (Whether or not this vision of the Ukrainian genius is
realizable, acceptable, or even intelligible from either the European
or Russian perspectives, is not at issue here; it is the myth, according
to Arjakovsky, of a people who desire to be a nation.)

In this discussion, Arjakovsky appeals to three further thinkers in
order to develop the "elements of a methodology" that would utilize
the "theologico-political key" adumbrated above to unlock the Russian-Ukrainian conflict. These thinkers are Raoul Girardet, a Parisian
historian and specialist in modern French nationalism, Gilbert
Durand, author of a very influential book, *Structures anthropologiques et l'imaginaire* (1969), and Charles Taylor, Canadian philosopher and author of *A Secular Age* (2007). Girardet, author of *Mythes
et mythologies politiques* (1986), is known for his position condemning contemporary political science for its ignorance of the imaginary,
symbolic, and mythic dimensions of modern political life, marked
by, in actuality, a "mythological effervescence." Arjakovsky quotes
Girardet's own summary of the basic features of the mythic consciousness stemming from the French Revolution that binds together
the French nation: ". . . with its ritual, symbols, and rhetorical lyricism [the French Revolution] is a new form of political religiosity
that was brought to completion by being reconstituted around a relatively coherent system of collective values: cult of Right, Justice, Liberty, and Solidarity, celebration of the Homeland, faith in human
Progress, in the advent within consciences of a new morality authen

ticated by Reason."[6] According to Girardet, political mythology, of course "legendary" and false, objectively speaking, mainly serves an "explanatory function" which means that it "furnishes a certain number of keys for understanding the present," and thus in actuality constitutes "a screen through which the disconcerting chaos of facts and events can appear ordered" and meaningful. This explanatory function, he observes, also serves a "mobilizing" function.

A last feature of political myth in its meaning-bearing and mobilizing roles in a culture is its fundamental "ambivalence."[7] Myth, therefore, cannot be understood according to the rules of "Cartesian" understanding, comments Arjakovsky, for its logic is closer to that of dreams for which the unfolding chain of images respond to one another in a free manner that escapes the grasp of rational control. Girardet appeals to the classic juxtaposition of the sons of Zeus, Apollo and Dionysus, made famous in modern thought by Hölderlin and especially by Nietzsche in *The Birth of Tragedy*: the former serving the daylight function of sobriety, reason, restraint, and control; the latter representing the shadowy side of human nature and experience, emotion and instinct, the subconscious, emerging in dreams and feasts, laughter and pain, joy and suffering. Both the drive to order and the encroaching chaos are ever-present in us and to us in the interlocking worlds of nature and culture. Hence, concludes Girardet quite soberly: "Dionysus remains a shadowy god. At the end of the day it is wise to recognize his place—his just place—rather than attempt to muffle his voice."[8] Arjakovsky rightly sees the limitation of Girardet in his affiliation of myth with the Dionysian dimension alone. On the one hand, Girardet is correct to see the permanence and "effervescent" presence of myth in human existence. On the other hand, he "follows Durkheim too closely" in considering myth in light of the concept of "*anomie*," in opposition, generally speaking, to law and moral standards, and specifically, in the social-political context, to the state of a break-

---

6. Girardet, *Mythes et mythologies politiques* (Paris: Seuil, 1986), 189 (Arjakovsky, 32).

7. See Girardet, 13 (Arjakovsky, 32).

8. See Girardet, 191 (Arjakovsky, 32).

down of norms that guide social life and underwrite the social order, leading to the experience of unrest and alienation of individuals in society (the principal concept in Durkheim's work on suicide).[9] But *lógos* does not determine the essence of *mûthos*, which can only be understood by accepting its own self-determining intelligibility. Myth "explains" the inexplicable precisely by allowing it to remain such through the explanation itself, capturing the sur-human aspirations of peoples, their desire to participate in that which is greater than themselves, which takes on human form precisely in the political domain, a domain intended to embody and to make possible the aspiration toward higher, divine ideals, especially Freedom and Justice. Myth is as much "Apollonian" as a separated rationality partakes of the "Dionysian."

In order to explicate this profound clarification of Girardet, Arjakovsky turns to Gilbert Durand. Durand's major insight, according to Arjakovsky, is the acknowledgment of the turning face of a single human social reality that manifests as *mûthos* and as *lógos* through the ebbs and flows of cultural events. "Durand," says Arjakovsky, "has shown that the logic of myth should be grasped" when one considers that "mythological constellations" are always present *in potentia* in the background, which "are able to enter into history in times of latency and violently resurge when a collective soul is profoundly troubled." The point Arjakovsky emphasizes in light of Durand's work is that myth is not merely a convenient fiction appealed to for stability in times of crisis, and used by politicians simply to motivate the masses. "It is probable," he concludes, "that in times of crisis *mythos* prevails more often over *logos* whereas in times of peace logic prevails over the mythical." This is crucial to understanding human history, the human present, and the human future. But only a misunderstanding of myth (and of human societies and cultures) would believe the massive myth that myth and rationality do not "interact permanently and are indispensable to one another." Myth, he concludes, "lies at the heart of institutional mechanisms and of the practices of contemporary societies."

Here Arjakovsky appears close to Hans Blumenberg, for example,

9. *Le Suicide* (1897).

34

from his famous *Work on Myth*.[10] For Blumenberg, myth and reason are two modes of the same basic human enterprise, that of coping with the "absolutism of reality." According to Blumenberg (after
Gehlen), human evolution (and the passage from the canopy of the
forest to the unprotected, open savannah) led to a strange "deficit"
in the basic "coping" mechanism that every kind of animal develops
in order to survive and flourish. Humanity evolved in excess of its
own instinctuality. No longer able to cope "naturally" with its
unprecedented situation, it turns to the symbol-making capacity
that makes it unique in order to mediate, to humanize, the open
world in which it is now exposed. This requires humans to develop
creative mediating structures to place between themselves and the
overwhelming harshness of experience ("absolutism of existence"),
its crushing and final fragility that perpetually threatens nascent
humanity. These structures comprise human culture and at their
center are social institutions that reinforce the mythic-ritual narratives at the base of culture (originally generated out of the basic
human experience of anxiety, which turns into fear, which is then
managed by ritual, which generates myth). According to Blumenberg, modernity is no less mythic than antiquity, but has only
increased the "deficit of instinct," thereby, in actuality, requiring
myth all the more radically. The modern, secular account of self-
sufficient reason is at least as mythic, then, as the guiding narratives
of the most primitive of peoples. Arjakovsky, of course, believes in
"universal values" tied to the Judeo-Christian revelation,[11] and considers them to be knowable in an objective way, that is, not (crassly)
reducible to one's comprehension of them, but as norms (necessarily) mythically structured, constructively revealed to us by the basic
stories we tell, norms which therefore require the consent found
through the practice of faith, norms which can be debated, reasoned about, and proposed to others as true and worthy of consent
and practice.

10. *Work on Myth* (1985).
11. See Arjakovsky's comments in "The Putin Illusion: Mythology, Irrationality
and the Russian-Ukrainian War," trans. W. Chris Hackett, *ABC Religion and Ethics*
website, July 24, 2014.

Myths, it seems, express and cultivate common desires of groups of people; they define the social order, making collectivity, and therefore the higher forms of society, possible. Arjakovsky describes this desire at the heart of myth as "an aspiration to participate in a comprehensive mystery, to incarnate a particular vocation, to work towards the advent of a kingdom of justice." Arjakovsky, speaking in defense of Ukraine against Russia, is richly redolent of classical political theologies of the Christian past, especially St. Augustine's *City of God against the Pagans.* This is disconcerting to a Western, secularized Christian who suffers the era of the decay of his own national, cultural, and civilizational myths, for whom Christendom and its heirs have been long dead, and for whom the best hope for peace is the conquest of technological abundance that, in pacifying the stomach of those rising zealous collectivities that thirst for power and desire to wield it on the global scale, will also make them too lazy to imperialize, that is, to disrupt his own comfort. Those who do not enjoy the enslavement of prosperity, and who embrace and are carried along by the desires incarnate in their myths (religious, political, religious-political) are madmen (some may well be), and it is the single task of our governments to neutralize their aspirations by making them into the image of ourselves.

Whatever the case here, Arjakovsky makes explicit that the logic of the "kingdom of justice" at the heart of the Ukrainian struggle is indeed inherited from Judeo-Christian revelation, which, he says "gives a specific mission to the nations, all the while framing them within the larger perspective of the advent, promised by Jesus Christ, of the Kingdom of God on earth." According to Arjakovsky, the determining myth of medieval *and* modern politics alike is the vision of the Kingdom of God preached by Jesus Christ, that is, the reign of divine charity over all things and through all things, involving the realization of the Creator's plans for the world, centered on humanity, which will involve a resurrection of the dead (accomplished in principle, ahead of the end, within history, in the appointed man, Jesus of Nazareth, who, as the "New Adam," is the entrant of the Kingdom of God in person, the *autobasileia* as Origen said). In this myth the terminus of the resurrection is a final judgment, where all of humankind will appear before the Creator, in the bodies through which they lived on the earth, to be judged according to the Creator's perfect justice through the regnant Lord Jesus himself. It culminates in the renovation of the world, a "New Heavens and New Earth" wherein there will no longer be any separation between God and humanity, and the temple-paradise of the beginning will be restored, advanced, and completed—extended to the point of coincidence with the entirety of the cosmos by means of the collaboration of the renewed and justified and perfected humanity that is heir to the Kingdom of the Christ. The Kingdom of God is a myth, the Christian myth. In it, through the resurrection of Jesus Christ, there is (the promise of) a final translation of mythic spirituality and ultimate meaning into the body of human life on earth, an eclipse of world, myth made history (or history made myth). The Kingdom, for Christians, is the hidden aim of the Creator from the beginning, and its day is "hastened" through faithful activity of Christians in the present who live here and now as citizens of the Kingdom that is coming. This separation of the kingdoms of the earth from the Kingdom of God, ruled by Christ, means that the kingdoms of the earth are in fact altogether "secularized" and cannot be underwritten by an identification with the sacral register; they are servants of a higher kingdom which they can only anticipate, but for the sake of which kingdom and in light of the final judgment *that kingdom will bring*, they have a vocation to serve. Hence, as Arjakovsky has said elsewhere: "While it is necessary to distinguish between the Kingdom of God and the Kingdom of Caesar, these two entities can no longer be simply separated. The Church believes that what confers rights and responsibilities on each person is the fact that he is created in the image and likeness of God. The Church also believes that all power in heaven and on earth has been given by God the Father to Jesus Christ, as stated in the Gospel of Matthew (28:18). Consequently, the Church must relativize the role of the state while orienting it towards the responsibility they hold in common: to make the Kingdom of God come on earth."[12] The myth of the Kingdom of God, at the heart of Christian

12. Arjakovsky, "The Role of the Churches in the Ukrainian Revolution," trans. W. Chris Hackett, *ABC Religion and Ethics Online*, March 7, 2014.

faith and spirituality (Jesus taught his disciples to pray that the Father's *basileia*, his kingdom or reign, his just and universal rule, would "come on earth as it is in heaven"), certainly compelling in Arjakovsky's Ukraine, where the culture remains highly religious, is to Western European Christians like a faint echo of their own most sacred myth that has suffered high "spiritualization" or "internalization," a slow and persistent deracination of the Myth from the social and political and cultural domains. What is left in the case of the Western world is hardly any longer even a "secularized" myth, but rather only the emotive convictions of such a vision that manifest themselves in a detached way, often in so-called liberal or progressive social agendas, which many Christian "intellectuals" reinterpret as advancements of the Kingdom itself, although these are born from out of a wholly post-Christian, even anti-Christian, socio-intellectual context.

But judgment is not ours to lay down, here or elsewhere. Whatever the case, Arjakovsky follows Charles Taylor's juxtaposition of the medieval and modern conceptions of the Kingdom of God. "The Middle Ages," he says, "established a continuity between truth and justice, whereas in the Modern Age the true, the good, and the just have been distinguished." Continuity, on the one hand, and discontinuity, on the other, are defining features of these "ages." The present era, which self-consciously asserts itself against the medieval through a decomposition of what it unified, is marked by a "progressive awareness of the limitations of the two preceding periods"—the Middle Ages and Classical Antiquity. If the previous era of "Christendom" involved the "progressive suffocation of human freedom in the name of an objectivized vision of God as *Pantocrator*," then the Modern Age will assert itself as "the progressive suffocation of divine freedom in the name of an objectivized conception of Reason as self-sufficient." This assertion of the human over-against God, seen, ironically, as constricting its "nature," is also finally a turn against itself, since the stability of meaning, especially of the human self, requires an orientation towards a transcendent that it cannot capture (reducing it to itself) or avoid. The increase of this "modern" project of the "suffocation" of the divine is the source of the increasing ambiguity of the present modern social order, inasmuch as it is predicated on the erasure of a *transcendent* end or aim as the "final cause" of human flourishing for the sake of a bare, conditionless movement of *transcendence*, which at its most intense is the feeling of freedom. If the Middle Ages located this feeling of freedom in the ecstasy of worship, the Modern Age finds it in autonomous self-assertion, which Nietzsche called the will-to-power. Both ages are lacking, it would seem to go for Taylor, inasmuch as they perform an objectification of that which they idealize: for the Medievals (and this becomes apparent only in early modernity) it is the objectification of God, the face of the transcendent, the Transcendent as such, as the means through which they secure their own immanent projects; for the Moderns this objectification concerns the movement of transcending itself, which rejects *a priori* any possibility of a transcendent term that would, by its own moral intelligibility, define the human project for humanity. In religious terms this idealization or objectification is called "idolatry," whether of a concept of God or of Reason. The passage of transcending, as the feeling of self-empowerment, collapses and exhausts itself without the goad of the Transcendent that calls it forth, ever eluding it, which is given nowhere but by Myth.

With this repetition of Taylor, Arjakovsky concludes his description. He does so without comment. For him there is no need. Neither Ukraine nor Russia is "modern" in a straightforward or uncomplicated manner. They are not Germany, France, or America. To expect them to understand themselves according to the myth of liberal freedom would be similar to expecting the invasion of Iraq to install a Western-style democracy in the heart of the Middle East (once the people have tasted freedom…). The "Iraq War" itself quickly broke down the myth, which only reasserted itself in a cogent and pressing manner as a response to 9/11. The Ukrainian myth and the Russian myth are in accord, Arjakovsky says, on one thing: the need for transcendence, in its double-meaning (as I want to make clear) of transcending passage and transcendent rest: "The truth within the 'Russian myth' is that a rationality without god is as dangerous as an irrational god—whether it be a matter of class,

race, sex, or the nation."[13] This is an indictment of the myth of
Western secularism, which *until* it sees itself as a myth and comes to
terms with its origins, making peace with them through an appreci-
ation of them, however critical, will remain at the level of *ideology*.
Ideology does not consider its mythic conditions and is therefore
irrational.

Arjakovsky's project here is highly specific to unfolding political
events in Eastern Europe. And, building on the tradition of "political theology" (for which modern political concepts are "secularized"
religious concepts), it is revolutionary for contemporary political
theory and international relations. His presentation is brief, elementary, and synthetic. But the reader must make himself see the
force of his descriptions for any account of rationality as such and
hence any account of the philosophical in its quest for itself and its
understanding of the humanity of man. A few closing words to that
end:

Only *in time* is the object of myth—identified as the beginning,
the Source, and the end, the Goal—distinguished. "Where do we
come from?" "Where are we going?" These are questions at the
heart of myth that bring the Absolute into bicameral focus. This
separation gives the meta-logic of history and is its fundamental
condition. The Book of Genesis is an eschatological passage that
serves as the paradigm of sacred history: a divine conquest over
nothing that unfolds according to the poetic logic of freedom. The
inclusion of man and woman in the divine plan to repeat and mag-
nify this conquest of darkness through the fruitful multiplication of
the image of God—with the mandate to extend God's "reign" over
the face of the earth, to make the earth fruitful, redounding in an
ever-increasing lavishness that mirrors the divine beauty itself, to
extend the borders of the Garden, to guard and protect the basic but
contingent holiness and goodness of all that is—is itself a part of the
original act of creation: the divine "rest" is an enthronement at the
heart of the world, the beginning of the Creator's plan to unfold his
reign through the cosmos by means of a formal collaboration with

---

13. From the closing lines of Arjakovsky, "The Putin Illusion."

humanity, come hell or, indeed, high water. The Creation is already "eschatological" as the "Beginning"; the End is the completion of the Beginning, a "world without end." The temporal separation of Beginning and End contains the entire drama of humanity as a finite but God-like freedom and my human history, and it unfolds from within the primary narrative intelligibility of myth. The eschatological end of the beginning is necessarily expressed for me in mythical terms: "[T]he real result of our earthly existence is manifested on the other side of death in an event which, in symbolical language, is called 'judgment of the dead.' This event is not accessible to our imagination: it is not something that we can [presently] experience. It takes place between the divine and human sphere, outside of historical time" and beyond the conditions that frame my present manner of consciousness, of knowing, of perceiving.[14] Theologically speaking, these conditions of our historical intelligence are determined by the interposition of a distance between me and the divine Reality called history (always mythically, because narratively, comprehended). On the subterranean mythic plane, where my historical consciousness first becomes aware of itself in a unified, intelligible world, the human story that I live begins in a "banishment" from the Garden, a disenfranchisement from my proper home, which is in fact *this* world, but, through the passage of eschatological judgment opened in Jesus Christ, liberated and renewed, no longer restricted by the form of death, and united, replete with and held in God, as the End, the infinite and eternal Source of all that lives.

14. Josef Pieper, *The Platonic Myths*, trans. Dan Farrelly (South Bend, IN: St. Augustine's Press, 2011), 30.

# STUDY 2

WORD: Transcendence, Mythography, Synecdoche
NAME: John Milbank
STYLE: Commentary
MATTER: Commentarial Fragment on a Passage from
  John Milbank, *Beyond Secular Order* (2014)

THROUGH A CAREFUL READING of a difficult passage from the preface to *Beyond Secular Order* (2014), John Milbank's much-anticipated sequel to *Theology and Social Theory* (1990), we will find that the revolutionary character of biblical religion when fused with Greek thought at the beginning of Christianity is found in the seriousness and dexterity with which it inhabits Greek categories, using them (*chrēsis*) for its purposes, and in the perennially open revision this requires of our image of reason. To reach and sustain the richest point of contact with the passage, we must first contextualize it the best we can. This work is done by means of a patient exposition in three parts, leading us through twelve pages of text to the passage in question, four dense paragraphs on the idiosyncratic character of the biblical religion. The exposition is preceded by a brief apologia regarding its use of the "commentary" form.

## APOLOGIA

I am aware that the following "commentary," or set of critical annotations, though doubtlessly a philosophical and theological form of research substantially hallowed by various intellectual traditions of the world and, in the West, from the greatest students of Plato and Aristotle onwards, is all the same rather unique in contemporary academic writing (outside of New Testament studies, which has its own distinct customs proper to it, and which remains obvious in any case). An apologia of sorts, therefore, appears necessary. I provide one here with some reluctance, rather wishing the form to speak for itself.

Granted the ancient pedigree and the self-evident justification (at least formally) that most would be compelled to grant this form, the following brief commentary on a chosen fragment from (to whatever degree we grant this) an authoritative contemporary master of theology, is nevertheless clearly different from, say, an academic essay that concerns itself with the same material. How so? In the first place, the modern essay or academic article must have a clear *thesis*, one supported by a logical *argument* in distinct or measurable steps—must, that is, be dominated by a conceptual progression distinguishable by a reason that at each step recognizes its own principles, that is, *its very self*, within it. Now, the *image* of reason behind this form is widely contested in both contemporary philosophy and theology at least since Kierkegaard: how can a reason already ever transparent *to itself* actually discover anything "new"? We can therefore encapsulate this problematic image of reason by reference to the cult of *originality*, alive and well, and, accompanying it, the relentless equation of that which seems original with "valid" research. The commentary form recovers—again, at least formally—a more ancient conception of "originality," and therefore challenges us to be *less* "modern" (in my opinion only an intensified scholasticism) and *more* original. Besides, there is no cosmic law that scholarly writing must conform to a singular *formal* standard, but only expectations shaped by normative practices. This is perhaps sufficient. Differences with contemporary norms in *expressed content* are left to be discovered by the reader. What matters above all is the truth of what we say, not how we say it, though to be sure, how we say something gives the truth differently.

Here, in the following, the author sets for himself and for the reader a modest task. We would like *to understand* more clearly the meaning of what appears in a dense passage of a recent book.

*Understanding.* That is the most important justification for the following study. But the justification comes at the end: the reader must judge (and think) for himself—and that happens most powerfully through sustained and careful dialogue with the difficult notions of others. If I must be held to a "thesis" to be proven, let that be it. If we let the following critical annotations do their work, that will resolve itself.

The structure of my commentary, concerned with pages 1–13 of John Milbank's *Beyond Secular Order,* is as follows:

1. Orienting Remarks
   *On the intellectual background and context of Milbank's wider intellectual project.*
2. Beginning: A Formal Contextualization (1–3).
   *On the "hermeneutical" situation of historical humanity "between theory and practice" and the central place of religion for human existence and its irreplaceable role in our understanding of human being.*
3. Continuation (1) Distension: Intimations of "Myth *and* Reason" (3–11).
   *On questioning the modern* mythos *vs.* logos *principle.*
4. Continuation (2) Intensification: An Adumbrated "History of Religions" (11–12).
   *On the common religious logic—theo-logic—of myth and philosophy.*
5. A Metaphilosophy of Revelation: Commentarial Analysis in Four Frames (12–13).
   *On the paradoxical way biblical religion distends and intensifies human rationality. The heart of our analysis. An attempt to "freeze-frame" four terse paragraphs of Milbank's text in order to elucidate their basic meaning.*
6. Concluding Comment.
   *Summarizes the results of the foregoing commentary.*

## 1  Orienting Remarks

The passage for our annotation is found in the preface to the successor volume to Milbank's *Theology and Social Theory*.[1] We begin where the author does. The task of this present volume, *Beyond Secular Order*, is stated on its first line: "to deepen [*Theology and Social Theory's*] analyses" (1).[2] This is straightforward enough. Contemporary scholarly readers are certainly sufficiently familiar with the argument of the first volume by this contemporary theological master that no comment appears directly necessary, besides stating its thesis in the simplest terms: the fundamental assumptions of "modern" life and thought, most importantly our defining concept of "secularity," were made possible by and lie in intelligible continuity with specific decisions made in medieval theology. The critical elements of this thesis, at any rate, will be recalled as the commentary unfolds. As an initial orientating question we can ask: how is this analytic deepening meant to take place?

Structurally and thematically, I observe the following:

In the course of this preface to the sequel, Milbank proposes a third and final book entitled *On Divine Government*. The second and third volumes, then, will develop his hallmark genealogical investigation of the concept of the secular in the philosophical and political domains (the two parts to the present book) and in theology and the history of religion (presumably the two parts to the proposed third volume). Clearly the development or "deepening" of what *Theology and Social Theory* concerns involves a structural clarification absent from the first volume, though perhaps already implied in its title: two divisions, one theoretically concerned with human theory, the other theoretically concerned with human practices. There is philosophy and theology on the one side, and politics and the history of religion on the other. We will see shortly that this is only a structural artifice that is heuristically important as a dis-

1. John Milbank, *Theology and Social Theory*, 2nd ed. (West Sussex: Wiley-Blackwell, 2006).

2. John Milbank, *Beyond Secular Order* (West Sussex: Wiley-Blackwell, 2014), 1–18. References to this text are cited in-line.

tinction to be maintained as much as transcended or problematized. But let me adumbrate the schematic here through further elucidation of the formal structure of his analyses.

Later in this preface Milbank will suggest a clearer description of
this scheme, as far as it relates to the latter two volumes: the two
halves of the present book concern metaphysics and political theory, while the third book concerns religion and theology, where theology is defined "precisely" as the "coincidence of political theory
with metaphysics" (13), that is, one theoretical discipline (rooted in
and expressive of a religious practice) that underpins them all, in
their theoretical and practical ends. The genesis of the modern theoretical domain, dominated by the fundamental category of the *secular*, is found paradoxically rooted in theology above all, since
theology is historically and ontologically concerned with the totality of reality in an analogous way to political theory's concern with
history: they touch on and can elucidate the deepest aspects of
human existence. Both theology and political theory "blend" theory
and practice in a way that brings us into renewed contact with the
depths of reality. But it is precisely this access and contact that possess a perennial difficulty that remains intrinsic to any attempt to
conceive it.

Before following Milbank's examination of this difficulty there is
surely a question to ask, if only for the sake of better understanding:
whether the theoretical half, or a "blend" clearly dominated by the
theoretical dimension, is *inevitable* for any approach to the questions he is asking. Can, in other words, theory understand itself precisely as (granted, pro-leptic) preparation for the liturgical "real
thing"? (And ultimately—though this is only a question I rhetori-
cally pose as a student would to a master—whether this prioritization is the most appropriate for human being... Though of course
this is certainly the case on the Dominican "intellectualist" account,
especially when the question is framed as a matter strictly of a
choice between either a Dominican intellectualism *or* a Franciscan
affectivism that leads from voluntarism through transcendentalism
to nihilism. Perhaps the truth is that these two representative forms
ought to be "antinomically" held together. It is true that Milbank
himself has already begun "blending" even these in his rehabilita-

tions of an intellectually charged feeling through imagination.[3] And what is of specific concern for him is the traditional unification of the will/affect and intellect, defended and developed by Thomas Aquinas and the Dominican tradition after him culminating in Meister Eckhart, and the "Franciscan" innovation that separated will from intellect, reducing the scope of intellect to what pertains to this world, and affect to what exceeds it—union with God and all things; divine being asserted to be extrinsically beyond the reach of the intellect—thus laying the foundations for Kant.[4]) My parenthetical gesture here only intensifies an initial conclusion: the domination of the theoretical is surely not necessarily the case in the reality of human material actuality (though necessary in the ideal domain signified in books), for theory could understand itself as a handmaid to the essential act of worship (viz., sacrifice), as arguably theology (and philosophy as "spiritual exercise") does paradigmatically in the Classical-Patristic periods most acutely.[5]

We would have to pose this question, as the parenthesis indicates, to Milbank's own seemingly intellectualist position, however inflected

---

3. See for example, John Milbank, "Hume versus Kant: Faith, Reason and Feeling," *Modern Theology* 27.2 (2011), 276–97.

4. As Milbank points out in *The Monstrosity of Christ*, ed. Creston Davis (Boston: MIT Press, 2009)—and as he reminded me in a private communication—Eckhart himself sometimes speaks of the soul in its totality as will. In the same communication Milbank observed that Eric Voegelin makes a similar if perhaps more radical criticism of the Franciscan tradition in his *History of Political Ideas* (*Collected Works* vol. 20), observing that St. Francis's attempt to imitate the humanity of Christ was a Nestorian foundation for modernity, separating the humanity of Christ from his divinity and creating the conditions for modern secularity and its delusions: atheism, materialism, communism, etc.

5. The postmodern or "deconstructionist" critique of Milbank, viz., that his thought is dangerously "totalizing" inasmuch as it pursues a new postmodern and post-transcendentalist universality, is rooted precisely in the turn of primacy to the affective dimension as the domain of truth—a sort of "secularization" of modern mysticism. For a clear statement of this viewpoint, see John D. Caputo, "What Do I Love When I Love My God? Deconstruction and Radical Orthodoxy," *Questioning God*, ed. John D. Caputo et al. (Bloomington, IN: Indiana University Press, 2001), 291–317.

it has come to be in particular not only by his initial emphasis on the priority of ecclesial practice but also by a romantic-imagistic strain that steers contemplation/theology back into the waves of the liturgical, into concrete, embodied practice and into affectivity. We would have to ask whether the theoretical (as, precisely, a practical "exercise") serves to gesture towards and prepare the mind for sacramental-liturgical practice itself, which takes the mind paradoxically beyond its own native resources, as in Dionysius the Areopagite or Aquinas, for whom the "blending" of the theoretical/speculative and practical is less a matter of theological reflection (though the theological half of the pair can name and describe it for the sake of better understanding and therefore a greater blending) than it is a matter of sacramental participation.[6] We would have to ask, in other words—as already appears to be the case in both of these major figures—whether "theology" is not in the final analysis *ancillary* to the latter speculative-practical blend in embodied action that is soteriological-liturgical adoration of the Creator God in the Trinitarian fashion through sacramental practice of sacrifice that inscribes the mind and body in act into the triune life of God through sharing in Christ's body.[7]

But regardless of the final answer to this parenthetical question, which is a matter of judgment and therefore always provisional, Milbank is profoundly right: the question of the proper relation of

---

6. On this reading of the Areopagite, I follow Timothy Knepper's controversial but compelling summary of his own research in "Ranks Are Not Bypassed, Rituals Are Not Negated: The Dionysian Corpus," *Modern Theology* 30.1 (2014), 66–95. The reading of Thomas Aquinas accords with the tri-part structure of the *Summa theologiae*, as is very well known.

7. Criticisms of Milbank typically are an expression of basic theological and religious differences with him regarding his interpretation of Christianity and its living significance today. The fundamental difficulty with this kind of critical assessment of his thought (which happens to be legion) is that it tends to reduce the significance of the open-ended and revisionary character of his writing, particularly inasmuch as it is an expression of his endeavour to transcend assumptions that poorly frame "party politics" in contemporary thought.

the theoretical and practical dimensions of ourselves is basic if we want to come to some kind of proper understanding of ourselves in our humanity; and this question of the proper relation of the theoretical and practical in human experience is most deeply answered only from within the theological-religious domain. Demonstrating this is the double task that runs through all of his works, and they center on the meaning of our human being as *historical*. Hence his work can be intelligibly conceived as engaging in what Louis Dupré once called the discernment and integration of the "valid spiritual insights" of modernity (most centrally those of continental philosophy concerning language, historicity, and finitude),[8] an exercise therefore of "right use," despoiling the Egyptians, although *these* Egyptians are "Julian" in their paganism, indebted implicitly and always surprisingly to the Christianity they have "superseded." (This is the first reason why it is rather inept to consider Milbank a paleo-medieval romantic, quixotically endeavouring to return Western civilization to a lost "Christendom," which is doubtlessly the single-most common critique of his thought.)[9] We now see this exemplarily by returning to the text.

## 2 Beginning: A Formal Contextualization (1–3)

The "intrinsic difficulty" Milbank observes regarding his task of analyzing the conditions of the modern condition (as "secular order") in order to pass "beyond" it, is the initial subject of this preface under our analysis. Its title: "The Hidden Dimension of Humanity." What is this "hidden dimension"? And why does it make the

8. Louis Dupré, *Passage to Modernity* (New Haven: Yale, 1993).
9. Yet this is a criticism that squarely hits that mode of theology which Milbank himself is most concerned to overcome: neo-Scholasticism. For expressions of this critique against Milbank's thought, see, for example, Douglas Hedley's view that Milbank's thought is best understood as "grounded in the fertile soil of Catholic reaction to the French Revolution," in "Radical Orthodoxy and Apocalyptic Difference: Cambridge Platonism and Milbank's Romantic Christian Cabbala," *Deconstruction Radical Orthodoxy: Postmodern Theology, Rhetoric and Truth*, ed. Wayne J. Hankey and Douglas Hedley (Burlington, VT: Ashgate, 2005), 99–116 (quotation on 114).

work of intellectual genealogy "intrinsically difficult"? The answer to the last question is provided by the answer to the first. It can be elaborated by the concept of history: intellectual genealogy is difficult because concepts are historical (*because*, most importantly, human beings are) and history is always "half-concealed": "we are unable clearly to see ourselves" (1), beings immersed in history for whom the historical constitutes the beings that we are. *In particular*, this "hidden dimension" (and now we are broaching directly the first question) is a result of the basic *two-fold character* of human beings as historical: we act and think. "Human existence is split between actions and verbal or other symbolic performances on the one hand, and reflexive verbal theorisations (in whatever degree of abstraction) on the other" (1). Although typically understood as wholly distinct, this split down the middle of human existence is at the same time the point of unifying overlap that marks human existence. But the character of this mutually intrinsic relation between action and thought is critical to understand: thinking, despite what it often proposes about itself, is always an historical action, it occurs in the world, and action in the world (an act, to speak somewhat abstractly, being the discrete building block of history) already depends on and implies an *intelligible* world of some kind, the provenance of theoretical reflection. "In reality, all our actions assume a mythical, metaphoric, or rational framework, while all our theoretical utterances and writings are practical interventions in human history, whether deliberately so or not" (1). The threefold distinction of the intelligible delineation of the spheres of human action as "mythic, metaphoric, and rational" is immensely interesting, and I only take note of it for now (we will return to it below). What we should immediately observe is that this manner of intrinsic constitution and distinctiveness is the source of the basic ambivalence of thought and action, of words and deeds, of *verba* and *pragmata*.

It would be interesting to bring these intuitions to bear on our concept of revelation vis-à-vis a fundamental text of Vatican II, *Dei Verbum*, which makes precisely this distinction when discussing the paradigm of revelation, Jesus Christ, who in his integral humanity, *through* historical "words and deeds," *is* the revelation of the divine Person of the Son, who *is* the intelligible *lógos* of reality, the divine Word. The most intensely metaphysical is also at the same time wholly beyond it: divine *Personality*—which is beyond the distinction between actuality and possibility, and can only properly be approached by equally privileging both the intelligibility of the world in God *and* divine freedom, which is what we would expect if we assume the abstract formula that God's essence is his existence properly as an indication, as an *idea*, of the living truth and not as the definitive truth, in itself, of *who* is God.

This situation of thinking carries the interesting implication for one that the distinction between philosophy and theology is both maintained and eclipsed at the same time, since if philosophy, as Schelling taught, is judged by the adequacy of its idea of God, it is at the same time a matter merely of the idea of God, even if these ideas are scientific principles of revelation itself (e.g., Trinity, incarnation, creation). When ideas become *names* we advance through philosophy into the higher domain of the liturgical, where we find philosophy "consummated." But this is a comment to be taken up elsewhere.

The genealogist's work is therefore twofold, Milbank observes, and unified through this doubling: "to reach a level where we can regard these actions in the light of their presuppositions and theories in the light of their practical tendencies" (1). The work of the genealogist is therefore to "penetrate these shadows" in order to shed light on them, to be sure; but, as all of the foregoing implies, *not the light of scientific conceptuality*, which is implicitly predicated on the separability of mind from action and the affirmation of the former as the fundamental reality on which the latter alone is erected. Rather, the elucidation of the truth of human historical existence "runs the risk," says Milbank, of an "abstruseness" that seems implausible, but which at the same time will be presumably a mark of "authenticity" for any investigation that discerns the basic "homology" between theory and action that is the twofold appearing of "the deepest substance" of history's own occurring, at local levels, say, this or that culture, and, yes, even at a universal level, since we must assume, he stoutly observes, that the human race itself somehow shares a single culture (and a single history) that makes it, precisely, human (see p. 2).

I let the reader catch breath... All this is to say that the philosophical and the political, the seemingly most intensely elucidary points of theoretical and active appearing respectively, enjoy a historical unity that is a crucial point of their irreducible, mysterious truthfulness that always eludes our rational focus, an elusiveness that comprises, let us observe, a fundamental element of its *deeply satisfying character*: if our historical existence did not possess this quality, how terribly banal and dismal it would all be, and how little motivation there would be for theoretical reflection in the first place. Philosophy begins in *wonder* (and contra reductive rationalities, whether materialist or idealist, it does not eclipse that wonder but only enters further into it).

Milbank concludes his initial description of the "formal dimensions" of his project on the third page: the point of his examination is the discernment of the shared point of basic intelligibility that metaphysics and politics share (ultimately, as we saw initially, intensified and brought into the greatest clarity in the religious-theological domain). As we indicated, his task is of course avowedly theoretical, and will itself lie within that side of the human reality: "Within the scope of theory at least," Milbank says, "it is intended to show how ideas about being coincide with ideas about human action" (3).

The acutely theoretical character of his task is banal, and yet important. For we have to ask (to pick back up a thread we have found ourselves grasping from the start in this brief commentary) is it possible to accomplish this entrance into the "hidden dimension" through the domain of thought, "within the scope of theory," even given Milbank's rare theoretical power and complementary intensity of intellectual vision? Or do we here find ourselves in an analogous situation to wrongly privileging the distinctive (and hierarchical) relation between the Person (or, to be precise, trihypostatic Personality) of God and the idea of God, which is, arguably, a defining feature of modernity?[10] Does this attempt mirror that of Husserl's formulation (say) of the concept of the *Lebenswelt* to bring into conceptuality the pre-conceptual domain of ordinary life? And has this distinction been sufficiently recognized by Milbank or—to express this more adequately—is this recognition sufficiently present and at work in his thought? But even with this acute clarification of the question, it remains a question I continue to leave open, for it is one to which in Milbank's work the judgment can only be determined as a matter of emphasis and implication (that is: is he faithful enough to his deepest intuitions?). This is a question we must ask every thinker, and the answer is of course always "not faithful enough"; and when that response is most excellently made, truly, humanly, faithful... Doubtless, we will have to acknowledge without reservation, along with Milbank, that the theoretical is never without the practical, not only in its origins and in its implications, but also as an event in history with real effects. Clearly the book itself is already a pragmatic intervention, as he explicitly notes, and Milbank's work has always had this ad hoc character of intervention and response (but it does so *as a theoretical enterprise*, sometimes bringing with it, to express this too hastily—though in order to make the question as sharp as possible—the strong impression that it is theory that will accomplish what the Church perpetually fails to do...).[11]

The theoretical and practical are therefore always already blended in reality, and the import for theory in particular is that it should

10. And which is the most acute expression of the arguably modern privilege of theoretical expression, an activity of the mind, over practice, an activity of the body, traceable back to the first completion of Suàrezian metaphysics in Descartes. What is at stake here, in other words, is some degree of complicity of his thought with the modernity he has done so much to overcome.

11. See, for example, the common trope employed by Milbank: "what is needed...," "what we need now...," etc., followed by a theoretical assertion. See for example, "Hume versus Kant: Faith, Reason and Feeling," *Modern Theology* 27.2 (2011), 276–97; the preface to *The Future of Love: Essays in Political Theology* (London: SCM Press, 2009), ix–xx.

acknowledge this to the appropriate degree *and* in the appropriate manner. But what is immediately important in this present commentary is that this very acknowledgment, lived out as it were in the life of theory, in our books, through *what* they say as much as *how* they say it and how they *feel* to us (in, that is, their fundamental attitude, which touches a region of truth that the conceptual surface of the page only points to at best, but which it *can indeed* point to, thereby manifesting it at every point), is the litmus test, as it were, of our overcoming of the modern, defined as it is by the illusory and ultimately nihilistic conception of an objectifying rationality transparent to its own ground, to use language not far from Milbank's own delineation of this situation in this text. He understands this, as we now see:

Milbank illustrates this inseparable distinction without division between word and deed in the depths of our historical being (for which it is now clear that there is no history without human being and no human being without history) by reference to Aristotle's fundamental insight (in the *Nicomachean Ethics* and elsewhere) that "essence" (*ousia*) and "function/work" (*ergon*) are always together: something is what it is because it does what it does; "what is seen is what is done or made," he says (3).

I would like to introduce here (in order to show how the theological/religious domain maximizes the humanly intelligible) a notion not at all alien, perhaps, to Milbank, but one which, to my knowledge, he has not ever directly addressed, viz., the Palamite antinomy of *ousia/energeia* at the basis of Russian sophiology and its just as controversial companion, so-called "onomatodoxy," based on an antinomical affirmation: God is God's energies; God's energies are not God (though *at the same* time, God *is* God's essence, and God's essence is *not* God's energies).[12] If there is necessarily a fundamental distinction between God's essence and energies (insofar as, in Eastern thought, God's essence is wholly unknowable), then the

---

12. See Sergei Bulgakov, *The Philosophy of the Name*, of which the sixth chapter appears in English in *Icons and the Name of God*, trans. Boris Jakim (Grand Rapids, MI: Eerdmans, 2013).

simultaneous identification of the two is likewise just as essential and these two affirmations must be held together in a religious, that is, *human* manner (in a way that recognizes that the truth of God transcends our historical being but also founds it most deeply). The functional analogy in the West is Thomas Aquinas's idea of real relations, which is a one-way street between the world and God.

From this perspective and in this way (of "antinomy") reason is simultaneously "grounded" and always overcome, being broken open from within in its quest for (itself in) God. This antinomy likewise expresses the basic "supernatural paradox" of creation from the divine side of the equation that has fundamentally shaped Milbank's own thinking (indebted here to Henri de Lubac of course),[13] expressed pithily in Thomas's paradox of "real relation" that serves as an expression of the fundamental situation of our creaturely contingency: there is no "real relation" between *God* and the world, but only between the *world* and God.[14] Ultimately the human paradox, the hidden dimension of our humanity, is grounded in our relation to God, who is archetypally hidden in a way that we can understand analogously to our experience of ourselves in the world, the experience of our essential finitude which experiences itself most profoundly as an opening into the abyss of God (to speak like von Balthasar); or, expressed otherwise, as in David Hart's felicitous phrase, this opening itself becomes that which we have always already reached, finding ourselves passing through the divine interval, the "interval of the supernatural," in our very attainment of the "natural" itself.[15] Anthropological apophaticism is a path into theological apophaticism, and the former cannot be properly understood if it is not understood this way (*religion*, as the civilizational traditions of East and West testify, is *more philosophical* than what Blondel called a "separated philosophy"

---

13. John Milbank, *The Suspended Middle: Henri de Lubac and the Debate Concerning the Supernatural* (Grand Rapids: Eerdmans, 2005).

14. *Summa theologiae* Ia q. 45 a. 3.

15. See Hans Urs von Balthasar, *The Glory of the Lord V*, conclusion, and *Theo-Logic III*, section VII, and David B. Hart, *The Experience of God: Being, Consciousness, Bliss* (New Haven: Yale University Press, 2014).

that is itself not consumed by the perennial questions lived in religion)...[16]

## 3 Continuation (1). Distension: Intimations of "Myth *and* Reason" (3–11)

In reaching this point, we have come to understand how the "formal" dimensions of Milbank's work, sketched out in the opening pages and elaborated here, relate to the "substantive" argument that is familiar from *Theology and Social Theory*, which I can now restate: The concept of the secular—a principal concept of modern social theory, politics, and metaphysics—is thoroughly theological; intellectual genealogy discloses it to be thoroughly suspect on the hidden theological grounds proper to it. Theoretical or ontological secularism, as it were, coincides with political (or socio-historical) secularism. Uncovering the common theological root of these domains (uncovering the *radix* of "modernity," which is a basic set task of "radical orthodoxy"—a second reason why it is shortsighted to consider Milbank merely a wistful romantic for a lost Christendom) demonstrates this. If the former volume focused on social theory, the central point of his present volume is that political philosophy is best understood when it is seen to "disclose a concealed, more ultimate 'context'" that is most radically theoretical and practical at once. This ultimate context, again, is religion, the liturgical-theological domain—to state the essential, driving thesis of Milbank's entire oeuvre, which is at once so humanly obvious and equally so startlingly profound.

This leads Milbank, on pages 3–4, into an analytic elaboration of the four assumptions of *modern* ontology: (1) a univocal conception of being, replacing the earlier analogical conception; (2) representationalist epistemology, replacing paradoxical "identity"; (3) a prioritization of possibility, replacing the classical prioritization of actuality as controlling metaphysical image and category; and (4) a

16. For an acute expression of this viewpoint relative to a different philosophical toolset see Jean-Luc Marion, *Certitudes négatives*, chap. 1 (Paris: Grassett, 2010), 21–86.

conception of causality as "concurrence," replacing the earlier participatory notion of "influence." Rooted as they are in late medieval theological aberrations introduced principally by Duns Scotus and infecting later Scholastic, mainly "Iberian" interpretations of Thomas Aquinas, these four assumptions chart the coordinates for a trajectory in every case toward a "rationalist reduction of real mystery"—a reduction of the real, the necessarily wonder-ful, from mystery (and thus so eminently interesting and valuable, as we noted above, being worthy of a life lived in its pursuit, instead of, say, spending our time smoking marijuana, updating social media and watching trash television like, it seems, everyone else) to the rationally transparent or exhaustible (illusorily so—such is the argument of a believer, the *clairvoyant* and lover of the world in its transcendent mystery). I set aside the further sketches of the basic contours of the sequence on politics and the far-reaching set of eleven theses set out on pages 4–11, demonstrating, convincingly, the "revisionary" rather than "reactionary" character of Milbank's thought introduced here.[17]

Now, with what I have already commentarily summarized above, we can now begin to set our sights on some direct preparations in order to make our own pass through the ultimate passage of interest, four brief paragraphs on pages 12–13 articulating in Milbank's typical breathless fashion a set of remarkable far-reaching theses precisely regarding the nature of the Christian religion (our own, and Milbank's fundamental concern, as believers), conceived (as we have seen) as liturgical-theological *and therefore as* most radically metaphysical and political. In that section I will freely interpolate my comments in the text, thereby slowing down almost frame by frame his rapid thought in order to catch some of its brightest flashes, contemplating them and expanding on them—in order to see what they mean for our understanding of ourselves as religiously engaged in thinking about ourselves as religious, as beings in the world for whom the world does not exhaust the meaning of our-

---

17. Does the sting of Milbank's critique of our own comfortable modern "liberalism" manifest itself within the force of our own critiques of Milbank's backwards romantic "medievalism"?

selves, but which always offers out to us an ever-elusive transcendence. But that remains a few pages away. Further introduction is still necessary:

We must first observe that this passage to be analyzed in section 4 below emerges as the high point of a summary reflection on the main contours of the sequel to the present volume, mentioned above. This volume, in being concerned with the religious, with the *Divine Government*, with the logic and events of God's activity vis-à-vis the world, centered on human history from the meta-historical vanishing points of creation and resurrection, will show forth all the more directly, says Milbank, the homology between the ontological and the praxeological with which we are now familiar, *inasmuch as* its subject matter is all the greater than the regional "matters" of politics or social theory—even "ever-greater," we could add, thereby noting for one the fact that these "regional" disciplines are not closed off from that with which the theological is concerned.

The mystery of God, as modern thinkers from Hegel onward knew, though not radically enough—and to sound again the distinctive chord of the manner of thinking we discern here—discloses to us the deepest mystery about ourselves. Milbank here explicitly divides religious "discourse" into two complementary and surely perennially conjoined halves, the *mythic* and the *theological*, whereas religious action is conceived in the familiar way as liturgical or ritual. This introduction of the distinction and union of myth and theology *as con-jointly rational* is a truly post-modern starting point for reflection, and we can trace this recognition of the rationality of myth on its own terms—at least in the modern period—to Schelling.[18] It may be that Milbank suggests a new rapprochement between myth and theology, that, after Heidegger, but here already beyond him, recognizes the universality of the mythic in all of our reasoning—*particularly* when we are reasoning about reason itself.

18. Schelling, the father of modern mythology, for whom, *after Vico* (a major figure in Milbank's formation), myth is considered on its own terms, not merely as a confused proto-rationality anticipating philosophy or science (as in Aristotle or Hegel) but rather as coincident with its own logic in the very form in which it appears. See Milbank, *The Religious Dimensions of the Thought of Giambattista Vico* (1668–1744), vols. 1–2 (Lewiston, NY: Edwin Mellen Press, 1991/1993).

We will have to see if there are intimations below of the nature of the relation of the mythic and theological, and subsequently their necessary co-existence and collaboration vis-à-vis the ritual domain.

For the moment, though, we already have enough here to fulfill the obligation gestured to above with a brief, interpolary comment on the threefold distinction of the intelligible into mythic, metaphorical, and rational modes.

On the one hand, there is the basic distinction between the mythic and the rational with which we are familiar as inhabitants of an Enlightenment mythology of *Logos vom Mythos*; on the other hand, the supplementary distinction between the metaphoric and the rational emerges from the primary distinction, and harbors, if properly understood, a way of overcoming the Enlightenment's own mythic space for the sake of fidelity to the relation of language and reality in ourselves. In short, the recognition of the ubiquity of myth for and within reason requires that we rethink the metaphysical priority in the supplementary distinction. Instead of saying with Nietzsche that our truths are "dead metaphors," which is where we invariably end up within the Enlightenment mythology, we would have instead to entertain the seemingly remarkable but at the same time more self-evident idea that the metaphorical is the site of our greatest encounter with the truth of things—that living metaphors manifest to us the truths that transcend us, especially our conceptual grasps. The meta-phoric in this meta-physical sense is a third way, beyond the opposition between the merely mythic on the one hand, though recognizing it as a perennial and necessary dimension of reason, and the merely rational on the other, though recognizing the religious validity of its purification of our thinking. In short, the highest way is to see the deepest roots of our reasoning as human and historical precisely as metaphorical *and*, as such, the deepest path into the divine (the metaphorical here being understood, of course, as paradoxically "realist"). We will have to keep this basic taxonomy in mind when we undertake the direct commentary on our passage below, which will explicate what we only anticipatorily and hence incompletely adumbrate schematically here.

Presently, Milbank only more acutely sounds his inaugural thesis that a remarkably intensified correspondence between the theoretical and practical is found in religion, and which is therefore the ultimate key that fits the lock to the "hidden dimension" of our historical being, and which, most radically, he believes—he is "Christian" after all—is found in Christianity. He thus states: "These observations begin to suggest that religion is always the most fundamental domain of human history and specifically human experience. Here the hidden but assumed [finally] emerges partially into the light" (11).

A subsidiary comment again appears necessary. This, which happens to be Milbank's signature assertion, is so utterly traditional a conviction and ought to be so uncontroversial to historically sensitive readers that I continue to be amazed at the way this pseudo-issue has become so remarkably faux-dramatic among theologians in particular, for does not the believer have the right to believe that religion, and even in fact his own religion, possesses a unique pride of place? And if one's religion does not, then one's metaphysics does—these coinciding at this level, where one symbolizes one's otherwise invisible relation to the ultimate conditions of one's existence. Is not the conviction itself the mark of belief and its intensity itself the measure of the authenticity of one's faith—so intense perhaps, as is the case at least for Christianity, to give one the capacity to see the one Creator God involved, even soteriologically, in and through the religions of his neighbors? I only ask the question with some perplexity, but I do not express myself lightly. If Milbank's fundamental thesis as a genealogist regarding the secular is right, then this traditional conviction is back on the table, and the critic must be willing—at least in an imaginative manner, which is the means toward a higher and richer manner of *critique*, through, that is, understanding the best one can something from within its own logic, a manner of critique that is in the first place an extension of Augustinian *charity*—to face this possibility head on and measure one's thinking by it at least in intellectual practice, if only better to grasp the implications of this very engagement. Surely, despite all appearances, this is not asking too much from serious, or at least aspiring, intellectuals today?[19]

Let it be said as well that this Christian perspective on the whole ought not to be controversial for one determined to speak within the horizon of his own faith tradition, to be faithful to his faith (the greatest and most engaging task for thought), and determined not to take a facile shortcut and feign a sort of god-like master position outside of "religions," able somehow to determine them all in a grand intellectual scheme vis-à-vis one's own laughably limited position (Milbank's thought is in this way, perhaps, more humble than the latter faux-humility of rationalist Christian theologians and masked, secular political theologians who use religion as a means to confirm their bourgeois academic irreligiosity as authentically religious, or for the sake of its socio-political power as a means to the accomplishment of a predictable socio-political agenda).[20] Is this all theology really is?

## 4 Continuation (2). Intensification: An Adumbrated "History of Religions" (11–12)

As we make a final approach to our intended passage, we first must descend through the clouds of a mini-history of religions in three paragraphs (11–12) meant to sketch the basic lineaments of the rise of philosophy within religion—which gestures towards the (impossible to prove) shared inheritance of a number of the major faith-

---

19. Note I do not say "academics," or specifically, "*mere* academics," who are too often hopelessly ideological mouthpieces for the status quo—equivalent to the "assistant professors" castigated by Kierkegaard. I say this, recognizing first in myself this very tendency... Although, laboring in a warehouse full-time and attempting to retain some intellectual life as an adjunct professor does temper in oneself what classical thinkers called intellectual "pride."

20. I could refer the reader to Milbank's own comment at the beginning of his contribution to *The Monstrosity of Christ*, noted above, and to his essay "The New Divide: Romantic versus Classical Orthodoxy," *Modern Theology* 26.1 (January 2010), 26–38.

civilizations and even moments of foundational interaction of Indian, Ancient Near Eastern, and Greek-European worlds. This is a thesis that was already exposed long ago tantalizingly if also necessarily incompletely by linguists, and always returns dramatically into view through the most suggestive scholarship. The sketch Milbank provides is quick and broad, as is his fashion, but its lineaments are clear and suggestive, resting, I think, on a few valid insights. I reproduce the logic of them here in further adumbrated fashion, but expanded, again, with commentary.

Beginning with the important observation that all religions are *not the same*, Milbank notes that their irreducible differences are nevertheless in actuality expressions of various approaches or responses to a universal situation, an ultimacy that defines humanity as such, as we will shortly see: the relation to the "reserve" of the ultimate. This defining situation, Milbank rightly implies here, involves the cosmic whole (termed the "world" by modern philosophers), the totality of all that is in its implicit unity, vaguely intuited at the root of consciousness. There is also involved, as a second step, already implied as a possibility within the first, the understood necessary "question" of the reason for the whole (though only conceived as such through explicit reflection), the meaning of being as such. Myth is an ineffable grasping of the ineffable mystery of creation, the living intuition of the contingency of what is. Religion mediates this grasp and makes possible, and even requires, "philosophical" reflection on the whole. This basic "question" that defines the second step, which is the negative form of the native recognition of mythic consciousness, that we in our finitude are not ultimate, is *existential*, and most importantly, it seems to me, irreducibly *religious and philosophical at once*. It was expressed, let us observe, classically by Leibniz and then Schelling and Heidegger (at one stage) as essential: "Why is there something rather than nothing?"[21] This is

---

21. Leibniz, "The Principles of Nature and Grace, Based on Reason," *Leibniz: Selections*, trans. Philip P. Weiner (NY: Simon and Schuster, 1957), 527; Schelling, *Philosophie der Offenbarung, Ausgewählte Werke* (Darmstadt, Wissenschaftliche Buchgesellschaft, 1990), t. I; Heidegger, *Introduction to Metaphysics* (New Haven: Yale, 1959).

the way philosophy invariably understands myth. But the question immediately arises: how do we describe these approaches to what we now call *philosophical* questions that religions already most acutely imply? And what is the form of their basic implications? This is the task of Milbank's mini-history of religions.

"Many religions," says Milbank, "relate themselves, both theoretically and practically to a cosmic level which they take to be less than ultimate.... Effectively they deal with metonymic or synecdochic substitutes for this ultimacy" (11). We will examine directly these specific *figures of substitution* below, and remain directly engaged with their general character here. What is this "substitution"? To elaborate—and this seems to be restating a basic insight of Mircea Eliade—the polytheistic religions understood or understand themselves as utilizing material or worldly means to reach the gods that transcend them—requiring, in order to be a living religion, a sustained distinction between the material idol of wood or stone and the god itself. But also, to take this one essential step further, firmly implied within the logic of this figurative "substitution" is the additional distinction that the gods, being understood as cosmic powers, always directly raise: their existence raises the question of the ultimate divine behind them and to which they are permanently— *like* the humans they terrify and thrill—finally subject.[22] This distinction in other words, to return to Milbank, is articulated through mythical narration, and typically if not universally involves a *violent* rending at the origin of the cosmic order (as in traditional creation accounts of India, Greece, and the Ancient Near East—Israel excepted, though the Genesis account itself of course depends on earlier traditions that bear this stamp of a primordial violence with which it is critically engaged). There seems to be a persistent if not ubiquitous shadowy awareness of some nameless ultimate, *more* negatively manifest through myth: the wars of the gods created the present cosmic order, but what is *their* reason for being? What logic, law, principle, governs the initial cataclysm behind the present order, and in many accounts, the endless cycles of order and disorder? In this way there opens up, says Milbank, "a reserved

22. See Eliade, *The Sacred and the Profane* (Orlando, FL: Harcourt, 1987).

space of mystery that is sometimes occupied by a posited but unknown"—and let us add normatively *unknowable*—"'high god'" (11).


In anticipation of the further steps to be made, I can mention here the resonances of this starting point (and the logic that follows) with that of St. Paul on the Areopagus in Acts 17, "arguing every day with the Jews and the God-fearing pagans in the Synagogue and with whoever happened to be in the agora" (v. 17). The Epicureans and Stoics, explicitly mentioned in Acts, considered that he spoke "nonsense," seemingly advocating "strange deities," *Iesou* (Jesus) and *Anastasia* (resurrection) (18). But when allowed to make a formal address, Paul appeals to the scrupulous religiosity exemplified by the various temples and idols with which the city was so alarmingly replete (16), focusing his attention famously on the altar to the Unknown God, proposing a correlation between their worship of a? the? god that is not known and the one Creator God who is the covenant Lord of the people Israel, who created all in heaven and earth (24), and, being absolutely unique, does not dwell in temples and cannot be represented by the products of human artistry (25). What the biblical author accomplishes here is a remarkable correlation to make, and it is difficult not to see a profoundly theological point made through this dramatization of an encounter between the Apostle to the Gentiles and the cradle of Greek culture and philosophy. To suggest that the Greeks "unknowingly worship" the God of Israel by virtue of this exemplary instance is to say that the broader truth is only synecdochally represented by the physical altar dedicated *Agnósto Theō*. Pagan polytheism is an anticipatory form, a "groping after" and "seeking" (27) the God who is always evident through the intelligible order and beauty of the cosmos (26). This "natural theology" of paganism, tending towards the one Creator God and blindly brushing into him at every point but always tragically incapable of finding him, is set in bold by the Apostle's appeal to the witness of pagan poets (28). God, the absolute source of "life and breath" for all things (25) is himself "not far from any of us" (27): "in him we live and move and have our being" (28). Because the Creator is not far off, being evident in the basic intelligibility that pervades everything that is, and because he is the source of our life and we are his "offspring" (here the Apostle appeals through a pagan poet to the Genesis account, which calls Adam the "son of God" and to its theological anthropology of image found there), *therefore* we ought not represent God with "images formed through skill and thought" (29): God is not like *these* things, says Paul; instead, *man is like God*. To think of the divine in mere polytheistic terms is *ágnoias*, "ignorance" (30); to put the created thing before the Creator, to misplace one's worship, is to denigrate, grossly, one's own humanity. The God "unknowingly worshiped" in paganism's best moments, albeit in ignorance, only manifests the crisis situation for humanity that the Creator graciously resolves through the resurrection from the dead of the "righteous man he appointed" to judge the world (30–31) *and* his sustaining a period (the present era of Apostolic preaching) for all humans to "repent" before the impending dread day of last judgment, funneled through the "man appointed," Jesus, Israel's Anointed, when the pure fire of the righteousness of the finally *Known God* will be revealed to all. To know this God, for the Apostle, is to believe in his consummate act in the world, the resurrection of Jesus.

This entire narrative is clearly a summative account of the earliest apostolic preaching in its essentials. The metaphysics of God and world forms the necessary backdrop to understanding the historical activity of God that reaches its decisive moment in the death and resurrection of the Messiah of Israel, meant to bring the entire creation into its originally intended but inchoate destiny in the eternal life of resurrection that renews all things.

What matters in the present context are the following dimensions, which agree with Milbank's sketch here: the enchanting but necessarily unfocused proto-monotheistic unitive mystery behind the mythic horizon penetrated in a shadow way by philosophy, giving birth to an unfolding (one could even say "dialectical") account of the mythic and philosophical modes of wrestling with humanity's ultimate situation, and the basic role this "space of reservation" plays in the [logic of the] history of religions. The latter will be presently elaborated.

It is this reserve toward the absolute, a sacred humility and aware-ness of human finitude before the unknowable, basic to myth, says Milbank following some indications from Thomas McEvilley's mag-num opus, *The Shape of Ancient Thought* (2002), that serves as the condition and means for the emergence of "philosophy," as it did in both ancient Greece and India—philosophy that claims for itself the capacity to deal with this level of reserve, the ultimate reality presup-posed by but beyond mythical vision, and to be present to it through a fundamental intuition. This new boldness toward the reserve in myth led to a transformation within myth itself, which came to identify the transcendent unapproachable shadowy mystery beyond the whole *with* the all of the cosmos, as *en kai pan*, "one and all."[23] Milbank, like the great Russian philosopher Alexei F. Losev, identi-fies as fundamental to much myth, and to the cosmology of ancient thought shared by myth and philosophy (through the fundamental myth inside of philosophy), the envisioning of the universe as a human body, the concept of the "cosmic man" or *Macranthropos* (common to Indian, Ancient Near Eastern, and Greek civiliza-tions).[24] The earliest philosophy in the West (that of the so-called "Pre-Socratics") is likewise defined by the question of this domain of transcendent reserve, but, in identifying this domain with being as such, is marked by a tendency to "reserve" being itself, understood as the original showing forth of that which is as an object of contem-plative knowledge separable from rituality and ascetic practice, the form of intelligibility of which is mythic narration. Both the cosmic man and this separation of being from the embodied mythicality of ritual led to a radical immanentist monism, which replaced the "rule" of figurative substitution basic to mythic consciousness with an evacuated monistic conceptuality or proto-conceptuality.

So myth always harboured the possibility and even necessity of philosophy, and contained within itself in narrative, quasi-allegori-

23. Thomas McEvilley, *The Shape of Ancient Thought* (NY: Allworth Press, 2001).
24. See Losev's "Twelve Theses on Antique Culture," *Arion* II/1, 2003, 55–70, and McEvilley, *The Shape of Ancient Thought*, chapter 2.

66

cal and imagistic modalities, a sort of proto-philosophy, but harboured it "negatively," as it were, in a sort of negative theology *avant la lettre* by means of the fundamental mythic attitude of reserve toward the shadowy ultimate expressed through myth. Philosophy arises within myth as proto-theology, claiming to deal "rationally" with the absolute, to penetrate into its paradoxes and to express them. But both myth and philosophy tended in this very same reductive direction—the former through the macroanthropic identification of the beyond with the whole, of the "high" with the "all," and the latter through the defining separation of rationally contemplated being from the practice of embodied (ritual) encounter with the totality of the cosmos in its fundamental living principles and through them brushing up against the unfathomable donating Source of the all, the unnameable Life itself. This latter separation for the sake of grasping the unnameable source by a (philosophical) rationality that aspires to a monotheistic or proto-monotheistic grasp of the root of the world's intelligibility was only possible at the cost of replacing the dense intelligibility of figurative substitution— more proper to transcendent reality conceived as *living*, but also always risking anthropomorphic reduction—for a conceptual identification seemingly requiring a univocal monism and, I could add, a reduction of the life of the Source to abstract idea.

The choice between violent myth and reduction of mystery, between figurative encounter and rationalist monism, seemed absolute, although the way out is anticipated *by means of* the common monist reduction of mystery shared by myth and early philosophy, since philosophical and religious integrity depended on a fundamental reaction to this reduction—a way out that was already enacted to some degree by the Platonic-Aristotelian current(s) of Greek thought in their "proto-Christian" philosophical monotheism.[25] The passage from myth to "critical rationality" is one version of *lógos*. Logos$_1$ or the philosophical *lógos* passes through critique

---

25. For a statement of the critique of Milbank's contradiction of his metaphysics of peace, see Gavin Hyman, *The Predicament of Postmodern Theology: Radical Orthodoxy or Nihilist Textualism?* (Louisville: Westminster John Knox, 2001), 73 ff.

(monism) to meta-critique of reason itself in favor of the divine "reserve" that, reason discovers, can only best be signified through figuration. The other version, logos$_2$ is the stream of divine revelation that culminates in the incarnation of the divine Word. It too pursues a remarkable criticism of the mythic inheritance of humanity that it absorbs, but its passage through is founded on a lived faith in the living God, who transcends every conceptual grasp, exposing the farthest strained reaches of rationality as in need of similar reform as the mythic itself.

The choice between an "ontology of violence or peace" is a classic expression of Milbank's approach. Since *Theology and Social Theory* at least, he has argued for the Christian vision of metaphysical "peace," rooted in the gift exchange of the Holy Trinity that founds *creation ex nihilo,* as the only viable alternative to the "metaphysics of violence" of paganism and that behind contemporary postmodern nihilism, only the unveiled mask of modernity. Although Milbank has been accused of proffering a hermeneutical violence onto the tradition by means of errant interpretations of key figures (Plato, Augustine, Thomas), these do not reach the vision itself, only Milbank's presentation of it. Besides, as we see here, the proposal is one of "blending" (of Greek and Jewish traditions) and transformation from within over time through the leaven of revelation, a transformation that includes the modern age, however aberrant it has, at moments, become.

## 5 A Metaphilosophy of Revelation: Commentarial Analysis in Four Frames (12–13)

The stage now set, we enter directly into the cradle of *Christianity* (and Rabbinic Judaism and Islam too). My promised "frame by frame" commentary on the passage of interest now follows.

The reader may benefit from a continuous reading of the critical passage under analysis. Since the original text is so brief, I thought it would be useful to set it out here in its original form before the four-frame explication:

> By almost unique contrast with other cultures, the ancient Hebrews refused what they saw as the "idolatry" of metonymic or synecdochic substitution. Instead, they risked an open-ended metaphoric tension with the ultimate, whereby figurative substitutions of finite for infinite had also to be suspiciously negated, since they were not simply of part for whole or effect for cause, but rather of obscure symbol for obscurely symbolized. In consequence, new and more adequate substitutions had to be constantly sought and then negated in their turn. Thus neither the exclusive worship of the high god, nor the refusal of "idolatrous" substitutions is what truly marks the novelty of Israel, but rather its invention of not just a mythos, but also a restrained cultus of the ultimate. The ark of the covenant may have been unspectacular and frail, but *that* was Israel's crucial invention.
>
> Precisely because its ritual referred to the one creator God, there developed in Israel no "philosophy" since reflexivity was not here alienated to the level of abstraction. Instead, because it was retained at the level of linguistic tropes, reflexivity was also doubled, since the import of metaphorical rule is that the ultimate as "being" lies both (as for philosophy) beyond action and contingency, and yet also (unlike philosophy) not beyond, since in only action and event is reality ever manifest. As Hebrew rituals peculiarly claimed to reach the absolute, the blend of representation of being with enacted norm proper to ritual was naturally never negated even in the projection of transcendence.
>
> When, with Philo and others, the Jewish tradition met with Greek philosophy, it arrived at an explicit third moment of reflection beyond its own implicit double reflexivity from narrated action to being and back again to action. As it had so far tacitly taken God to be being (as in Exodus) and his law to be an ontology of the Creation (as in Numbers, Leviticus, and the Wisdom literature), so now it openly proclaimed that Greek being was in fact God, and the Greek order of the cosmos was a matter of divinely willed legality. Christian and later Islamic thought duly followed suit.
>
> But as we have already intimated, this synthesis of *nomos* with *ousia* was only possible because Plato and Aristotle had already to

some degree, by reinvoking a mythos of a transcendent realm "activated" the ultimate *ousia* and in Plato's case identified the ultimate source more as the active source of radiating normativity than "abiding" being. This new note of peaceful donation of the cosmos contrasts both with the violent generative break with transcendence enshrined in earlier myth, and with the alternative myths of sacrificial partition of the cosmic man that continued to inflect the perspectives of the first immanentist philosophy. However, the first philosophical mythographers of transcendence had not quite arrived at the monotheistic sense of God as an outgoing will and self-deliberating intelligence.

Here I interpolate my annotations in insets following portions of the full text cited above.

## FRAME 1

"By almost unique contrast with other cultures, the ancient Hebrews refused what they saw as the 'idolatry' of metonymic or synecdochic substitution."

The mythic character of Ancient Near Eastern religious consciousness (shared in common with Greek and Indian civilizations, making the "history of religions" possible at all), characterized, as we have seen, by a sacred reserve and figurative substitution as in other civilizational loci, was originally critiqued within the religion of ancient Judaism itself from the beginning, albeit based on a monotheistic exclusivism that deepened through the development of Israel's faith through the drama of her history. This is so commonly observed in academic exegesis of Genesis 1–3 that it needs no further comment. It is highlighted by the fundamentally non-violent character of the creation myth as is well known. (Whatever traces it contains of such Ancient Near Eastern creation myths, this violent cosmogony is not foregrounded, and this is precisely the miracle.) The point, in other words, is that a unique horizon of religious reasoning, of "wisdom," is already found intrinsic to the character of the faith of the biblical people. The original "enlightenment" by logos$_2$ in other words, the discernment of the free origin of creation and therefore its unique intelligibility, and a simultaneous liberation from the oppressive, violent

powers, the gods, who controlled through fear, is here, in ancient
Israel, identified with religious, ritual faith and its origin myth.[26]

"Instead, they risked an open-ended metaphoric tension with the
ultimate, whereby figurative substitutions of finite for infinite had
also to be suspiciously negated, since they were not simply of part
for whole or effect for cause, but rather of obscure symbol for
obscurely symbolized."

> These substitutions are seen as necessary, but the development of
> Israel's religious consciousness as seen in the later prophetic litera-
> ture—which itself can be understood as a constant religious medi-
> tation on the creation-exodus narrative(s), and already within the
> reconstructed history of the redaction of the Pentateuch itself,
> unfolding from this "beginning"—means that these substitutions
> are always at the same time not enough. They must be kept in play
> and at the same time *and with the same fundamentality* rejected.
> This is the basic *antinomy* of such religious awareness, and it
> exceeds the rationalism of *mere* philosophy, that is, any reductive
> philosophical rationalism (dialectically excluding the divine from
> the totality, thereby instituting an ontology of "competition"
> between divine being, reduced to the force of will over against the
> world, in conceptually-driven reaction to the monistic identifica-
> tion the divine with the world), and at the same time exceeds the
> stasis of mere figurative substitution, capturing and sustaining
> therefore the best of both pagan polytheism, with its awareness of
> the living, personal character of the highest realities, and philo-
> sophical proto-monotheistic critique, with its simultaneous con-
> tradictory rejection of anthropomorphic reduction and reinstating
> of a veiled and more pernicious reduction of rationalist transpar-
> ency of the ultimate. This is possible because it already transcend-
> ing them from the beginning.

"In consequence, new and more adequate substitutions had to be

---

26. On this identity of an "original" enlightenment and liberation with the biblical religion, see Joseph Ratzinger, *In the Beginning: A Catholic Understanding of
the Story of Creation and Fall* (Grand Rapids, MI: Eerdmans, 1995). See also, of
course, though from a different perspective regarding the continuity of this primal
enlightenment with the modern, European "Enlightenment," Moses Mendelssohn's
*Jerusalem* (1783) and the later Neo-Kantian Hermann Cohen's *Religion of Reason
Out of the Sources of Judaism* (1919).

constantly sought and then negated in their turn. Thus neither the exclusive worship of the high god, nor the refusal of 'idolatrous' substitutions is what truly marks the novelty of Israel, but rather its invention of not just a mythos, but also a restrained cultus of the ultimate."

> The mythos and "restrained" cult at the center of Israel's life already inscribes within it the highest reaches of philosophical, critical proto-monotheism, *and* a higher critique of them precisely through a figurative substitution that directly knew itself as such and knew that this was necessary in order to be related to the living God, the free source of life.

"The ark of the covenant may have been unspectacular and frail, but *that* was Israel's crucial invention."

> The unapproachable Creator God, who is by his free action at the same time approachable; the God of Israel is invisible *and* visible. To see him is both death *and* life. The way of abstraction (mere philosophy) and the way of substitution (mere mythology) are both dead-ends when pursued alone, and only when held together simultaneously by the higher revelation are the unique path forged by ancient Israel and to which the Jewish people today are a *miraculously* enduring witness.

Before passing to the second frame, an extended comment on the schematic of linguistic tropes implied by the discussion.

Synecdoche and metonymy are figures of speech that are closely aligned. Synecdoche is commonly the figurative substitution of a part for the whole or the reverse; metonymy is the substitution of an attribute, an aspect or an affiliate for that about which one is speaking. Synecdoche: "My Husserl is sitting on the shelf," or "Can you drink the cup that I drink?" Metonymy: "The English crown has determined to go to war with Spain," or "Heaven will judge the truth." Both can probably be considered to be sub-species of metaphor, if we understand the latter classically, that is, to be essentially a matter of substitution, viz., putting an identity in play between aspects of analogous things in order to illumine the character of one thing in light of another. Metaphor is the intensification of the basic mechanism in play in all signification. Developing this awareness, when most radically conceived, however, in a way that exceeds the classical context from Aristotle and Quintilian onwards, that is, when we consider the religious context as fundamental and perhaps paradigmatic for all meaning, *therefore* considering metaphor no less than ontologically, involving, that is, a real "expansion" of human awareness regarding fundamental reality and as such an "expansion" of reality itself, since reality is the holistic intertwining of being and consciousness (as Jüngel puts it in his famous essay), then we enter into a fundamental revision of these accepted hierarchies of meaning. Here, in religion (as in the best art), paradoxically, the most "literal" is the most figurative, which is why the poets always exceed philosophers in matters of truth, and figures grasp the real in greater ways than concepts.[27] In terms of religious signification most generally speaking, we can say that metaphor is the use of inner-worldly categories, native to ourselves as historical beings, to signify that which exceeds the world and its categories. Insofar as metaphor recognizes its essentially illicit character, inasmuch as the inner-worldly is always essentially inappropriate for the Absolute, and simultaneously recognizes the necessity of this substitution, it is *analogical*, containing within itself the entire pathos of negative theology from critique to metacritique by excess. And metaphor, as a result, is the normal, everyday form of that which at a rigorous conceptual level is considered [the doctrine of] analogy.

Milbank is using these figures of speech less as kinds of religious signification, and more as types of understanding of relation with the ultimate that results in religious signification. If knowledge proceeds from the better-known to the lesser-known, and we know the lesser known by reference to the better known (as Aristotle put it), then metaphysics is always the opening up of the unknown through metaphorical knowing. Concepts emerge out of embodied experience: the empirical unfolds itself through experience in which comparison with what is already given as known gives rise to conceptual fixing of an identity to what is sought to be known: the lesser-

27. Eberhard Jüngel, "Metaphorical Truth," *Theological Essays,* vol. 1 (London: T&T Clark, 2000), 16–72.

known becomes better known, but only by analogously partaking from the already-known based on the *metaphysical wager* that what is already known is grounded in the unknown-but-to-be-known *because* more knowable in itself. The transcendent God is known by reference to the immanent world of experience, and through this experience inasmuch as this world can propose itself as a plane of separation between the self and God, a plane that becomes transparent to the divine as a point of contact, a medium of communication. The world, while remaining wholly itself in its integral coherence, can become hieroglyphs of the higher, divine world and thereby expose its deep religious character, as the ancient traditions of human culture attest together. And to grasp this, according to the religious vision, is to grasp the world itself.

## FRAME 2

"Precisely because its ritual referred to the one creator God, there developed in Israel no 'philosophy,' since reflexivity was not here alienated to the level of abstraction."

> Or rather, we could simultaneously say that for Israel cult was philosophical and simultaneously beyond it, and by extension daily life in Israel was philosophical, since cult, the worship of the one Creator God, extended from the priestly-caste-led sacrificial system centered at the Jerusalem temple in creatively overlapping tension with the royal house of David and his heirs, into the whole of life. For the priestly caste was, despite its prerogatives, only one family among equal families of the sons of Israel, that of Levi, albeit for whom a special role was apportioned (though again balanced with the fact that they had no land inheritance, since "the LORD himself is their inheritance"). Josephus therefore only somewhat surreptitiously called the various movements within Israel "philosophies." In fact, if what I have already explicated is correct, this cult was more than philosophy and certainly no less than philosophical, probably best called *hyper-philosophical*, to use a key Christian theologico-philosophical theme: the Temple cult in its gestures contained and surpassed philosophical reflection. In other words, in this biblical tradition, the one God gives himself an opportunity to be known: logos$_2$. This knowledge is of the

highest kind, one of personal "face to face" presence, a companionship and collaboration, an Edenic intimacy established by God, lost by humanity, and sought for by God through sacred history. This tradition is carried forward in Christianity. The logos in God is transliterated, normatively, into the world as the man whose identity is divine.

"Instead, because it was retained at the level of linguistic tropes, reflexivity was also doubled, since the import of metaphorical rule is that the ultimate as 'being' lies both (as for philosophy) beyond action and contingency, and yet also (unlike philosophy) not beyond, since in only action and event is reality ever manifest."

As we anticipated above. It is worth quoting Milbank's footnote attached to this sentence: "One might remark here that philosophy is perfectly capable of apophaticism, but not of 'mystical theology' in Dionysius the Areopagite's sense: that is, not of the negation of the negation, of the surpassing of negation as well as affirmation." And let me italicize the concluding sentence of this note: "*For affirmation of what lies beyond the unknown requires an appeal to* mythos *and* symbolon."[28] Yes we are dealing here with the defining religious miracle at the heart of biblically-inspired reflection: *affirmation*. This affirmation is double and irreducible; if we can, following Bulgakov and Florensky, let's try to bring this into a higher clarity: the highest "yes" beyond the "yes" of synecdochic or metonymic affirmation, and the "no" of later (late Antique) critical negation that rejected and affirmed the monism (affirming because positing beyond it solely the Ineffable, but rejecting it as the highest by positing the ineffable there). It is an affirmation that affirms both the "yes" and "no" at once, witnessing to the higher divine freedom (that is paradoxically and irreducibly, again, *antinomically* one with its intelligibility). This highest as affirmation is higher than a highest as negation because it recognizes the freedom of the highest to overcome the rational strictures of both substitution and critical negation *and* the absolute monism that sustains them both. Beyond the unknown, the hyper-unknown is more radical than the most radical negative theology of the philosophers: say, Damascius, who was the radical terminus of pagan Neoplatonism. It is more radical because the speculative is *more*

28. On page 12, note 18.

*speculative* when "blended"—let us say, "held together irreducibly as mutually reinforcing"—with the presence ritually "made" present, and with the practical "appeal to *mythos* and *symbolon*" that it requires for speculation to continue *through* the ritual encounter. Divine freedom in the biblically-inspired ritual meta-philosophical faith is compelled to become manifest through the covenant "binding" brought about in ritual "renewal" of the original covenant even at the heart of logos$_2$.

"As Hebrew rituals peculiarly claimed to reach the absolute, the blend of representation of being with enacted norm proper to ritual was naturally never negated even in the projection of transcendence."

> The mythic-ritual-philosophical impulses are *uniquely* held together in a total theological horizon that is embodied and enacted in the ritual encounter itself. Understood as expressing the personal knowledge given in a companionship- and collaboration-type presence that is given as promised, as a symbolic place-holder for a finally given presence at the end, that is, sacramentally and eschatologically, this mythic-ritual-philosophical impulse expresses the full picture of logos$_2$.

We have now penetrated in this commentarial explication deeply into the result of the encounter between this tradition of the Hebrews and Greek civilization after the Alexandrian conquest (conditioned by these mythic commonalities elaborated above) for the sake of elaborating Milbank's intuitions anticipatorily—following his lead through his introduction of the Areopagite in a note. Presently, however, he directly introduces the upshot of the encounter.

## FRAME 3

"When, with Philo and others, the Jewish tradition met with Greek philosophy, it arrived at an explicit third moment of reflection beyond its own implicit double reflexivity from narrated action to being and back again to action."

The encounter with the Greek tradition was not merely one of critique but of development through which what is already contained in the dynamism of Israel's faith and her reflection on it is uniquely brought forth. This productive encounter is already intrinsic to the literature of the biblical corpus itself (e.g., in the Wisdom literature and of course the New Testament). To summarize acutely, a new "name" of God, as it were, is introduced, or rather, made explicit:

"As it had so far tacitly taken God to be being (as in Exodus) and his law to be an ontology of the Creation (as in Numbers, Leviticus, and the Wisdom literature), so now it openly proclaimed that Greek being was in fact God, and the Greek order of the cosmos was a matter of divinely willed legality."

In Exodus God reveals his name: "I am," and the passage of reflective return to its sources that elaborates on its fundamental themes from Numbers/Leviticus to Wisdom literature (and made explicit in the later rabbinical commentary) recognizes the Law itself to be an expression of the intelligible framework that holds together the creation, its underlying logic or "metaphysics." The first identification, made explicitly thematic in Aquinas and famously defended in the 20$^{th}$ century by Gilson, is of course controversial, given the possible interpretations of the revelation of the Name to Moses in the Exodus passage (as the refusal of a name at all: *I am who I am*; as the promise of faithful presence: *I will be* who I am; etc.). And yet it is a product of the LXX: *ego eimi ho on—I am the One Who Is*. Given all that, the point to be brought out here is not merely a matter of the traditional place this "correlation" of God and being has in Christianity, but rather the fact that it was first possible and remains essential to it that the "identification" is principally conceived metaphorically or symbolically, that is, mythically, and not *merely* figurative-substitutionally, on the one hand, or *merely* abstract-conceptually, on the other, but somehow including the sense of both in a higher or more fundamental mode: beyond critique there is the return of the "rule" of metaphor over divine signification that is meta-critical, and which requires the resulting inhabitation of a new "naïveté." That is to say, the identification of God and being, taken as a "metaphor"—and as metaphor understood in a radically *realist* sense—is made possible by the recognition of the absolute character of God as Creator, not only as freely correlated himself with the creation but also as both like and unlike the being of creation, and both sides equally.

"Christian and later Islamic thought duly followed suit."

> In the case of Christianity (and in fact Islam too), the identification "openly proclaimed" between God and "Greek" being, the path of thinking God through metaphysical categories, means that God can be called Being, eminently, and at the same time "beyond Being"; God can be rightly conceived as "nothing" (as in Erigena among others) *and* as the "not-other" (*non-aliud*), as in Nicholas of Cusa. Thinking in regard to God is equally unsettled wherever it lands and only the holding together of extreme opposition leads us to what we can call the truth of God captured (in an uncapturable way!) by the finite mind: the history of Christian dogma in the Patristic era throws this in our face again and again, demanding that we make this *coincidentia oppositorum* a principle of our reasoning about the divine. Thinking God as the Creator requires an *eclipse of the world*, the assertion of an absolute "difference" between God and the world that exceeds the basic categories by which we can think in the world, like same-different, part-whole, etc.[29]

## FRAME 4

"But as we have already intimated, this synthesis of *nomos* with *ousia* was only possible because Plato and Aristotle had already to some degree, by reinvoking a mythos of a transcendent realm 'activated' the ultimate *ousia* and in Plato's case identified the ultimate source more as the active source of radiating normativity than 'abiding' being."

> The height of pagan reflection reached forward into this domain, as the Church Fathers, following Philo and other Jewish-Hellenist thinkers, were certainly convinced. Plato in particular saw and enacted the necessarily mythic manner of approach, the collaboration required between myth and philosophical contemplation, and the ever-unfinished character of such reasoning: one must

29. See Robert Sokolowski, *The God of Faith and Reason* (Washington, DC: Catholic University of America Press, 1995).

always return to re-immersion in the ritual enactment of the mythic embrace of the whole that opens to the Most High God. This embrace took the paradoxically necessary shape of something like the contemplative "concept" of creation *ex nihilo*, or at least the major notion within it that creation is not understood as cause and effect on the same plane, as in our everyday experience of cause and effect, for which the cause is equal to that which it effects, but rather that the effect is ever contained wholly within the cause and therefore the cause pervades the whole reality of its effect which is by reason of the simultaneously transcendent-immanent presence of the cause with it. The Cause most eminently *is*, but only because it is at the same time most eminently *beyond being*. Only myth run through critical rationality and returned to as the expression of the higher truth ritually lived, after all, is capable of expressing this highest truth. The great philosophers anticipated this:

"This new note of peaceful donation of the cosmos contrasts both with the violent generative break with transcendence enshrined in earlier myth, and with the alternative myths of sacrificial partition of the cosmic man that continued to inflect the perspectives of the first immanentist philosophy. However, the first philosophical mythographers of transcendence had not quite arrived at the monotheistic sense of God as an outgoing will and self-deliberating intelligence."

What is lacking of course in the world-picture of these "first philosophical mythographers of transcendence" is the freedom of God the Creator and the concomitant radical contingency of the world, which did not *have* to be. Yet the point here seems to be that Plato and his followers, before and more acutely after the advent of Christianity, had intuitively anticipated in their philosophy major aspects of the account of the God who is revealed in Scripture. This is why the tale of the encounter of Moses with the fathers of Greek philosophy in Egypt was presented and defended with such verve in the writings of Jewish and Christian Hellenist thinkers. Logos$_2$, if it is indeed a fundamental break from philosophical rationality even in its highest, monotheistic form—since that latter could, through its abstract method of ascent, never arrive at the "personal" account of the divine as is found in the biblical faith, and especially the tri-hypostatic Personality flowering in the

Christian account, yet also, at the same time—lies in an elusive continuity (within discontinuity) with the "natural theologies" of history's greatest philosophers.

I can only mention here the case of the more recent recognition of analogous "points of contact" with the great philosophy-religions of the East, with non-dualism, for example.[30] What is clear in this case, similarly with the case of the so-called "Abrahamic" religions, is that the work of properly inhabiting the space of discontinuous-continuity among these traditions is not the work of a single generation of scholars. What is required in any case, as Sara Grant acknowledges well, is faith's *a priori* recognition, on the one hand, of the primary and ultimate but normatively "insufficient" character of the Christian revelation, while at the same time the demand to recognize and to give full justice to the religiously valid intuitions, concepts, and symbols of these great religious-philosophical traditions—hence of an *orthé chrēsis*. I will have to return to this more fully elsewhere. But these surprising points of fundamental continuity between reason and revelation are what we would have to expect if the God who is revealed is the very Creator of the world, if humans in the world enjoy in their very being a special connection with this God, being made in his "image and likeness," and if this God has destined the world for "deification," participation, and enjoyment of his life and love and knowledge, in, as the ancient prayer says, a "world without end, amen."

## Concluding Comment

In this commentarial analysis on portions from the first thirteen pages of John Milbank's *Beyond Secular Order*, we first examined the "formal contextualization" of his argument found on pages 1–3. Here Milbank provides an elaboration of the contemporary recognition of the problematically historical character of human exist-

---

30. See for example Sara Grant, *Toward an Alternative Theology: Confessions of a Non-Dualist Christian* (South Bend, IN: University of Notre Dame Press, 2002) for a primer.

ence. This recognition, articulated as the interplay between theory and practice, is a variant of a basic insight of contemporary Continental philosophy regarding the "hermeneutical" situation of human being. Ultimately, according to Milbank, it is religion itself—*with* its paradoxical claim to possess a unique and irreplaceable and necessarily "universal" truth in revelation—that actually inhabits this historical hermeneutical space in the richest manner and becomes the most radical means toward understanding it. The two "continuation" sections of our commentary exposited, first, the intimations of a revision of "myth and reason" that appeared as the upshot of his hermeneutical explication regarding the "difficulty" of theoretical access into human existence (3–11) and, second, an adumbration of the history of religions that demonstrated the common historical-theological horizon, and perhaps common logic, of myth and philosophy, two modes of basic intelligibility that are clearly both most acutely found within the religious horizon (11–12). The first "continuation," of the commentary therefore sought to adumbrate and expand upon Milbank's unique recognition of the "ubiquity" of myth, an extension of the contemporary Continental discovery of hermeneutics. If it is the case that myth pervades rationality due to our essentially historical character, then our conception of rationality itself must be renovated in light of this. Here we found the essential thesis suggested that theology (with the *primacy it accords to the truth-bearing capacity of figurative modalities*) has always harboured the possibility of this renovation of reason. The second "continuation" laid the groundwork for showing the uniqueness of the religion of Israel on the world stage, specifically the manner in which it wrestled with the fundamental problems, part and parcel of human existence, that it shares with the universal modes of human intelligence, myth, and philosophy. In the fourth and final section we finally reached our goal, the "frame by frame" analysis of four paragraphs on pages 12–13, in which the "philosophical mythography of transcendence," if realized by the theologian-philosophers of ancient Greece, was also (so to speak) outperformed by the biblical religion that evolved no distinction between philosophy and myth, but rather fused them both in a higher, more excellent way—which requires nothing less than an ever-more radical revision, a *meta-critique* that transcends both our understanding of concepts and of the concepts by which we understand by means of the dense intelligibility of the symbols they initially transcended.

# II

# WISDOM

T HE GOAL OF PHILOSOPHY, logos$_1$, is inseparably the goal of theology, logos$_2$. Both are determined (finally, and therefore firstly) by God. I am speaking of wisdom (which, as we saw in the preceding chapter, means knowing fused with doing, in such a way that a human life is lived in a paradigmatic way, which is ultimately a gift from above, comprehended in mythic intelligence and sifted rationally in order to be more fully consummated, as it were, liturgically). Wisdom is determined by what faith first gives to see: "In the Christian faith," says Robert Sokolowski in the opening lines of *The God of Faith and Reason,* "we are told about ourselves, about our history, and about the world. We are told both how things are and how they ought to be." Theology deals with what is believed to be "true myth": revelation. In the Christian sense, revelation is trans-historical: it depends on true events that determine the meaning of human history as such, although they are not reducible to the historical alone (paradigmatically so, the resurrection, the Archimedean point on which the entire 2000-year edifice of Christianity balances). Here we are given the all-determining context for ourselves, for a final account of reason and for the final meaning of that which is. If revelation is beyond reason, it is not without reason; it is *expansive* of reason. Philosophy and theology (if we are to keep the terms, and, why not?) are, at the very least, inseparable. Heidegger (for whom such an inseparability was a square-circle) did not think this way, and I have no right to demand that he square any circles, *unless* he sought through his thinking a fidelity to the truth of Christianity, that is, to the resurrected Jesus as the definitive truth of the meaning of God, myself, and the world, as the disclosure of our human destiny. He did not. I would like to. Sokolowski continues: "But these teachings are coherent only when they are taken within a setting provided by a special understanding of God." God is the key—and if God is real and if God matters then he is (almost by definition) absolutely real and he matters in an absolute way. All this depends on the peculiar nature or character or intelligibility (pick one) of God. The attentive reader will have already grasped a difficult paradox. "What we are told" in Christianity—the primary mythic order—itself is a wider "setting" that makes them finally coherent. This setting is the theme of theology: "a special understanding of God." Theology, like philosophy—and there is no strict reason to distinguish them here—plays with mythic data, but crucially transposes them onto a new, conceptual plane. But for neither is this transposition an end in itself: the end, for both, is an understanding, lived. For Christianity, at least, conceptuality is prohibited from negating the given mythic data: it can only explicate it. This is the case because Christianity is not an esoteric religion: it finds the truth in the divine mythic form, which is a matter of God's own historical "words and deeds" and in Jesus Christ above all, who is wholly and singularly identified with the Creator, appearing, strangely, within the order of historical becoming. Revelation is first a matter of human testimony to an historical event: the resurrection of the Nazarean prophet. Theology and philosophy, or the singular work of Christian intelligence in pursuit of the defining human truth to be lived, cannot exceed the mythic given: the data is given (as "wisdom from above") and sacred; it is divine speech. Yet the work of religious intelligence wants to identify, explicate, and seek ultimately to unite, intellectually and personally, with the Reality who acts and speaks in this data. Yet with Arjakovsky's explication of myth, above, we have clearly grasped that myth or narrative understanding is the permanent setting of human activity and intelligence, although conceptual intelligence always finds itself competing with the mythic for the same territory, namely, *the total human reality.* On the one hand conceptual intelligence does in fact exceed the mythic, albeit without departing from it, inasmuch as it identifies and explicates the intelligibility of the realities about which myth speaks (God, the world, humanity). *And yet* it cannot accomplish this excess but by remaining within the circle of the myth.

Sokolowski continues: "God himself, as God, does not appear in the world or in human experience. He is not the kind of being that can be present as a thing in the world. And yet, despite this necessary absence, he is believed to be that which gives the definitive sense to everything that does appear in the world and in experience." One crucial upshot of this basic conceptualization of God is that religion is not a-philosophical; it is richly and acutely philo-sophical. Where do I meet this God? The answer is everywhere and nowhere, but "first," that is, most acutely, even paradigmatically, "in the course of Christian living," in sacramental experience, in the Scriptures, through addressing him in prayer and responding to him in my actions. It is from out of this… milieu… that we think about God, and his relation to the world, looking for the disclosure of "necessary elements and structures" that pertain to this God of faith (and reason). We practice intellectual attention to what Chris-tianity tells us about the most elemental things from within the practices of Christianity itself. Sokolowski calls this discernment and elucidation "theology," but here, precisely where the essence of the theological is grasped I think we have to add that it is also a mat-ter of concern to logos$_1$. If (as Sokolowski proceeds to indicate through this opening chapter of his little masterpiece) reason works through making basic distinctions, through *affirming* and *denying* predicates or attributes, by clarification of the meaning of the idea, which, for faith, is inseparable but not equal to the manifestation of the intelligibility of the reality (the intelligibility of things arises for me most acutely when contrasted with what they are not: this exposes the limits of my reasoning, but simultaneously the proce-dure of its advance), then God—most especially the most divine God who has revealed himself and the mystery of the world in "these latter days" once and for all by raising Jesus of Nazareth from the dead—contemplated, considered, and loved (in the intellectual mode) is the most radical thought-project possible, one that finally defines the philosophical as such because it promises to accomplish the spiritual quest that defines philosophy, *gnōsis*. God's essence of course cannot be known in this way, and hence by human reason; God's existence, however can be known—not "proven" in the ratio-nalist sense, but known by being (my words are carefully chosen) *felt through reason*, as, if you like, a "carnal acknowledgment" or affective "being drawn to."

It is tempting, and I bow to the temptation here, to suggest that, on analogy to the core roots of Indo-European languages, a common feature of Indo-European religion and society is a shared sense of order and its relation to disorder. The idea traditionally called "cosmos," that of total order shared by nature and society, has in these archaic societies a divine origin and is protected by the gods. Yet, this cosmos is vulnerable, unstable; it must be *protected* by benevolent gods (of fertility, nature, victory in war, and of stable social relations, from the family to various classes up to priesthood and the royal house itself), who guard it from maleficent, destructive forces, personified by other gods who rule over this dark face of nature— flood, famine, war, death. Human society plays a role at the *center* of this cyclical play between order and disorder: rituals must be performed, the gods *must be* placated, in order for the cycle, framed by and centered on the agrarian order, to be maintained and renewed, for order, sustenance, balance to be maintained.

It was not so much that this contingency was conceived as determined by human freedom as that human action was simply a part of *what must be*: the cosmic-socio-political order as it is is essentially *immutable*. Variations on this basic theme are found in the origin myths and religio-political practices of peoples from India to the Ancient Near East: I refer only to the set of cultures Norman Cohn studied in *Cosmos, Chaos and the World to Come*: "Egyptians, Sumerians, Babylonians, Indo-Iranians and their Indian and Iranian descendants, Canaanites and pre-exilic Israelites" (but not merely: think also of the Meso-American civilizations of the Aztecs or Mayas and of the Chinese cycle of civilizations).[1] One could argue that this conception of the world formed the basis, and stability, of the archaic civilizations built on the foundations of the agricultural revolution, which transformed tribal nature religion into a highly stratified and intensified order of relation between gods and humanity, a divine hierarchy reflected in the social order itself. Cohn's study is about the transformation in this conception of the world that occurred first in the Iran of Zoroaster (around 1500 BC), who seems to have first made a fundamental transformation of the

---

1. Norman Cohn, *Cosmos, Chaos and the World to Come: The Ancient Roots of Apocalyptic Faith*, 2nd ed. (New Haven: Yale University Press, 2001), 232.

combat myth at the basis of the Indo-European conception of the world order, where the forces of benevolence triumphed over evil at the beginning. In Zoroaster and increasingly in the Hebrew prophets this combat becomes linearized and focused on a *final end* where the static order of cosmos, perpetually challenged by forces of chaos, reaches an apogee and then ultimate, permanent resolution. An *End* appears to the founding myth that parallels the absolute character of the *Beginning*: a final battle will be waged that will bring about the completion of the primordial conquest that was left unfinished at the beginning; humanity will be divided along the lines of the gods, between good and evil, and the wicked will be relegated to utter destruction, whereas goodness, peace, and stability will finally reign forever, to be enjoyed by the just.

There is little doubt that the teachings of the Persian prophet Zoroaster influenced Jewish diasporic thought, which became a central feature of post-exilic thinking in Palestine, especially in the new and influential genre of apocalyptic literature. But the eschatology of the Hebrew prophets of exile and return, beginning with Ezekiel and Deutero-Isaiah in particular, was itself the internal crucible through which the transformation of this main stream of a Jewish vision of the world primarily developed. The razing of Jerusalem, the destruction of the Temple and exile of the social elites (especially the priestly class and royal family) at the hands of the Babylonians in 587 was singularly interpreted by the prophets, Jeremiah, Isaiah, Ezekiel (and all the rest) as God's *just* but overwhelmingly terrible judgment on his people. It was not interpreted, as was expected and as was typical, as the defeat of Israel's God by the god of the foreigners. God did not lose his earthly throne—from which he was supposed to reign on earth as he does in heaven—but willingly renounced it, because of the gross infidelity of the people to remain faithful to YHWH alone. God's king, his chosen representative on earth, his "image" and his "son," was made to watch the execution of his own sons, was blinded and brought in chains to Babylon; and yet this, however remarkably, was not interpreted as Israel's god's defeat by the god of the Babylonian king. Rather it was the Creator God's judgment on the family of David, and all the people, for their idolatry

and infidelity to the covenant he forged with them at their beginning through the exodus from Egypt. Exile was in actuality the
central element in the mixture that forged the radical eschatological faith of major movements within exilic and post-exilic Judaism—and, then, Christianity, which, historically speaking, is the
Jewish "sect" that continues this apocalyptic strand of Judaism
after the destruction of the second Temple in the seventieth year
of our era.

The end of the first Temple, of land and of kingdom, was understood by the exiles in Babylon to be temporary: the prophetic vision
paradigmatically found in key passages of Isaiah and Ezekiel elaborated the core conviction that God was going to bring about their
return, was going to lead a new exodus from bondage that would
result in a worldwide glorification elevating Israel to its proper
place (given its direct tie to the Creator-God) over the nations
(originally apportioned to lesser gods), bringing about the defeat of
her enemies, the restoration of the temple cult, and the exaltation of
Israel's God as king over the nations and their gods. God would
reign as the one true Lord, and the entire cosmos would be transformed. Exile was a judgment, but it was a means, a pathway to the
great and final restoration: judgment itself, the revelation of God's
righteousness, will bring about Israel's salvation, and through this
act somehow also that of the nations and even the entire natural
world order that in its very essence longed and panted for liberation, brought about through the final and complete reign of the
God who created the world as his material inhabitation, his cosmic
Temple. Of this universal reign and revolution the Jerusalem Temple (and the Law, the Land, the Kingdom) was not the *telos* but
rather a sort of launching point in the midst of history.


Out of these remarkable themes that construct the core mythic
background to Christian self-comprehension, through the story of
Israel between the first and second Temples, roughly a thousand
years from David and Solomon/the erection of the first Temple to
Christ/the destruction of the second, I want to focus in particular
on the phenomenon of kingship—exclusive rule tied to exclusive

worship, or at least its prioritization, and the acute proximity of the God and the king.[2]

In Archaic society the king *is* the high priest of the high(est) God: he is the focus and principle of order in nature and society. If there is a differentiation between the royal house and a priestly caste—as there almost invariably is—the priestly caste is subservient to the royal household: the king's decisions are divine decisions, which the priesthood serves. The cosmos and the state in this ancient formulation of order are analogous. The king is the human *par excellence*, the natural or adopted "Son" of the God who rules the cosmos. His essential role is now that of humanity writ large: to maintain the harmony of the cosmos, to enforce justice in the social sphere in order to guarantee cosmic good. The traditional role of ritual—to meet, mingle with the divine life-giving source(s), and thereby sustain and renew the features of the natural order of things, the return of spring, etc., to secure blessings and stave off curses in the domains of nature and war, is now centered on the king.

In Egypt the king reigns by virtue of knowledge or wisdom, *sebayit*. His divine status guarantees his access to the *sebayit* by which the gods rule. He thereby reaches *maat*, the divine order englobing the cosmos, the inner law of reality. The ruler's own divine access to *maat* guarantees that his words and deeds are manifestations of the divine cosmic order itself. He incarnates justice. His rule, and therefore by extension his "house" (including future sons, but also his vice-regents, emissaries, and whoever else speaks in his name or is identified with his rule and protection, up to the entire "divine" people of Egypt) participates in the eternal divine *maat*.

*Maat* is personified, in fact, as the daughter of the Sun-god Re, whose regular circuit in the sky is *Maat*'s most powerful manifestation. This prefigures the hypostatization of Wisdom, *Hokma*, in later Jewish wisdom literature.[3]

---

2. See for some main contours of the following paragraph, Francis Oakley, *Kingship, the Politics of Enchantment* (Oxford: Blackwell, 2006).

3. See Helmer Ringgren, *Word and Wisdom: Studies in the Hypostatization of*

It has been remarked regularly, from within the general schema that I have followed here, that the transition from Archaic to Axial eras involves a trend of "world renunciation," which seemingly involves a radical differentiation, even break, within manners of conceiving the world as a whole, or at least the raising of the question of the absolute unity of that which is, shared by the gods and humans, as communicated by the myths (which may be answered by a radical reassertion of the traditional "monism" at a theoretical level, as in the "metaphysical monism" of the Upaniṣads or Parmenides) and which develops radically in times of political upheaval in particular.[4] This social trend is, in other words, corollary to the manner of articulating this transition in the context of "wisdom" already given. The renunciant sees that "all existing institutions stand under divine judgment" which means the royal house of the king and the priestly caste and its activities.[5] Think of the Buddha in India, or the great ascetic teachers of the Tao in China. This new "dualism" is classically formulated in Plato—very much a political philosopher (of justice in the polis through radical revision of founding myths paired with rule through theoretical reflection) and purveyor of the path of true salvation (in escape from this world to the soul's native world of the gods), as much as he is a metaphysician (of the Forms). But there is also a formulation of wisdom in Ancient Israel: if Plato offers the philosopher-king as the path by which justice may be incarnated, Israel proposes something distinct but analogous: God, the Free Creator as the only true King. God alone in this vision is Israel's King; society is founded not on a royal figure who unites in his person and/or function the differentiated domains of Heaven

---

*Divine Qualities and Functions in the Ancient Near East* (Lund, Sweden: Haekan Ohlssons, 1947), for texts and summary analysis.

4. In 1963 Bellah was already speaking of "the emergence in the first millennium B.C. all across the Old World, at least in centers of high culture, of the phenomenon of religious rejection of the world characterized by an extremely negative evaluation of man and society and the exaltation of another realm of reality as alone true and valuable" ("Religious Evolution," 359).

5. Bellah, "God and King," *The Robert Bellah Reader*, ed. Robert Bellah, Steven Tipton (Durham, NC: Duke University Press, 2006), 362.

and Earth, the worlds of the gods and humans, but is founded on a *covenant* between the incomparable God and the people of his choosing. This is the socio-political essence of the Exodus.

And yet Israel had a human king.


Before addressing that feature, let me note a third threefold classification to shed another angle of light on the three keys for a Philosophy in Word and Name that this sketchbook intends to promote. The passage from myth to wisdom to the hyper-wisdom of apocalypse reaches the End where it touches and perfects the Beginning. In it protology and eschatology are joined through wisdom, wisdom that sees their unity and defines the task of human, historical life and culture as enacting in oneself and in society this union. This third scheme may be represented by a threefold progression of the concept of kingship in Israel.

This progression is represented by three biblical personages: Saul, David (and Solomon), and God. Saul is the king who is first chosen. He represents the desire for Israel to be like the nations; he falls short of the kingship in Israel because he acts again and again like the pagan kings that surround them. What is required is a king "after God's own heart," who knows that God is Israel's true King, a man who represents the people to God, who serves as God's central instrument of activity in the world, whose will is one with God's own, a will extinguished in God's will through love. This bizarre and beautiful portrait of ideal kingship is very much the image of David portrayed in the books of Samuel and Kings. With David and Solomon the Temple is built, the two kingdoms of North and South are unified under one rule and one cult, and the kingdom of Israel expands into neighboring kingdoms, which become, along with their gods, subservient to it.

Along with the institution of kingship in Israel there also comes, importantly, a royal court, with professional scribes, advisors, prophets. A wisdom tradition develops, very much through interaction with surrounding nations. Israel is *like* the nations, having a temple, a central, national god who is ideologically elevated above the other gods, a king who is this god's central means of rule in the world, and with imperial ambitions that match the status of their god in the heavenly realm. But Israel is also *unlike* the nations: she has the Law, she is the elect of the one God who increases in ascendancy as the "YHWH alone" movement grows in intensity from the time of the discovery of Deuteronomy during the Temple renovations under the reign of Josiah (649–609) in the Kingdom of Judah. And her Temple has a throne on which sits, uniquely, no image, but instead concentrates the manifest presence of God himself. This God is King; how he will become the King that he is is a matter of increasing perplexity for Israel's wisdom and prophetic traditions, and hence of intense speculation. Ultimately, with the genre of apocalyptic, the reign of God becomes a matter of a final revelation. The realization of the kingship of YHWH in the death and resurrection of Jesus Christ may be taken as shorthand for the Gospel of the Christian sect of Judaism in the middle of the first century.

It used to be popular to speak of "comparative philosophy." This went out of vogue when the danger was recognized that the traditions of intellectual reflection of civilizations outside of the purview of the Greek legacy might be being read through the constrictive lens of this Greek legacy, and even more, through the implicit canons and norms of subsequent Western thought (philosophy's distinction from theology, as academic discourses, for example, hermetically sealed from one another). Yet there are clearly family resemblances among the wisdom traditions of the world. If I can retain the term "philosophy" to name the intellectual traditions of full-blown civilizations, namely the members of the set called "Axial Age" (born in China, India, Israel, and Greece), I may then observe that philosophy derives directly from the canons of critical reflection on the intelligible content of the symbols that primarily inform the religious practices in these contexts. The "philosophical" critique of ritual in the Upaniṣads, and its internalization through the expansion of its conception of interior, metaphysical connections between disparate parts of reality into a universal principle of identification, *Brahman*, does not make them any less "religious" texts. There is at

94

least an analogy to be made here with the texts of Plato—despite the way they are normally read by modern scholars. The Axial revolution, as has been observed by all of its defenders, is a religious revolution (Lao-Tse, the Buddha, the Hebrew prophets, the early Greek philosophers). The comprehension of the forms of religion as *symbols* raises the question of their veracity and validity, calls for the reorganization of our relation to them, and creates—in the various manners unique to each Axial case—the first step from myth to wisdom.

Religion has been defined as "a set of symbolic forms and acts which relate man to the ultimate conditions of his existence," apart from which I cannot express these conditions or my perceived essential link to it that comprises the condition of both myth and ritual.[6] If it is true that here I have at least the rough sketch for a useful definition of "religion" that sheds light, not only on the Axial cases or on the various cultural systems that comprise human collectivities, *but also* on the philosophical questions we are compelled to formulate and to try and understand by virtue of our human situation itself, then it is worth dwelling for a moment on the concept of the symbol that informs this reflection.

The symbol is a sign; it is always a sign, although it may be more than a sign. A symbol from this point of vantage is a sign that not only points to what it signifies (indication) but also "represents" what it indicates. From both of these vantage points, the concept of sign, therefore, is crucial to the comprehension of the character of symbols. A sign is an entity that stands for another; it may be linguistic, but it does not have to be. Smoke is a sign for fire and fever is the sign of illness: a sign brings to mind something other than itself. It performs an act of reference. Symbols have two basic functions, a "presentification function" and a "separative function."[7]

6. This is the Geertz school definition, from his famous essay, "Religion as a Cultural System." I draw it directly from Robert Bellah, as articulated in "Religious Evolution," 359.

7. For the following distinctions see Lucien Scubla's preface, which nicely draws together some main aspects of Camille Tarot's *Le symbolique et le sacré: théories de la religion* (Paris: La Decouverte/M.A.U.S.S., 2008), 22–24. The notion of "disjunctive conjunction" is a riff on Levi-Strauss, *Mythologiques* III.

The presentification function is one of *mediation*: symbols make present something that is absent. The separative function is one of *distinguishing*: symbols separate things present to one another. This separative function is involved with the presentification function in the symbol: presentification depends on separativity and separativity depends on, is conditioned by, presentification. The word, the linguistic symbol, a sign, is interposed between self and the cosmos—it enacts a "disjunctive conjunction" that constitutes the possibility of conceiving a self over-against the world, within it but partially, problematically transcending it, and it constitutes the world over-against which one is oneself constituted. The word is interposed between self and cosmos like a tool (whether conventional or natural, it does not matter). A tool is interposed between the hand and the object of its action. The tool is an extension of the hand but it is not the hand; it joins and separates. Yet the tool-character is not the essence of a symbol. Tools do not constitute worlds, they instrumentalize what is given. Before its tool-being, signs enjoy a constitutive-being. We understand the world through the use we want to make of it; we approach it through symbols. Religious symbols (first ordered in ritual and comprehended in myth) are the least instrumental of all; they want to associate us with the power(s) that transcend us and that constitute the world as it is, in its wholeness.

A sign, in short, partakes of four parts: signifier, signified, meaning, objective referent and... intelligible referent. Take the example of smoke and fire: smoke is the signifier, fire is the objective referent, the meaning or sense is the idea of their connection of causality (fire causes smoke) and the intelligible referent is the general conception of causality as metaphysical reality, which implies (according to the interpretation) a "meta-cosmic" significance and hence the possibility of an open and pluralized signification that transcends the "immanent" or "earthbound" order of meaning, natural-cultural, given with the sign itself.[8] A symbol is all these things. It

---

8. For the basic distinctions of this paragraph I summarize the main contours of Jean Borella, *Histoire et théorie du symbole* (Lausanne, Switzerland: L'Age de l'Homme, 2004). This fourfold theory of the sign is his, as is this example (205–6).

establishes a relation between a signifier and a signified thing; it orients thought to an object by means of a meaning attached to a sign. But I can now say that a symbol is the integration of two degrees of sign noted above: natural and institutional signs. A symbol presupposes the innate semiotic character of the natural world, the world of experience—the world that gives rise to or serves as the context of the cultural world, the world of institutional signs. For natural signs the signifier is related to the referent by virtue of a natural relation (as in the smoke's signification of fire), whereas institutional or cultural signs involve a relation of signifier and signified resulting from a choice (as in language); the institutional-cultural or conventional sign breaks the order of causality of natural signs— or rather, more precisely, it *reverses* it: the sign itself enacts the activity of the appearing of the invisible, not as an effect or emanation of its referent, but by an act of human-linguistic creation: *this* sign brings to mind *that* reality.

There is also a third genre of sign, the mixed, partly natural and partly institutional—a sign that is conventional but at the same time resting on the nature of things (sacraments being the first example: the water of baptism partakes of the "natural" semiotic propensity of water to provide the dense and multifaceted signification[s] it does in the ritual domain). For a proper understanding of the symbolic sign, the "natural" sign must be understood as an "epistemic" sign: it augments our knowledge by creating a passage from the visible to the invisible (visible lactation is a sign of invisible pregnancy; miracles are the sign of the presence of the invisible God). Within this purview I must be willing to acknowledge the fourth "metaphysical" dimension of signification that stands in excess of the objective referent, and creates the possibility of the institutional *interpretation* of the natural sign. This act of transformation is the domain of symbolic signs. The symbolic sign, then, enacts a pluralism of reference, a pluralism that points to a "cause" transcending the plane of visibility, strictly, of the order of cause and effect intrinsic to the worldly plane conceived as a whole.

A *metaphysical symbol* therefore points beyond the order of the "earth," by *saturating* that order with meaning. Take the sacrament of the Eucharist: under certain conditions wine and bread visibilize

97

*through* their natural and cultural significations the invisible presence of the Eschatological Reality of the Resurrected in a manner that transfigures our most disciplined orders of signification (as in "transubstantiation," through which the Aristotelian theory of substance/accidents breaks down: accidents are "impossibly" detached and associated with another substance than what they give to appear!). Yet the symbol possesses no objective reference properly speaking: the third dimension of the sign is evaporated: there is no "objective" reality there corresponding to the signifier on its ontological level. To be precise, the objective referent is less evaporated than "delayed"; it is anticipated and intended, but present in a way that the sign as such cannot "grasp" or contain. Symbols break apart signs from within, and they point into another order of being—I will call it *eschatological being*, which it invariably is for Christianity—that partakes of a meaning that the order of the sign (both natural and conventional) that is at my disposal in the present order of finitude (what I have just called "earth") does not pertain to except perhaps like shadows to realities. I wonder if I may even dare the formulation that the symbol (in the Christian context) enacts a "conjunctive disjunction" between being and being-to-come. With this example, and this observation, I reach the point where the semiotic description returns to deepen the phenomenological one with which I began this digression.[9]

A symbol, says Jean-Yves Lacoste, enacts a "redistribution of the field of experience."[10] Symbolic redistribution rearranges the given furniture—whether naturally or culturally given, it does not matter—of the world of experience, a world of given meanings, in order to signify what this world does not contain. Symbolization, as a species of signification, must happen by means of the use of the given

9. See Jean-Yves Lacoste, *Experience and the Absolute*, which contains the following definition.

10. Lacoste seems to refer here to Jacques Rancière's celebrated expression, "le partage du sensible," from *The Politics of Aesthetics*, which is concerned with the aesthetics at the heart of politics: distinctions between what is visible and what is invisible, what is sayable and unsayable, what is meaningful and what is not in public discourse, is forged through political action. I would argue that its source is myth and its first site is ritual. Politics is grounded in religion.

order of meanings contained in the world. As symbolization this signification can make present a meaning that draws this world to a transcendent order, an order that pertains to it but which it cannot give except through this symbolic presentification. The primary form of this distribution is ritual—coincident, perhaps, with the origins of language. For it is always already a *re*-distribution, since at the origin of human communication and the formation of meaning the natural order was primordially redistributed into conventional signification, perhaps first in gesture, re-enactment, and then utterance (such as primitive song, first mimetic, an echo of the natural, and then conventional). The order of "play," of culture, plays with what is given in the order of survival, running through numerous redistributions of that field to create cultural institutions, like mimesis, language, and music (ritual) that mediate to me the conditions of my existence through forms that do not dissolve away when the signified is reached through them, but are taken to embody, to presentify in and through themselves the higher realities that are inaccessible but through them.[11] The function of the symbol is separation and control, but its first separation only gives birth to the human self over-against the world in which it finds itself problematically immersed. This entire order does not exhaust the possibilities for human understanding, but rather may signify an entirely other order that is nevertheless supremely present in and through the orders of the given, both natural and cultural. One may dwell "liturgically"—which partially means *delaying* the interpretation of the given world, of the self, in light of the very possibility of interpreting the given otherwise, of a reception of the ways of redistributing the given that never come to an end within it, but which may even give, under their veil, in the very form, precisely, that they take in the world, another reality to come. In Christianity this *delay* comes from God, who opens up within the world of earth the symbolic order of heaven, principal of which is Christ, the symbol of God *par excellence*, and promises that this symbol will find its referent, in the form of a "parousiac presence" that draws the symbol to

11. For the notion of play, *mimesis*, song, communication, I refer to Bellah, *Religion in Human Evolution*, 145–46.

its end in the reality it anticipates, at the end of time, when time, history, the entire order of my given finitude is surpassed, transformed in light of the things that ritual and mythic redistribution vaguely signify.

Ritual enacts the primary form of redistribution of the field of experience but it claims to repeat and activate anew, to manifest the being and power of the hidden order of intelligibility underlying human experience. Ritual "redistribution" has two basic dimensions, a *reordering* part and a *reparative* part. It symbolically reorders the furniture of the world in order to make a "key" that fits in the keyhole of reality, thus opening the door to the transcendent font of intelligibility behind experience. By entering into a unity with this hidden order through signitive repetition of its basic features, humanity renews or repairs the field of the given, on which humanity depends for material sustenance. Conceptual and theoretical rationality—originating from meditative reflection on the ritual realities themselves, intensified through the crucible of sociopolitical change—will come to see that it is itself based on a higher order, and ultimately (as is very common) a radically unifying principle—in other words, that the intelligibility can be discerned in itself through theoretical reflection with its drive to unity in explanation. In the Upaniṣads, for example, this means that the absoluteness, and even necessity, of the Vedic sacrifices is called into question: the essential, which lies beyond the cosmic-divine order, may only be reached through renouncing that order, and ultimately renouncing the scriptures themselves once what they give is given: the knowledge of the Self (as in Sankara's interpretation).[12] In the Bible this means that God alone is King, that his reign, the liberating reign of charity, is come in the Crucified, and therefore that the reality which the shadow of the Law signifies is here, present in a parallel order that has opened and that will finally draw the present order to a close.

12. See Sankara's commentary on the Brihadaranyaka Upaniṣad: *Brihadaranyaka Upaniṣad with Sankara's Commentary*, 3rd ed., trans. Swami Madhavananda (Mayavati, Almora: Advaita Ashrama, 1950), I. 3, 28 (85–91).

In the path from myth to wisdom there is the recognition of the distance or differentiation between the order of nature and culture, a gap that, I have found (following Borella), the symbolic sign bridges by tying these orders together, by reference to a transcendent *par excellence* that cannot be contained in the given forms of nature and culture, but which is never absent from these, but rather absent by virtue of a radical presence in excess of the entire order of differences and similarities by which human intelligence works, and which comprises its world, its basic intelligible milieu, signification. This transcendence means that culture—based on human action of "redistributive" reordering and repair in ritual, and the socio-political forms it reciprocally creates and underpins, forms that rule and condition human life—is a primary product of the human response to the transcendent order only partially comprehended.

Theoretical intelligence critiques the mythic, but it does not question its normativity until the modern era, which is defined by the attempt to eradicate and replace that normativity with the particular theoretical intelligence of modern science.[13] The ever-possible potential excess of the semiotic sign, the possibility of "metaphysical" interpretation of human experience through a transformation of the given order that constitutes a perceived meaning that cannot be established within that order, since its intelligible referent escapes that order, but promises to found it, to bring about that founding anew and perfectly at the Omega-point of an absolute end, means that an absolute theoretical eclipse of the mythic can only be brought about by an *a priori* determination of the possible that rules the metaphysical referent (of Origin and End of the given communicated in mythic symbolization) out of bounds. This may always be questioned.

Wisdom may be essentially derived from the myths of the investiture of royalty with the gifts of the gods; in Egypt the Pharaoh was (ritually) present when the highest god made the cosmos; he observes his activity and understands. He rules as a god among men

13. See Bellah, *Religion in Human Evolution*, 40–43.

for the sake of the extension of that wisdom into the human cultural sphere. In Israel Wisdom, *Hokma*, is personified as a queen-like figure at God's side, who observes and even enacts his creative intelligence; she embodies his knowledge by which the world is made and possesses even his very power. In both cases from antiquity, wisdom is as much a gift of the divine as are the myths themselves, the sacred stories that contain and communicate wisdom. One may even say that wisdom, partially detachable from myth, is the path of critical intelligence by which it may reach that core of intelligibility *by which* the myths are sacred. It is certainly such in Plato and his pupil Aristotle. What does wisdom find when it touches this core intelligibility, however?

In the Ancient Near East, wisdom often finds only a growing perplexity: if the incarnation of justice is the highest human achievement, the goal and purpose of kingship, then why do the poor suffer at the hands of the wicked? Why do the wicked prosper? Why is human striving for knowledge (of right living) so futile? So much about the gods is unintelligible to humanity. From within this matrix the traditions of wisdom come to discern a two-fold tendency that more and more acutely threatens to bring the entire edifice of archaic religion of which wisdom is a part into serious question. There is a *monotheistic tendency*—the drive toward unity of intelligibility, a principle, and more fundamentally an all-powerful God that actively ensures justice. There is also the *existential tendency*—the recognition that the good suffer and the evil prosper.[14] These two tendencies drive in opposite directions: it is classically formulated in the problem of evil, which for wisdom in Israel only intensifies in its problematicity to the degree that the justice of God is fiercely held onto, that is, uncompromisingly, even especially when it falls squarely on Israel herself. The rational response in Israel is that God will intervene at a chosen time known only to him

---

14. See Louis Bouyer, *Gnosis: La connaissance de Dieu dans l'Ecriture*, chs. 6–7. I borrow from his description of this twofold tendency, 84–88. I am also indebted to his discussion of the progression from wisdom to apocalypse at the heart of the biblical revelation in this text.

that will reveal his great justification as Lord of the Covenant and Creator of the Cosmos. Just as wisdom originates only in God, so also may its terminus be divulged by God. It is the end or ends of wisdom that only apocalyptic, the disclosure of a (final) wisdom from above, can bring to resolution. It is out of human hands.

The primitive Christian confession is that Christ is the *Son of Man*, the chosen representative of all of humanity before the *Ancient of Days*. The crucial source-text is Daniel 7. Daniel, the legendary sage among the Babylonian exiles,[15] the ultimate picture of the faithful Jew under the circumstances of the divine judgment of Israel through exile, faithful to the God of the covenant with all patience and fidelity, is given the gift of wisdom, which is God's alone to give. Among all the wise men of the peoples brought to the court of the king of Babylon, the "mystery is revealed" (cf. 2:19) to Daniel alone. Daniel's wisdom (in chapter 2) is the capacity to discern the speech of God in the elusive, symbolic forms in which it is given to humans, as humanly unknowable apart from the charismatic gift of interpretation. In this chapter he is given a share in the divine wisdom in order to interpret the king of Babylon, Nebuchadnezzar's dream of a statue of a man composed of four parts: a golden head, breast and arms of silver, belly and thighs of bronze, legs of iron and feet of iron mixed with clay. Suddenly a stone cut from a mountain by non-human hands strikes the feet of the image and it crashes, dissolving into dust: the stone grows into a mountain that fills the entire earth. Daniel 7 is a more detailed and extravagant presentation of the same teaching. It is stylized as a written report at Daniel's hand of a dream-vision of four monstrous animals emerging from the primordial sea. Assuming again the common trope in the Ancient Near East of four kingdoms in succession, these beasts represent the succession of kingdoms that rule the world of the Jews, from Babylon to the Seleucids, a subset of the vast Greek empire established by Alexander the Great.[16] When this succession of superhuman beastlike

15. Spoken of in Ezekiel chs. 14 and 28.
16. See J. J. Collins, "The Place of the Fourth Sibyl in the Development of Jewish Sibyllina," *Journal of Jewish Studies* 25 (1974), 365–80.

power out of the "sea" (that is, the chaos, and gentile nations) reaches its apex of blasphemy, of evil, ignorance, and injustice, the scene suddenly shifts: "As I watched," reports Daniel,

> Thrones were set up
> and the ancient of Days took his throne.
> His clothing was white as snow,
> the hair on his head like pure wool;
> his throne was flames of fire,
> with wheels of burning fire.
> A river of fire surged forth,
> flowing from where he sat;
> thousands upon thousands were ministering to him,
> and myriads upon myriads stood before him.[17]

This great theophany of the God of Israel, symbolizing, in what is now called apocalyptic imagery (and rightly so), the absolute rule of God over-against that of earthly kingdoms that rise and fall before him, is a remarkable conception of the final resolution of the drama of creation, in a final confrontation with all the forces of disorder that threaten the good creation through a final judgment of God: the Ancient of Days takes his throne to judge these successive kingdoms of man. This judgment sets the context for what in nascent Christianity will be called the "good news of the Kingdom of God,"[18] viz., that Israel's God has unveiled the manner in which he will establish his kingship, wherein the exile of Israel is ended and her God is finally bringing his lordly reign, his justice to bear on the whole world. This passage of victory and enthronement of Israel's God over his enemies is understood in early Christian self-understanding to be definitively enacted in the death and resurrection of the Messiah. It is the final unveiling, the revelation of the mystery of God's fidelity to his righteousness in the created order. And Jesus becomes explicitly the son of man of Daniel 7: "As the visions during the night continued, I saw coming on the clouds of heaven,

17. Dan 7:9–10.
18. Luke 4:43.

> One like a son of man.
> When he reached the Ancient of Days
> and was presented before him,
> he received dominion, splendour and kingship;
> all nations, peoples and tongues will serve him.
> His dominion is an everlasting dominion
> that shall not pass away,
> his kingship, one that shall not be destroyed."[19]

Norman Cohn for example has argued that this vision does not take place "in heaven" but "on earth"—or perhaps better, at a time, the end of time, when the "distance" between earth and heaven is finally eclipsed, which is the very point of the last judgment in biblical terms: the beasts emerge from the sea, the fourth beast tramples over the same land as they (Palestine). And the setting up of thrones of judgment—and the final enthronement of the Son of Man—occur in the same locale.[20] This famous vision of the Danielic Son of Man is a temple theophany: the Ancient of Days has finally returned to his throne on earth, the Jerusalem Temple, in order to bring about his just rule over all the earth, which is mediated through the rule of his beloved elect.[21] If this is the case, then the "coming on the clouds of heaven" of the Son of Man would be an image of descent instead of ascension, or to do away with the perhaps misleading spatial direction imagery, of a glorified human figure born by the divine glory-cloud before the Last Judge to receive judgment, to be vindicated, to receive his just reward. He is given a universal and everlasting kingship over the earth.[22]

The rest of the chapter doubly repeats the interpretation of this vision that "terrified" and perplexed Daniel. Here Daniel is not the

---

19. Dan 7:13–14.

20. See Norman Cohn, *Cosmos, Chaos and the World to Come: The Ancient Roots of Apocalyptic Faith*, 2nd ed. (New Haven: Yale University Press, 2001), 169–70.

21. Cohn rightly points to Psalm 96 (among the Psalms of enthronement) and passages in Zechariah (14:5) and Joel (3:12).

22. See N. T. Wright's corrective to the "spaceman" imagery as "good first-century metaphorical language for ... the defeat of the enemies of the true people of god and the vindication of the true people themselves." *Jesus and the Victory of God* (Minneapolis: Fortress Press, 1996), 362.

interpreter, but the perplexed dreamer, who relies on an angel to instruct him of the dream's meaning. Understanding, as before, had to be given from heaven to one who dwells in the field of ignorance, on earth: "I approached one of those present and asked him the truth of all this; in answer, he made known to me its meaning": "The four beasts stand for four kings which shall arise on the earth. But the holy ones of the Most High shall receive the kingship, to possess it forever."[23] The Son of Man represents the kingdom destined to inherit the everlasting dominion of God himself; like Moses the great deliverer, like the high priest on the Day of Atonement, he is drawn into the presence of God in the clouds of theophany that surround him, with striking contrast to the terrifying beast-creatures of pagan rule by death that arise out of the sea of chaos and melt back into it.

The second, longer response focuses on Daniel's trembling query about the great "horn" on the last beast that raised the violent persecution of the "holy ones of the Most High" to an unforeseen degree—an element central to the author and original readers of a text substantially composed and/or finally redacted in the Maccabean period. Here is Daniel's repeated description of the event of definitive divine judgment and the reception of "the kingship" of "holy ones," those faithful to God's covenant through the era of persecution and violent suffering, martyrdom—the era of waiting on God's final act. Daniel's final description of the end of the era of the succession of kingdoms is a remarkable expression of late Second Temple Jewish hope in the Antiochene era and of the Maccabees. It is placed on the lips of the angelic being explaining to Daniel the meaning of the dream:

> But when the court is convened,
> And his dominion is taken away
> To be completely destroyed,
> Then the kingship and dominion and majesty
> Of all the kingdoms under the heavens
> Shall be given to the people of the holy ones of the Most High,

23. Dan 7:17–18.

Whose kingship shall be an everlasting kingship,
Whom all dominions shall serve and obey.[24]

In this dream-vision, "holy ones" is a technical term: it partakes of
the traditional meaning of the word, the angelic beings who faithfully serve God, denizens of his royal council. In the vision there are
countless numbers of these beings ministering before his throne. It
is at the same time a name for the people who are represented by
these beings, beings that mediate between the unapproachable
divine and the human world. There is no contradiction; it is a both/
and. In an apocalyptic cosmology, the angelic holy ones are the
heavenly side of one and the same reality of which the people Israel
and the nations that surround them are the earthly side.

Similarly, like the Suffering Servant of trito-Isaiah, the Son of
Man is both a Messianic figure and the collective community of the
People of God. The head stands for and represents the collective
community, and the collective community partakes in the share of
the head's rule, just as a head and a body relate in organic unity: St.
Paul will make much of this imagery, with his core conviction that
the reign of God established by and enacted through the resurrected
Jesus is shared by the "holy ones." Here he is clearly following
Daniel. But there is a difference. "Do you not know that the holy
ones will judge the world? ... Do you not know that we will judge
angels?" he asks the Corinthians with exasperation.[25] Here, as in
Daniel, "holy ones" is still a title for the people of God in the final
reign of God. This time however they are no longer conceived primarily as the earthly pendant of the angelic representatives in the
royal divine court. Now it is humans who will judge angels. From
the time of Daniel to St. Paul, something has fundamentally
changed. The difference is significantly determined by the intensification of the Messiah figure in the Pauline apocalyptic (which is, as
I see it, a fine name for the "theology" we are perhaps glimpsing
*through* the letters themselves), an intensification required by the
meaning of the death and resurrection of Jesus in Paul's thought.
Briefly, for Paul the death and resurrection of the Messiah created a

24. Dan 7:26–27.
25. 1 Cor 6:2–3.

covenantal revolution on the scale of that change from before and after the call of Abraham (or that from before and after the giving of the Law to Moses on Mt. Sinai, or the investiture of a permanent dynasty at the center of God's plan for the house of David, etc.). The apocalypse of the final justice of God in the "Christ" (technically, God's appointed world ruler) brings about a definitively epochal change for St. Paul, in continuity, on the one hand, with the former "age," precisely as its *telos*, its completion, its fulfillment, its goal and purpose, but as such it is also a radical refiguring of the character of the Creator's covenant with his world, though (always) *through* the mediation of his elected people, Israel. Not only is the covenant opened to the nations, the Law itself is transfigured, and the other great symbols that determine Jewish identity are similarly refigured (Temple, Land, King): all become centered on and refocused by the disclosure of God's final act of faithfulness to the covenant with his people Israel. Angelic mediation belonged to the order of world that is "passing away," mediation of Law as well as cosmos. The new order, hidden in God from the beginning, a "*mustērion*" now unveiled (*apocalypsis*) is mediated by a renewed humanity, made one under the leadership of Israel's anointed.[26] A theological interpretation of advanced technological discovery, precisely in its radically ambivalent and truly apocalyptic character, finds its starting place here. And Incarnation, likewise (and Trinity, by consequence), is a dogmatic concept that finds its biblical origins in precisely this Pauline vision.

*This* faith in human co-regency with God, seeded in the world already through the institution of the Church (the "sacrament of the Kingdom"), is so hard to maintain in these days of *rampant* clerical sex abuse of children, but was it any easier to believe in the apostolic days themselves?[27]

---

26. See the proems to Colossians and Ephesians, as well as the first and last chapters of Romans, for a start.

27. See 1 Cor 5:1–5.

# STUDY 3

WORD: *Sacra doctrina. Sapientia. Similitudine.*
NAME: Thomas Aquinas
STYLE: Exegetical Comment
MATTER: Reflections on the Distinction between
Theology and Philosophy from the Vantage of *Summa
theologiae*, quaestio 1

"Let the mind worship the uncreated God; it is after all written,
'Behold the worship of God is wisdom' (Job 28:28)."
— St. Augustine, *De Trinitate*, 383 (Hill trans.)

MUCH LIKE THE GOD of Nietzsche, the "conflict of the faculties," an invention of the Middle Ages and a fundamental principle of modern Western intellectual culture, is dead. Powerful institutions and those who unquestionably think within their conditioning strictures laid down like the law in the hearts of any who desire to gain sustenance from this business, may act for a long time yet as if this intellectual framework is not obsolete, but it is. I will not argue this perspective here except to assert another point that at least explains the pathos of the position: the permanent, pressing human questions demand the transcendence of this procrustean bed that has only done humanity the disservice of burying her basic questions in a heavy winter's slumber: religion, whether true or not, is the site where the human questions are most intensely lived and interrogated. Philosophy has to awaken to itself again here. If the conflict is dead, the question "what comes after the conflict" is alive. The following would like to contribute to that question through an observant rereading of the opening question of

Thomas Aquinas's *Summa theologiae*. First some broad historical remarks to orient my reading, ever in the light of the motivating concern, just expressed, that brings me to this text.

The distinction between theology and philosophy is a Christian invention, and in fact is made concrete only very late, in the high Middle Ages to be precise. It begins to emerge, we could say, in the thought of Peter Abelard in the twelfth century (the first to use the word "theology" in the modern sense, which for Abelard involved simply the application of the dialectical method to acute problems within the *lógos* of religious faith, *problematic in a purely rational sense*),[1] but gets institutionalized in the distinction of "faculties" in the medieval university as a working compromise after the intellectual crisis brought about by the West's second discovery of Aristotle that took root just after Abelard's death. Before this time, Christian thinkers almost unanimously conceived of themselves as *philosophers*,[2] and in fact it is a way of conceiving what Christian thinkers do and what Christian *life* and *thought* is (understanding, therefore, Christianity in a properly *philosophical* unity of word and deed) that extends at least into the 14th century, in the writings of late Byzantine thinker Nicholas Cabasilas in the East (*The Life in Christ*), and even the 16th century by Erasmus or John Calvin in the West (for example in the preface to Erasmus's *Enchiridion*, or in Calvin's *Institutes*): arguably expressing the core of the Christian tradition from Justin Martyr, these authors conceive of the Christian practice of prayer and discipleship (which includes an intellectual component in continuity with this dynamism) as the "true philosophy." Yet the distinction is nevertheless assumed by many today, heirs of the

1. See the prologue to *Sic et non*, wherein he proposes that the dialectical method can be the central means to allow us to sift the often contradictory assertions of the Fathers and Scripture in order to arrive at the truth, which is "resolved by logic."
2. As Balthasar points out in one of his best essays, "Philosophy, Christianity, Monasticism," this is the determinative understanding of the Fathers from the second century and is extended in the West in the self-understanding of monasticism.

"conflict of the faculties," and it is assumed to be found, to take the most important example, in the thought of Thomas Aquinas in the 13th century. Let us ask ourselves: how did Thomas conceive of this distinction? Is his conception ours today? The most obvious place to turn for such a seemingly introductory question is Thomas's *Summa theologiae*, a text itself introduced by means of clarifying this very problem in its opening question.

The first question of the *Summa* is divided into ten articles. I recite the concern and scope of this question, addressed through ten distinct steps, in Thomas's very own words:

> To place our purpose within proper limits, we first endeavor to investigate the nature and extent of this sacred doctrine. Concerning this there are ten points of inquiry: 1. Whether it is necessary? 2. Whether it is a science? 3. Whether it is one or many? 4. Whether it is speculative or practical? 5. How it is compared with other sciences? 6. Whether it is the same as wisdom? 7. Whether God is its subject matter? 8. Whether it is a matter of argument? 9. Whether it rightly employs metaphors and similes? 10. Whether the Sacred Scripture of this doctrine may be expounded in different senses?[3]

To all these questions the answer is of course "yes": 1. Yes, sacred doctrine, beyond philosophical wisdom, is necessary (because human salvation, the fulfillment of human nature, requires knowledge of things higher than the reach of reason). 2. Yes, sacred doctrine is a science (because it "proceeds" in a properly scientific manner "from principles established in light of a higher science ... the science of God and the blessed"). 3. Yes, sacred doctrine is one *and* many, a unified multiplicity (because it treats everything under the aspect of God, that is, in light of the concept of revelation). 4. Yes, sacred doctrine is speculative *and* practical (because it is concerned with truth and the good, and eminently so in both cases, wherein it fuses these separate orders into one, specu-

3. ST 1,1.

latively considering the *most intelligible reality*, God, and practically concerned with the perfection of human happiness which is achieved *in* that very intellectual vision). 5. Yes, sacred doctrine is preeminent among all other sciences (because it includes them all within itself). 6. Yes, sacred doctrine is the same as wisdom (because, simply, it considers the highest principle of reality, which it can *most properly do* by thinking from God's self-revelation). 7. Yes, sacred doctrine (rightly, "scientifically") has God as its subject matter (because it treats everything that is in light of its reference to God, either revelation itself or creation seen as effect of the divine cause). 8. Yes, sacred doctrine is a matter of argument (because it reasons from first principles, the articles of faith). 9. Yes, sacred doctrine rightly employs metaphors (because this is the most naturally human manner of knowing divine things). 10. Yes, sacred doctrine expounds Scripture in a multiplicity of senses (because God necessarily speaks metaphorically, as we will see, that is, like a poet, through the signification of things through other things).

By addressing these topics in the manner adumbrated here the question of the "nature and extent" of sacred doctrine is to Thomas's mind "comprehended" (*comprehendatur*), and the task of treating "whatever belongs to the Christian religion" (the goal of the text, according to its prologue) is set on proper footing, that is, articulated in a "scientific" manner, by which Thomas means, *according to the light of intelligibility intrinsic to the* Catholica veritatis—in his words, "according to the order of the subject matter" itself (prol.). We will trust him with accomplishing that intention, and investigate instead *how* in particular he goes about doing so. Let me specify further now the motivating concern in the form that it will have through this exercise in interpretation: my particular question will be "modern" and it will be shared with Thomas himself: how does Thomas conceive of the relation of theology and philosophy?

Like Aristotle, Thomas affirms in the opening article that he sees "theology" as a synonym for "divine science," but *unlike* Aristotle, he goes on to say that he sees the divine science as requiring first principles that are naturally inaccessible to our mind and can only be revealed by God, and he therefore sees the divine science as something that is not (unproblematically) *intrinsic* to what is called philosophy as its culminating and completing activity. This extrinsic factor, "revelation" (if I may use an abstract conceptualization not clarified until after the Enlightenment), separates the pagan and Christian views of the distinction: for Christianity, God must give a share in the knowledge of himself he enjoys, which is shared in the here below through faith, for faith accepts principles of reasoning that transcend our ordinary rational capacity. Aristotle's "divine science," the "theology" of his *Metaphysics*, is a part, says Thomas in article 1, of a particular and particularly eminent kind of science, viz., the "philosophical science built up by human reason." By contrast, the theology "that is a part of sacred doctrine" is concerned with "certain truths that exceed human reason," that are "made known to him by divine revelation": it therefore *"differs in kind [differt secundum genus]* from that theology which is a part of philosophy."[4] The distinction between revealed theology and natural theology (the theology of philosophy) is birthed simultaneously with the distinction between theology and philosophy in general. But more important to note here is that this "extrinsic" factor (which is in actuality—or this is the case Thomas makes—finally more intrinsic to our nature than the naturally intrinsic principles of reason) possesses a peculiar quality: let me term it "excess" insofar as it fundamentally "exceeds" but nevertheless determines the ultimate character of human rational nature itself.

Hence, despite the "extrinsic" nature of this excess, at the same time this divine science of Thomas of course wholly incorporates the content of philosophical inquiry, as article 2 makes plain in what seems a strange way, viz., appeal to the primary and secondary bearers of the divine science, its bearer by right (God), and by grace (rational creatures, angels, and humans): if divine science is, most properly speaking, "the science of"—that is, the order of knowing proper to—"God and the blessed," and only ours here below, in the

---

4. ST 1,1,1.

form of "sacred doctrine"—that is, the teaching of the Church—in a "subaltern" manner—that is, by derivation from higher principles accepted by faith,[5] built on principles that only God could reveal (as opposed to ones that reason can grasp in their self-evidence)—then nevertheless this science of sciences *does not* oppose or contradict the intelligibility of the lesser domains. Paralleling, perhaps, the doubling of distinction within theology as between theology and philosophy, Thomas here affirms the incorporation of philosophical reason into theology by making a distinction between God and humanity (the divine science is God's own self-knowledge and humanity's by a perfecting elevation of the latter's nature through divine gift that realizes its nature as intellectual creature). And he makes a distinction in the modes of humanity's share: there are those who share "fully" (that is, according to their essence: for the known is always known according to the mode of the receiver) in the divine science (the *beati*), and there are those who share partially, through the mediation of embodied faith (believers here below, *in via*, who must ascend to higher realities through the mediation of the material world and must assent to the teaching of the Church). *Their* divine science is *our* sacred doctrine. And both modes of knowledge can be called theology (as they are in Pseudo-Dionysius): God's self-knowledge mediated by his very words (interpreted by the Church) and the human study and apprehension of these words. The former, of course, is theology properly speaking. The human speech to/about God is derivative, always evidencing a lack that only God's condescension can overcome. Speech about God (what, since the thirteenth century, we call "theology") is always a category mistake: humans cannot "properly" speak about God; divine speech is address to God. The former receives its vitality and reason for being wholly from the latter. In other words let me affirm: Thomas assumes the unity of human rationality. Hence if a distinction between discourses is shared between the medieval and modern it is nevertheless owned in two very distant manners, for this unity, presumed by Thomas, is itself made impossible for modern thought.

5. ST 1,1,2.

In Thomas it is this unity itself that he seeks to sustain and justify through the clarification of the distinction.

All this *even though*, I must immediately add, this unified divine kind of human knowledge may of course stretch and radicalize to the breaking point the best conceptual systems that human thinking can offer. Augustine observes this through an extensive discussion in *De Trinitate* (Books V–VII) concerned with the disruption of the Aristotelian categories when applied to the mystery of the Trinity. According to the bishop of Hippo we have to speak improperly when speaking of the Triune mystery, the rationality of which exceeds mere human rationality: we have to fracture, fundamentally, Aristotelian categories and elevate the category of "relation" up to the level of co-primacy with "substance" when speaking of God, since the divine essence and the persons are equally primordial in God. Even more radically, because the divine persons are distinct from one another, "in relation," but *not* distinct from the divine essence, we have to assert and deny the primacy of the category of relation—we have to speak "properly" and "improperly" at one and the same time. Thomas Aquinas has the same playbook. A frequently cited example: he observes something similar in regard to the Aristotelian doctrine of substance and accidents vis-à-vis the mystery of the Real Presence of Christ in the Eucharist. The "transubstantiation" of the bread and wine into the Body and Blood of Jesus Christ retains the accidents of the former substances. This is of course "impossible" according to Aristotelian theory, since accidents *can only* manifest the essence of something to which they refer. Clearly, for Thomas, we are dealing with a *miracle*, and therefore human rationality fracturing before divine things, in application to which the categories of human rationality can only stutter (it is quasi-miraculous that we actually have to point this out...). In both cases of thinking the Trinity and the Eucharist (and how many more? Christology comes readily to mind) the religious mystery breaks the laws of these rational systems, exposing their fragmentary and incomplete character. These three loci of theology point to the possibility that incompleteness of reason before the divine disclosure is a norm, and even possesses a unique manner of intelligibility, a "theological" intelligibility, where the intellect (theology speaks only for those with eyes to see) is suffused with the mystery it contemplates.

"The divine science is one and simple, yet extends to everything," says Thomas in article 3: it considers everything from the highest, most universal vantage point, that is, insofar as it is divinely revealed, insofar as it refers to God.[6] "In sacred science," he will elucidate later (article 7), "all things are treated under the aspect of God; either because they are God himself; or because they refer to God as their beginning and end."[7] For Thomas, divine science is a larger category than philosophy, and indeed, the most comprehensive scientific categorization (in Aristotle it was the other way around: an aspect, indeed the highest aspect, of philosophy was the "divine science" of "theology"). Here again, an excess that disrupts and refigures the Aristotelian expression of human rationality. Like philosophy, the divine science of Thomas Aquinas considers all things and all things in their relation to God, as their highest cause. But unlike philosophy, it *penetrates higher and extends more universally* by virtue of the unique revelation of God's knowledge of himself; theology therefore *includes* the philosophical, like every other science at least principially, *within* itself. Further, proof of this universality of theology, for Thomas, is the peculiar dual or blended character of theology as *both* speculative and practical, incorporating and perfecting the totality of the human order, whereas other sciences are divided into *either* speculative *or* practical domains (the concern of article 4).[8] Theology, I say it again, contains philosophy in principle.

With this point Thomas seems to have in mind the great eighth book of St. Augustine's *City of God*. In the fourth chapter St. Augustine famously opens with the classic Christian definition of "the true philosopher" as "lover of God" in order thereby to prove that the Christian, who loves God most truly, that is, with the fullest

---

6. ST 1,1,3.
7. ST 1,1,7.
8. ST 1,1,4. Cp. Aristotle, *Metaphysics* 1025b25, 1026a18–19, etc.

knowledge of God, is the most authentic philosopher and that Christianity is the truest philosophy. Here St. Augustine states that most properly speaking "the pursuit of wisdom consists in both action and contemplation" because wisdom concerns both the "conduct of life" and the "investigation" of truth, as well as the reciprocally informing relation between these (a holy manner of life prepares one for the reception of truth and the truth informs our way of life through our love of it).[9] Christianity accomplishes this twofold pursuit of wisdom because it *knows* and *loves* God as creator and redeemer, who reveals to us the true "pattern" of human life in the worship of the Father through Christ and discloses himself as the worshipful "cause" of existence and the "ground" of all our understanding. For St. Augustine, the pursuit of human wisdom, *philosophia*, centers on and is completed in God because, he says, "man has been created in such a way that, through that which is most excellent in him, he may attain to that which excels all else, that is, the one true and perfect God."[10] St. Thomas repeats this in his own specific key in the first article as we have seen: "man is directed to God as an end that surpasses the grasp of his reason..."[11]

There is more to the paradox. Further, as article 6 makes explicit, theology does not contradict or negate philosophy, but rather *intensifies* philosophy. We would have to say that for Thomas the divine science is in fact most philosophical, philosophy *par excellence*: now quoting St. Augustine's famous definition of the love of wisdom or philosophy as "knowledge of divine things" (*De Trin* 13–14), Thomas observes that "sacred doctrine essentially treats of God viewed as the highest *cause* [since God is not known in himself here below but only through his *effects*, whether in creation or sacred history]—*not only* so far as he can be known through creatures just as philosophers knew him . . . *but also* so far as he is known to himself alone and revealed to others." Both theology and philosophy treat God, and together they treat him in a specific manner, as the highest cause, the source and end of all things—but theology treats of

9. *City of God*, bk. 4, 316. Cp. also Book 8.1.
10. Ibid., 316–17.
11. ST 1,1,1 resp.

God in an even higher way than philosophy in this *natural* aspiration towards the knowledge of God, which, though *ultimately* definitive of the natural, only can be given by grace. From the vantage of Thomas's clear Augustinian grasp of Aristotle, the nature of man is, we can only say, "naturally supernatural" or "immediately supernatural": expressed in the precise language of Thomas Aquinas, man reaches his "perfect" end, that is, the fulfillment of his nature, only through "help from without," that is, by divine "grace," since his perfect end ["the vision of God's essence"] surpasses the powers of his nature.[12] To think properly the character of human being demands the thinking of an *exception* to the distinction between the natural and supernatural before it even gets established, and therefore also to the concomitant distinction between philosophy and theology, which are *therefore defined by the exception to their distinction.* This means that theology can only be thoroughly *philosophical* (that philosophy is already thoroughly "theological" is not in question on Thomas's terms, as we have seen). And it means further that philosophy's aspiration to utter *and* to live out the definitive human truth—ultimately a *divine* truth, a truth that is *given* by God—is a task that articulates the very meaning of human, creaturely nature, and which can only be accomplished through a gratuitous intensification granted by God that exceeds the "natural" humanity of man: man is a paradox; his most immanent truth is found "outside" of himself in God.[13] Theology responds to a disclosure of God *beyond* the order of creaturely being, *in excess* of the naturally knowable, a disclosure of the truth that God alone possesses and which he alone can reveal, according to his free determination to do so. Already the antinomical cracks of the Christian rational "solecism" begin to emerge here again, for this revelation, though unnecessary, is *at the same time* absolutely necessary for the fulfillment of the singular end toward which man is naturally

12. ST I-II 5,5, resp., and ad 2. The phrase "naturally supernatural" is Jean-Luc Marion's summary of de Lubac's supernatural paradox in his essay "Foundations of the Distinction between Theology and Philosophy."
13. ST 1,1,1, resp. again: "It was necessary for man's salvation that there should be a knowledge revealed by God besides philosophical science built up by human reason . . . man is directed to God as an end that surpasses the grasp of his reason."

ordered (but to which he is wholly disproportionate).[14] This fundamental disproportion of human finitude before its infinite end, and the concomitant impossibility of the knowledge of God that allows man to accomplish this end (since it cannot be directly known, only presupposed as given and thought from, as the principles of sacred doctrine), does not mean at all—if I can express myself a little colloquially—that theology is not philosophical, or even less philosophical than philosophy itself. On the contrary. Thus Thomas concludes (again, clearly echoing Augustine), "sacred doctrine is *especially* called wisdom" [*Unde sacra doctrina maxime dicitur sapientia*].[15]

Theology done correctly overlaps with and includes within itself all philosophical knowledge, the science of God built up from reason; it is *fully* philosophical, but at the same time it is distinct from philosophy, from *mere* philosophy. How can theology be both philosophical and not philosophical? The answer to this crucial question is simple. Philosophy and theology possess the same formal object, God. And although philosophy knows God insofar as he is knowable through creatures, and theology knows God—let me be very precise—as God knows himself as revealed to others, *at the same time* theology knows God through creatures as well, *though not merely*. Theological knowledge is paradoxical: God speaks *to* humans *through* creatures *as* God. This is the divine prerogative. And it is why theology does not contradict philosophy, and indeed any of the vast storehouses of human knowledge, but wholly incorporates it into itself. Theology therefore reasons in the same way that philosophy does but by means of a reason informed by higher principles imparted by faith. Hence, *maxime dicitur sapientia*: there is one *lógos*, one source of the intelligibility of the world that is the same *lógos* who became flesh. The God of the philosophers is the God of Israel; the Lord of the Covenant is the Creator God. There is more: God, by his own free initiative, performs the impossible, making what is not God, and in fact has no "proportion" to God,

---

14. See Augustine, *On Christian Doctrine*, bk. 2.13.19, for the new sense Christianity gives, for him, to the grammatical concept: divine revelation introduces such novelty into human language that it requires its rules to be transfigured.

15. ST 1,1,6. Emphasis mine.

communicable of God. God is beyond proportion and even disproportion; his "excess" makes the communication of himself radically,
startlingly possible.

Theology, says Thomas, *sees* creaturely things as divine signs, in
their "reference to God as beginning and end," as the speech of God
about himself. But, already, philosophy does this too. The difference
is that theology presupposes the articles of faith (as principles of reasoning participant in divine wisdom given by God), whereas philosophy, that is, *mere* philosophy, does not.[16] Theology confesses the
faith of the Church. Philosophy does not have to do so in order to
find the true God, in his unity, power, and goodness, and even, albeit
dimly, as the Creator.[17] Theology lies in (paradoxical) continuity
with the philosophy it presupposes and incorporates into itself: it
fundamentally exceeds such a philosophy, but it shares with it the
same object (God) *and* the same reason. Yet again, Thomas is
impeccably traditional here: in *City of God* Augustine affirmed that
it was the divine god of the pagan philosophers alone—because
it was rational—that was worthy of Christian interlocution (as
opposed to the irrational gods of the poets or of the public cult).[18]
*Philosophy and theology involve the same human reason.* Faith,
though fundamentally a matter of things directly inaccessible to reason, includes reason within itself; faith is not irrational, but rather
*most* (*maxime*) rational: and reason finds the God in which one
believes and to which one confesses as its own most intimate truth.[19]

We have seen that, for Thomas, on the one hand, philosophy

---

16. ST 1,1,8.

17. ST 1,1,1: In the context of arguing for the necessity of a theology beyond the
*mere* theology of philosophy: "The truth about God such as reason could discover
would only be known by a few, and that after a long time, and with the admixture
of many errors."

18. *City of God*, 8.1.

19. In *De veritate* Thomas makes a distinction between the "truth of the thing"
and the "truth of predication" in order to articulate how the way in which things
exist in the Word of God is greater than the way in which they exist in themselves,
most properly speaking; but according to the order of predication, the truth is the
opposite. That is, the predicate "man" is more proper to the created thing that is the
effect of God's word than the thing as it exists (more truly) in the Mind of God. *De
veritate*, 2.4, resp.

contains a theology within itself, the knowledge of God as cause, as beginning and end of all things, insofar as God is "naturally" knowable through his effects; and on the other hand, sacred doctrine contains a distinctly different theology, which thinks inasmuch as he reveals himself, inasmuch as he grants to humans the knowledge he has of himself (which, again, takes the form for us here below of the articles of the Catholic faith). But nevertheless the reasoning at the apex of philosophy and at the heart of sacred doctrine are both called "theology." What justifies this univocal denomination of two equivocally determined manners of thinking that, as we have seen above, "differ in kind"? The theology of "mere" philosophy approaches God from the outside, indirectly, as implicit ultimate principle of its knowledge, whereas in the theology of sacred doctrine, which is "fully" philosophical, God is *miraculously* made a direct object of human science, by virtue of God's revelation. Same God, same reason. The content is both the same *and* new: the same inasmuch as the God is known as creator, as cause known through his effects; new inasmuch as it is this God (truly, but incompletely known already in philosophy) who performs an intensification and dynamic expansion of reason, directing towards its completion in a new order the very theological knowledge, the human knowledge contained within mere philosophy.

It is not wrong therefore to say that theology is *eminently* philosophical, and that philosophy is *immanently* theological. The distinction is necessary, insofar as philosophy can exist and can say true things, can think the truth of God (as highest cause, as beginning and end of all things) and can think the truth of things (referred to God as their beginning and end), and at the same time the distinction is always already overcome, since theology is philosophy at its most properly philosophical, *the* highest knowledge of divine things, granted by faith's access to revelation. Theology and philosophy are irreducibly different and irreducibly the same; there is an absolute gulf of discontinuity between them, and one that *within the horizon of faith* is always already overcome. According to Thomas Aquinas we must simultaneously affirm both distinction and unity, or better, discontinuity as an expression of a higher unity. In other words, the relation of philosophy and theology is, to conscript a

word used by Kant, an *antinomy*. For Kant, antinomies were dead
ends discovered through reason's free play, and pointed to a resolution in rules for practical reason; for us, here, their aporetic character turns on the motor of reason, and points instead to the negative
presence of higher truth.[20] Just as the speculative and practical must
be solecistically fused in the transfiguration of human knowing in
divine science, so also must the freshly minted distinction between
theology (based on supernaturally given principles), and philosophy (based on naturally given ones, that is, ordinary human experience of the world) be at once eclipsed, that is, made an opposed
polarity through which the higher, unified truth may manifest itself
to fragmented human intelligence. This opposition is found in philosophy itself (understood, abstractly, as separated from theology)
in a way that is different from the manner it is found within theology, in the antinomic manner I have just adumbrated. Briefly, the
difference is articulated by Thomas himself in his description of the
radical limitations of "natural" reason. I quote more extensively the
programmatic statement in article 1: "It was necessary for man's salvation that there should be a knowledge revealed by God besides
philosophical knowledge built up by human reason. Firstly, indeed,
because man is directed to God, as to an end that surpasses the
grasp of his reason. . . . But the end must first be known by men who
are to direct their thoughts and actions to the end. Hence it was necessary for the salvation of man that certain truths which exceed
human reason should be made known to him by divine revelation."
There is a knowledge of God, Thomas admits, present and achiev-
able outside of the condition of the intellect's participation in divine
self-knowledge through faith in the Church's panoply of doctrine.
Yet this "natural" knowledge is strongly and emphatically conditioned, even marginalized. He continues: "Even as regards those
truths about God which human reason could have discovered, it
was necessary that man should be taught by a divine revelation;
because the truth about God such as reason could discover, would
only be known by a few, and that after a long time, and with the

20. See Immanuel Kant, *Critique of Pure Reason*, "the antinomies of pure reason," A451/B479–A497/B525.

admixture of many errors." The truth about God that reason can realize outside of the horizon of the Catholic faith, for Thomas, is hardly universal, but only realizable, in fact, by the greatest intelligences that humanity may boast, and even in them, mixed with many mistakes. Natural, philosophical knowledge of God is "indirect," an exposure of reason to its own radical limitations and, as such, involves a dim awareness of its possibilities in the abyss of intelligible transcendence that opens before it, but which remains, for it, a silent hieroglyph. Hence human intelligence, though ordered to the knowledge of God as its singular, final end and structurally "in" the truth in an *a priori* way precisely *as* intelligence, needs supernatural illumination for a "saving" knowledge of God, which is the first knowledge that ultimately, finally matters (this knowledge is a condition for love—since, for Thomas, we only love what we know, and yet this love surpasses knowledge as its ultimate, final, and therefore "first" principle). The abyss of silence speaks, it addresses humanity, and through this electing address humanity is made capable of hearing the speech that is eternal in God. Within the divine science, philosophy is included as, simply, human intelligence transfigured by divinely given principles, made capable of a "direct," or better, "personal" knowledge of God (that is, participatory in the eternal divine speech but still "according to the capacity of the receiving intelligence").

With these brief comments on Thomas Aquinas we have passed through the first eight articles of the opening question of the *Summa theologiae*. We have seen that in Thomas's mind philosophy is not something one gives up in order to practice theology, but it is rather continued in a more intense modality through the expansion of human rationality that occurs within the broader horizon opened up by faith. Can we specify any further the character of this radical wisdom, the theology of the Church, *sacra doctrina*?

There are of course two further articles to this question that can fruitfully be approached with this question in mind. Yet these articles (9–10) stand out by the fact that they first appear (to me at least) to be appended to the question without a compelling, intrinsic reason. If this is the case, then Thomas's entire purpose for writing this introductory text (as stated in the prologue) would be a failure, on his own account. In the famous prologue to the book he states his intention to write a book for students that does not "hamper" their learning, which does not militate against the very task a work of theological writing is meant to accomplish: namely, to increase the person's participation in the wisdom of God, but in a specific mode. It is worth pausing for a moment, then, to catch the significance of the distinction Thomas forges in the sixth article.

According to Thomas there are two modes of human participation in the highest wisdom, two kinds of the highest human wisdom, one through practice, the formation of embodied habits that incline us to (or rather: into) God, and the other, which is akin to the way in which "a man learned in moral science might be able to judge rightly about virtuous acts, though he had not the virtue" itself. The first manner is simply the practices of the Christian faith, initiation and immersion in its sacramental life. The second manner is called the way of knowledge "acquired by study" based on principles revealed by God. For Thomas, therefore, this academic mode of knowledge, "learning," is distinct from the other mode of knowledge, which he calls, quoting Dionysius the Areopagite (*Div. Nom.* ii), "experience of divine things."[21] With "learning," described, again, as the wisdom "acquired by study," one explicates as far as humanly possible (the practice of *sacra doctrina*) the divine uncreated Wisdom, "the highest wisdom," God's own self-knowledge (the *scientia divina*). These two "ways" of participating in the one divine wisdom are, for Thomas, not in competition with one another, and the priority seems to be with the one that possesses the wisdom through "experience." The "way of learning" is only a way, although a real way, of participation in the inner reality of God. But this distinction seems to have radical ramifications for Thomas's theology as a whole—particularly in its wholly epistemological atmosphere and orientation, which I cannot but flag here. Let me only say that, on the one hand, this distinction makes the entire theological practice of divine wisdom a complement and deepening

21. ST I 1.6. resp. 3.

of the way of Christian practice as wisdom (perhaps in a way not far from the one proposed in the *Areopagitica* itself), but also, on the other hand, it is itself relativized by this way of Hierotheus, "not . . . mere learning, but . . . experience of divine things." Dionysius's Hierotheus is "taught" just as are Thomas's own students, but the difference between them is like the one between someone who possesses the habit of virtue, and can therefore judge rightly, that is, the virtuous man himself and the man simply "learned in moral science" who knows what the virtuous action would be, but may or may not be capable of enacting it (presumably not since, in Thomas's example, he "had not the virtue").

Allow me to return from here to the potential reasons for failing the pedagogical task that form the negative reasons that Thomas wrote the *Summa theologiae* in the first place. Our glance at questions 9–10 appears to raise the question, at least, of a presentation of the way of learning that "hampers" student progress in(to) the divine wisdom. Thomas lists three causes for these kinds of failure; after itemizing them I would like to focus on the second: "Students of the science of the Christian religion have not been seldom hampered," he says, "by what they have found written by other authors": the first cause is "the multiplication of useless questions, articles and arguments"; second: "because those things that are needful for them to know are not taught *according to the order of the subject matter* but according as the plan of the book might require, or the occasion of the argument offer"; and third: "because frequent repetition brought weariness and confusion to the minds of the readers." It is these failures Thomas Aquinas will avoid by "setting forth whatever is included in this Sacred Science as briefly and clearly as the matter will allow." Thomas proposes therefore to present the very rationality of Christianity "according to the order" that the subject matter itself proposes, that is, according to no *extrinsic*, facile, or *a priori* scheme. In this first question "on the nature and extent of sacred doctrine," meant to place the "proper limits" on the investigation, Thomas fundamentally, as we have seen, defines its principles (the articles of faith, which are the divine self-knowledge mediated by the authority of the Church), distinguishes it, albeit in a highly paradoxical manner, therefore from the other rational mode of inquiry into the divine (philosophy) and other sciences (being distinguished by its universal investigation of things under the aspect of revelation, and by its potential or actual inclusion of all sciences in itself), thereby illuminating its necessity (salvation requires the revelation of truths that exceed human reason) (article 1), and shows forth its scientific status and the peculiarities of its unique "scientificity" (if I can use Eagleton's neologism from another context),[22] which is exclusive to its uniquely revealed character, but which is nevertheless intelligible by the standard of Aristotelian "science," or order of knowing of (properly) ordered knowing: "a sacred science learned through revelation" (article 2), possessing a unity and singularity (article 3), albeit an ultimate and all-inclusive character (articles 4 and 5), and even a paradoxical equivalence, or discontinuous-continuity, with philosophy that it transcends, or rather "sublates" (article 6), and is, finally, a matter of argument (article 8) from uniquely mediated (article 7) first principles.

But it is the last two articles that on the face of it seem not to unfold from the subject matter itself. These questions concern, first, whether it is appropriate for the sacred doctrine to utilize metaphors (article 9), and second, whether Holy Scripture "may be expounded in multiple senses" (*sit secundum plures sensu exponenda*) (article 10). The ninth article is answered by the obvious: Holy Scripture is replete with metaphors, making primary use of them to communicate the divine truth that exceeds rational grasp through conceptual clarification, and the tenth article directly asks about the peculiar character of this Holy Scripture itself (the "sacred Scripture of this doctrine" [*Scriptura sacra huius doctrinae*] as he puts it in the introduction to this question). But I do not think it is the case that Thomas realized (as if as an afterthought to a thinking fascinated by Aristotle) that Holy Scripture did not become thematic enough through the first eight articles of this question and then decided to append two questions that deal with Holy Scripture, which for any Master of Theology (who is only propaedeutically Master of Arts) is obviously the source of the raw data by which he expounds the elements of the Christian religion under the

22. *Criticism and Ideology* (NY: Verso, 2016 [1976]).

authority of the Church (which possesses and communicates the principles of theological reason).

Three comments are appropriate. (1) The question of Holy Scripture and its relation to sacred doctrine ought obviously to be included in this introductory question to the *Summa*. Holy Scripture is the primary source with which the student of divine wisdom primarily works. I do not have to argue this point. It is properly included in this initial question. But the manner of its presentation in this first question nevertheless still seems extrinsic to the very order of the subject matter as it presents itself despite the fact that Thomas uses Scripture as the authoritative proof in the *sed contra* of articles 1, 3, 5, 6 (and 9); or rather, precisely because he does this it ought to have already been directly addressed. Direct attention to Scripture remains outstanding, and it is addressed in the last two articles, on first glance to justify (that is, to explain or elucidate the intelligibility of) his previous utilization of Scripture in the previous articles, a use which exemplifies his view that Scripture contains the Divine Science, translated into fully human form. The question, therefore, is: How is the character of this book an appropriate form for the divine Wisdom addressed to humanity? Any "summary" of Christian teaching itself obviously ought to tackle the question of Scripture in the first place (even more so for the medieval Master of Theology, whose central task was commentary on Scripture). And this conspicuousness becomes blaring in the context of a demonstration of theology's scientific status, since Scripture itself does *not* obviously possess a "scientific" character itself, but in form and appearance is more like the unphilosophical myths of the poets. Does the uniqueness of the divine science of the Church allow for such a unique mediation of divine revelation as that found in Scripture? It must.

(2) Article 8 raises the question of Scripture as it unfolds, and Scripture then subsequently passes from being indirectly addressed (as the means to answering article 9) to being directly addressed in article 10. In the second objection to this article, it is proffered that sacred doctrine is not a matter of argument because arguments are made either from authority or reason. But if the argument that unfolds within sacred doctrine is from authority, then it seems that

Thomas's conception of sacred doctrine as the greatest science is belittled, since the argument from authority is the least compelling kind of argument one can make. On the other hand, if the argumentation contained in sacred doctrine is a matter of reason, then it seems that the goal or end of sacred doctrine is belittled, since reason cannot attain by its own power that which sacred doctrine expounds: the truths of faith. Thomas responds to this objection by acknowledging that the argument from authority is what is in play with sacred doctrine, but because of the majesty of the authority, namely God, this argument is actually the strongest one can make. Further, he continues, sacred doctrine makes use of the authority of the philosophers (just as St. Paul did when he quoted the pagan poet Aratus in his speech on the Areopagus in Acts 17) where it can, and it makes use of the authority of revelation made to the apostles and prophets, that is, Holy Scripture, which it takes as a given, and which it considers therefore wholly "incontrovertible."

Interestingly, in this article, Holy Scripture is conceived as exemplarily (and "scientifically") making specific *arguments* (he refers here to St. Paul proving the general resurrection from the dogma of the resurrection of Christ in 1 Cor 15). Most spectacularly, Scripture is conceived as *presently* engaged in argument through the mediation of the Master of Theology: "Hence, Sacred Scripture, since it has no science above itself, can dispute with one who denies its principles [the *regula fidei* or 'articles of faith'] only if the opponent admits some at least of the truths obtained through divine revelation; thus *we* can argue with heretics from the texts in Holy Writ and against those who deny one article of faith we can argue from another." He concludes here that since faith rests on "infallible truth" given by God, and because the "opposite of a truth cannot be demonstrated," then every possible and actual argument against the divine truth can be defeated: "it is clear that the arguments brought against faith cannot be demonstrations but are difficulties that can be answered" (...*non esse demonstrationes, sed solubilia argumenta*).[23] Here Scripture is recognized as possessing the very

23. ST 1,1,8.

authority of divine speech, and sacred doctrine as arguing from this authority in an exemplary *and* living fashion. The Logos of God (the content of God's self-knowledge), which the Master of Theology himself uses, is already inscribed within Holy Scripture itself, and it is touched, tasted, and seen in the liturgical order; arguing Christian truth is a matter of sharing in the very theology that is God's by right, and humanity's by means of a miraculous gift. One's fidelity to the divine truth contained in Scripture means that one becomes a means by which it is manifest in the world of human wisdom: the single task of a Master of Theology is to show forth its divine character.

Now this assertion regarding the scientific character of Scripture (which possesses the divine science itself as communicated to men) raises the acute question regarding the rationality of the form of this revelation, which is full of images, figures, parables, and narratives, a question that is an echo of the problem of the many "solecisms, barbarisms, and monstrosities" in Scripture that was of great intellectual concern from the second to fifth centuries, from the first apologists to St. Augustine.[24]

(3) Here we can finally come to see how article 9, on the obviously abundant use of metaphors in Holy Scripture, and article 10, on the recognition and delineation of the multiplicity of senses in Scripture, relate to the previous articles, all concerned, as we have seen, with showing the (supremely) scientific character of sacred doctrine, that it is, again, reasoning based on (the highest) first principles. These final articles are particularly set to show first, that when it is a matter of divine revelation, the metaphorical character of such is not an impediment but a virtue: "Sacred doctrine makes use of metaphors as both necessary and useful."[25] Second, these articles will show that a multiplicity of senses in Holy Scripture is a result of its *divine* source and appropriate to the divine manner of speaking. Together, these questions show the *uniquely* scientific

---

24. See Henri de Lubac, for example, *The Christian Faith: An Essay on the Structure of the Apostles' Creed*, trans. Richard Arnandez, F.S.C. (San Francisco, CA: Ignatius Press, 1986), ch. 8, "Christian Solecisms," 261–90.

25. ST 1,1,9, repl. obj 2.

character of revelation, that revelation is characterized by some *wonderful* idiosyncrasies that in no way detract from its scientific character and instead precisely express that very character in its comprehensive but all-encompassing distinction from other sciences (with theology, *maxime sapientia*, the philosophy *par excellence*, we are dealing, in other words, with human reason at its most spectacularly miraculous and profound, for its object is God as God knows himself—reason itself, in uncreated form—insofar as this can be communicated to man).

Article 9 observes the obvious fact that Scripture is replete with metaphors. This it holds in common with poetry, the "least of the sciences"; and in fact a majority of Scripture itself is poetry plain and simple. Thomas's remarks here are hardly taken seriously enough by his students. He observes that *this poetic expression befits the Scriptures because the very form of human knowing possesses what we can call a metaphorical form*: as compositely spiritual and material beings we know spiritual truth through the mediation of the material; we know according to our nature, compositely, in a spiritual-material manner.[26] Therefore the Scriptures, he says, "put forward divine and spiritual truths by means of comparisons with material things" (*divina et spiritualia sub similitudine corporalium tradere*) because "it is natural for man to attain to intellectual truths through sensible objects, because all our knowledge originates from sense" (*Est autem naturale homini ut per sensibilia ad intelligibilia veniat, quia omnis nostra cognitio a sensu initium habet*). It is natural for humans to know through similitude, that is, "metaphorically": For "God," he says, "provides for everything according to the capacity of its nature." Man as metaphorical animal.

I will quote two further sources to elucidate this perspective: Nicholas Cusanus, from 14th-century Germany, and the Pseudo-Dionysius, from the 6th-century Syrian desert. In his most famous work, *On the Vision of God*, Cusanus speaks from this principle that humans know divine things only indirectly through comparison, or

---

26. ST 1,84,7 resp: "The proper object of the human intellect, which is united to a body, is a quiddity or nature existing in corporeal matter; and through such natures of visible things it rises to a certain knowledge of things invisible."

by analogy with the world of human experience: "In order to trans-port you to divine things by human means," he says to the monks to whom this treatise is addressed, "I *must* use some kind of simili-tude."[27] In order to pass into "mystical theology," says Cusanus, a sensible image is necessary. The term "mystical theology" of course comes from Pseudo-Dionysius, Thomas's key authority in this question. (It is likely that Cusa has this article from the *Summa* in mind here in *De visione Dei*.) Cusanus defines "mystical theology" in *On the Vision of God* as "wonders revealed beyond all sensible, rational and intellectual sight."[28] It is the highest form of theologi-cal knowing according to the pseudonymous Syrian monk who coined the term, and, as Cusanus indicates, it requires the intensifi-cation and conversion of sensible, rational, and intellectual vision (the threefold order of human being) into something higher, which can only be articulated through paradoxical language that holds together opposites like "knowing-unknowing" and seeing a "daz-zling darkness." This is based on the fundamental conviction of Pseudo-Dionysius that "we [humans as opposed to angels] contem-plate the divine mysteries *solely* by way of the perceptible symbols attached to them."[29] For Pseudo-Dionysius, mystical theology is the passage *beyond* (mere) negative theology, which emphasizes the transcendence of God by rejecting the capacity of any sign (neces-sarily, for us, taken from the creaturely domain) to signify God truly, and therefore undertakes the passage through the "negation of the negations," into the realm of an affirmation beyond negation, which demands a fresh return to the very symbols, images, and metaphors that one rejected as merely creaturely in order to reach farther into the divine mystery. He famously concludes: "[The Cause of all] is beyond every assertion and denial ... it is free of every limitation, beyond every limitation."[30] For Pseudo-Dionysius it seems that the practice of various "theologies" are, in other words,

27. *Nicholas of Cusa, Selected Spiritual Writings*, ed. H. Lawrence Bond (Mah-wah, NJ: Paulist Press, 1997), 235, emphasis mine.

28. Ibid.

29. *Epistle* 9 1104B (281). Emphasis mine.

30. *The Mystical Theology* 1048B (141).

intellectual preparation ("spiritual exercises") for the liturgical experience of Christian sacrifice, which is communion with the living flesh of Christ, containing the highest reaches of divinity in the most ordinary humanity.[31] This reading of Pseudo-Dionysius may shed light on the distinction proffered by Thomas between two human paths in the one divine wisdom: the way of learning is a spiritual exercise, preparation for better initiation and participation in the "divine things" themselves, the sacramental mysteries of the Church. The former way is not meant as an alternative to the latter.

In the response to the second objection (regarding the obscurity of truth that is involved in the metaphorical form), Thomas makes the remarkable observation, following again Pseudo-Dionysius, that divine revelation, inasmuch as God is "beyond every limitation," has the unique property of somehow overcoming the opaque density of the material domain and expressing itself freely through it: "The ray of divine revelation is *not extinguished* (*non destruitur*) by the sensible imagery wherewith it is veiled, as Dionysius says (*Celestial Hierarchies* 1); and [even further] its truth *so far remains* (*sed remanet in sua veritate*) that it does not allow the minds of those to whom the revelation has been made to rest [merely] in the metaphors (*ut mentes quibus fit revelatio, non permitat in similitudinibus permanere*), but raises them to the knowledge of the truth." In other words, the metaphorical character of the truth is not reduced to merely literal understanding, but rather *remains precisely metaphorical*, and therefore enacted as a veiled, elusive (hence!) *true* revelation of the divine. It is precisely metaphorically that God is known, for he is known properly when known as unknown. The Areopagite will therefore say that whereas angels know divine things in purely intellectual ways, the proper manner of human knowing is through the symbols wherein divine speech is materially incarnate in worldly images made sacred. Thomas similarly privileges the meta-

31. For the reading of the Dionysian corpus implied here, see Timothy Knepper, *Negating Negation: Against the Apophatic Abandonment of the Dionysian Corpus* (Eugene, OR: Cascade Books, 2014).

phors (*similitudines*) of Scripture as the most fitting vessels for divine speech to human beings.

Thomas recognizes that in the Areopagite this elevation of mind to God occurs in and through the metaphors, *not* because the metaphors are *left behind* like husks once the intelligible kernel is reached by the intellect, but because the metaphors themselves "do not allow the mind to rest," and are higher means of communicating the divine truth than abstractions themselves. The response to the third objection refers to Dionysius's development of the Proclean notion that apparently less apt and grosser expressions are in actuality *more* apt and *less* gross when the reference is God, who exceeds the order of differences that articulates the hierarchy of creaturely being though all the while founding it, being immediately present at each level.[32] Thomas summarizes the three reasons that Dionysius gives in this context, and the second is the most interesting: Not only— reason one—do the gross material expressions have a pedagogical tenor, reminding us that there is no such thing as a literal description of divine things for humans, and that even the most critically purified forms of our reasoning are still only similitudes themselves, being of the same category as the grossest images (and hence the grossest possible images have the merit of being upfront about their basic anthropomorphic or worldly form, hence allowing us deeper passage into the highest knowledge of God that is possible here below), and not only—reason three—does the veiling of divine truth in metaphors hide the truth from those who are unworthy (by, as Dionysius makes clear, only becoming accessible to faith, and not to mere learning, which is so easily led astray by pride—since it tends to assume that it can reach the divine truths in themselves by its own power, and thereby fails to see that the highest conceptual knowledge of the divine is *of the same order* as the lowest, most figurative—namely, of the human, the anthropomorphic order), but also (and this is the second reason in Thomas's summary) because metaphorical expression of divine truth is the highest possible expression within the order of worldly embodiment that presently

32. See Dionysius the Areopagite, *Celestial Hierarchies*, 2, 3; following Proclus, *Commentary on the Parmenides of Plato*, I, 638.

determines all our knowing: "This is more befitting the knowledge of God that we have in this life," says Thomas. "For what he is not is clearer to us than what he is. Therefore similitudes drawn from things farthest away from God form within us a truer estimate that God is above whatsoever we may say or think of him" (*Magis enim manifestatur nobis de ipso quid non est, quam quid est, et ideo similitudines illarum rerum quae magis elongantur a Deo, veriorum nobis faciunt aestimationem quod sit supra illud quod de Deo dicimus vel cogitamus*). Thomas says elsewhere: "the highest knowledge of God is to know that we do not know God."[33] Here he says that the "metaphorical" mode of "comparison" is simply the highest expression of this unknowing because it includes "negation" and the eminent "negation of negation" within its very expression: metaphorical comparison *is* an affirmation that negates. It says yes and no and yes/no at once. To say "God my rock" as the Psalmist does is to perform a creative *identification* of God and the rock, but as a metaphor it also undoes the identification, since the metaphorical character of the expression depends first on the literal fallacy of the identification. But it also includes the further, tempered recognition that God (cause) and the rock (effect) possess some kind of common feature(s), that the rock is an appropriate way to signify something about God, namely his strength, consistency, fidelity, etc. If philosophy is the knowledge of the divine cause, indirectly through its effects, the theological knowledge found in Scripture deepens this indirect knowledge and elevates it through making divinely privileged (and hence sacred) metaphorical comparisons. The identity, although a matter (ultimately, we can say) of analogy and not (obviously) univocity, is not exhausted by the conceptual (literal) expression of that which remains contained in the metaphorical expression precisely because God contains the truth of the rock that signifies him in a manner that is infinitely more preeminent than the rock as it exists in itself. Precisely because, therefore, there is no common measure between God and creature, it is somehow truer of God to speak, along with Scripture, metaphorically of his "right arm" than to express the same thing conceptually by affirming his

33. *Questiones disputatae de potentia Dei*, 7, 5, ad 14.

"operative power"—although the recognition that the metaphorical expression is rightly conceived as asserting what can be conceptually asserted is essential to understanding it, and is, further, included within the scope of its metaphoricity in the first place.[34]

Like the way theology encompasses the philosophical, metaphors encompass conceptual truth; the latter is only an explication of what is more intensively contained within the figurative expression. Because symbol and metaphor are most "natural" to *human* knowing, we could even say that they remain when the conceptual explication is exhausted, and that conceptual "naming" is always already and always remains (therefore) intrinsic to the metaphorical order of knowledge by similitude.[35] All that matters is that one recognizes the metaphorical character of the expression in order that one may participate in the dense intelligibility of the similitude and be elevated from the sensible to higher reality. This recognition means that one has already passed into the negative order of conceptual critique. We can even say therefore that this inexhaustibility of the metaphor by literal abstraction of concepts from it *results from* the analogical character of the comparative juxtaposition. The lesser known is known by means of the better known; God, who eminently exceeds the order of distinctions by which we know things in the world, and the world itself as this context of distinctions in which we know through finite differentiation, nevertheless becomes known to us by means of comparison with the world of our creaturely being, which includes the highest manner of our knowing as much as the lowest.

The ninth article, which I have spent some time expounding, is concerned to show the truth-bearing capacity and necessity of metaphorical, poetic expression when it is a matter of divine revelation. The tenth article argues that the deepening and stretching of signification evidenced in the fourfold character of sense in Scripture likewise is fitting when it is a matter of dealing with the speech, logos, intelligibility, or word of God himself. This multiplication of senses is exclusive to the divine science alone, Thomas observes, since God

34. See ST 1,1,10, ad 3.
35. See ibid.: the "parabolic" lies at the level of "literal" signification.

alone has the power to signify by words *and*, in a sort of redundance of excellence, even further by means of the things signified by the initial words: "The author of Holy Writ is God, in whose power it is to signify his meaning, not by words only (as man also can do), but also by things themselves. So, whereas in every other science things are [merely] signified by words, this science has the property that the things signified by the words have themselves also a signification." The normal mode of scientific signification, shared by God and man, is the literal: signs stand for things. The further mode exclusive to the divine prerogative is the "spiritual sense," based on and presupposing the literal word-thing signification, and possessing a further thing-cum-sign-of-further-thing order of signification, which unfolds in the traditional threefold division (*allegorical*, in which things unveiled in the New Covenant are hidden in the Old; *tropological*, in which Christ's actions signify what we ought to do; and *anagogical*, in which present things signify the glory of the world to come). Because God is the author of Scripture, there speaking of himself and all things in reference to himself, and because God comprehends all things in a single intellectual act, Thomas points out, the multiplicity and depth of Scriptural meaning(s) is not only possible, but in fact makes sense—it is "not unfitting" (*non est inconveniens*),[36] even though a facile mind might be forgiven in its conclusion that it is unscientific—which it would be if we were not dealing with a wholly unique object of our knowing, *God's* speech in *human* modality. The major point made by Thomas in this article is an extension of the ninth article: the divine science is unique by virtue of the primacy of metaphors in its expression of the truth, and indeed its, if I can put it this way, *total metaphoricity*. Just as metaphors involve the pluralization of significations, so Scripture (God's speech) is neither univocal nor literal in signification, but the word of the Living Reality that exceeds the order of worldly contrasts by which things may have their own individual and relative meanings proper to them.

Again Thomas is following St. Augustine, now from his discussion of metaphorical signs in the second book of *De doctrina Chris-*

36. ST 1,1,10, resp.

*tiana*. In that text Augustine defines the major division among signs as literal and metaphorical. Signs are literal "when used to signify the things for which they were invented," that is, when a word applies to a thing. Signs are metaphorical, by contrast, "when the actual things which we signify by the particular words are used to signify something else."[37] Things understood through other things, is the basic character of human understanding. Signs, says St. Augustine, "are those things which are employed to signify something else";[38] and more acutely: "a sign is a thing which of itself makes something other come to mind, besides the impression that it presents to the senses."[39] According to Augustine, the essence of human religiosity (itself the essence of human existence inasmuch as the quality of human existence is a matter of rightly or wrongly loving things) is the proper interpretation of things and signs. Interpretation is the work of ordering oneself rightly to God (and then the world). St. Thomas expresses the same thing in his own way when he observes in the first article of this question that the realization of man's singular, final end, the accomplishment of his salvation, is a matter of "knowledge"—the knowledge of the end by which man can "direct his thoughts and action to that end" that is revealed by God and comprises the Christian religion.[40]

It is "natural," as it were, for God to speak things themselves as signs, like the poets. God's creative activity is like an artist's construction in this regard.[41] All the effects of God's creation, everything that is, speaks God, becomes a sign, a thing-as-sign, that refers to the Cause, present in and throughout his effects. Human knowing of the transcendent Cause is a matter of discerning this likeness of the Cause throughout his effects, which is a matter of seeing a particular similitude between the world and God (which is a likeness within a greater unlikeness, which is at the same time an all-the-greater likeness; the metaphoricity of God's speech means in

37. *On Christian Teaching*, II, 10,15 (37).
38. Ibid., II, 2,2 (9).
39. Ibid., II, 1,1 (30).
40. ST 1,1,1 resp.
41. ST 1,14,8 resp. and ad 3.

part that sacred knowledge, the highest wisdom, is not abstract, but the most marvellous way of human knowing, involving the awakening of the soul to the Living Presence of God, personally addressing it through a suffusion of its unbearable glory in created things raised to the new status of revealed speech, which does not contradict but builds on their *naturally revelatory character* of God as the One Creator and Lord, but which speaks something new). This discernment of similitude is metaphorical inasmuch as there is not a literal correspondence between God and the creature, but a dynamic one in which whatever the creature signifies of God, whatever can be read in this creaturely likeness, only God actually properly possesses, and that to an eminent and unknowable degree— just as metaphors, in order to work, must be understood precisely as non-literal, as a manner of speaking, as thing as sign of another thing. God freely assumes this natural context of divine signification in creation and "uses" it to advance his plan of salvation through revealing truths about himself necessary for the salvation of humanity, called to the infinite blessedness of intellectually beholding God (the Christian path as understood, at least, from the vantage of "the way of learning" that Thomas calls theology).

Looking back over the passage taken by this brief commentary on the opening question of St. Thomas's introductory *Summa*, concerned with the "nature and extent of sacred doctrine," a conclusion is worth stating: Only through an *a priori* acceptance of divine revelation in its given form, as absolute wisdom, can the human love of wisdom properly realize its final (and therefore first) aim, which can only occur by the inclusion within itself of the places where the divine truth *most humanly* hides itself: poetry, symbol, myth. These are various names for the site of primary human intelligibility, the lifeworld of pre-theoretical understanding wherein we first become oriented in the world. This realm of mythic understanding first provides the initial coordinates of comprehension of the totality of reality stretching between our "unknown" Origin and End. We inhabit this world—the world, the world of life, and as such the human world, the world that pre-consciously forms the possibility of our primary valuations, a world that we are born into and receive already oriented and ordered—through our practical action. The highest practical action is action in light of our contemplation of God, but this contemplation arrives through and returns to the symbolically deepened world of rite, of material worship, like the permanent rhythm of our breathing that sustains our life—and in a way *is* our life.

With that conclusion stated, it is worth revisiting one final time St. Thomas's distinction between knowledge by experience and knowledge by theory raised in article six. Later in the *Summa* he returns to this distinction several times and it becomes clear that his ultimate recourse is (again) to St. Augustine, in this case especially from Book XII of *De Trinitate*. I mention in particular IIa-IIae q.45 aa.1–3. Here Thomas refers again to Pseudo-Dionysius's comment regarding Hierotheus's "learning" and coordinates it to St. Augustine's concept of "wisdom," pertaining to the highest order of reason wherein divine things are "contemplated" and "considered," contrasting it with "knowledge" pertaining to the lower order of reason, which rises up to God as Principle, Origin and End, through the world of our embodiment. St. Thomas here tends to use the terms wisdom as [intellectual] virtue and wisdom as [charismatic] gift. Wisdom as gift contemplates the "sovereign good which is the last end" and involves "right judgment about divine things" (the result of divinely-given contemplation) leading to "judgment of human acts by divine things and the direction of human acts according to divine rules": it offers direction of human acts according to divinely-given rules inasmuch as it is, by contrast to wisdom as knowledge, "a kind of union of the soul with God." This union results from charity, the basis and content of the gift of wisdom. Astoundingly, St. Thomas says that "it belongs to wisdom as intellectual virtue to pronounce right judgment about divine things after reason has made its inquiry, but it belongs to wisdom as a gift of the Holy Spirit to judge aright about them on account of connaturality with them." He justifies this statement by reference to Hierotheus's learning through "suffering divine things." This is astounding, first because wisdom as intellectual virtue is first considered as the manner of theology according to philosophy ("attained by human effort"), whereas wisdom as gift (termed the "highest wisdom" in the question we have examined) is coordinated with the gift of new rational principles that form the intelligence of faith, and derive from God's own unfathomable intelligibility itself. In the second place, this perspective is astounding because connaturality indicates human participation in God's self-knowledge that is one with his absolute love as Holy Trinity. The distinction between the two separate modes of wisdom, which we have come to call philosophy and theology is here again shown to be a partial perspective, and this because, ultimately, our supernatural Beginning and End is somehow natural to us: charity is the divine being, and as a result is our own, inasmuch as we are. It is the essence of the Good to communicate *itself*. Hence St. Thomas can affirm: "Now sympathy or connaturality for divine things is the result of charity, which unites us to God. . . . Consequently wisdom which is a gift has its cause in the will, namely charity, but it has its essence in the intellect, whose act is to judge aright." Charismatic union with God is a condition for right knowledge about God, for God's self-knowledge (the basis of sacred doctrine) is coincident with his self-union. But here again Thomas is only faithfully explicating Augustine's proposal, all-determining for Christianity, that the love of wisdom is, after all, the love of God, full stop. In Plato, *phrónēsis* was not yet separated from *sophia*, as in Aristotle, and we see here, perhaps, St. Thomas amending Aristotle, and profoundly even transcending the limitations of his Scholastic context wherein divinely revealed truth tends to be "epistemically" rendered on the model of what the de facto a priori discipline of "philosophy" determines.[42] What we may call the *gnōsis* of St. Thomas, the ultimate identity, by the grace of finite participation in the infinite, of our knowledge of God with God's knowledge of himself, is far closer to the concept of knowledge (*jñāna*) of Vedantic India than the gnostic modes of para-Christian practice that have not ceased to haunt Christianity from its beginnings. Plato was aware, perhaps in a way more directly or personally "religious" than Aristotle, of the primacy and pertinence

42. On this see Jean-Luc Marion, *Givenness and Revelation* (Oxford: Oxford University Press, 2016).

of an originally given revelation at the basis of the tradition of human knowledge, and serving as its condition, and which shapes the intellectual practices we undertake—including, as a fruition, the very form of our writing.

Thomas's sacred doctrine therefore unites in a new and "dazzling" manner what was only ever fragmented in the aspirations of human reason for God, but which the greatest intuitions of the greatest philosophers always somehow knew, as for Aristotle who still maintained that "the lover of myth is in a sense a lover of wisdom, for myth is composed of wonders."[43] Christianity, for Thomas, begins to see just how right he was. "Myth," says one theologian in a very apt way, "created the language in which every act of speech touching on divine things must be expressed in order to speak to humanity, even divine speech itself, since this language is native to humanity."[44] In the ultimate disclosure of God in the Incarnation of Christ—or rather: in the eschatological opening of humanity to experience of divine things, to the "wisdom from above" to which we are asked to dedicate the work of our minds in order to show forth the divinity of the things believed—a recovery and new appropriation of the "mythic" speech of God is enacted, divided from which the human love of wisdom was always radically impoverished and incomplete. This method outlined here by Thomas Aquinas may be expanded to include, through the privileged principle of "*chrēsis*," all of the places the wisdom of God continues to hide, not just the philosopher Aristotle.[45]

"Wisdom," said St. Augustine, "is the charity of God."[46] And what does not find its being and truth in the divine charity?

---

43. Metaphysics 1 (A) 982b 19–20.

44. Louis Bouyer, *Gnosis*, 64.

45. A first attempt at expanding this Patristic principle of the "use" (*chrēsis*) of pagan ideas and concepts within the Christian intelligence, for its own aim of understanding and showing forth the divinity of its sacred teaching, was sketched by Indologist Paul Hacker in a profound but dated book, *Theological Foundations of Evangelization* (Nettetal: Steyler Verlag, 1980).

46. Ep. 120.

# STUDY 4

WORD: Philosophy, Theology
NAME: Friedrich Schelling
STYLE: Essay
MATTER: Contributions to the Elimination of the Notion
of a "Conflict of the Faculties"

"The point at which *every* philosophy will find itself either in agreement or in conflict with *common* human consciousness lies in the
manner in which it explains the Most High, explains God."[1]

## Introduction

I t IS SURELY A PLATITUDE to continue our consideration of
wisdom, now in the modern period, with the observation that
modernity is marked by various dualisms. I will risk the platitude, not only because platitudes often harbor deep, overlooked
truths, but in order to introduce my theme. First what is overlooked: Modernity's dualisms are determinative of what we mean
when we say "modernity." Its dualisms are, further, *indexes* of what
is wrong with modernity, marks of its failure (to speak as a philosopher) to account properly or adequately, *with fidelity*, of and to the
humanity of man, the worldliness of the world and the divinity of
God.[2] It follows, therefore: these dualisms ought to be overcome.
These three dimensions are typically contained in any intellectual

---

1. Schelling, *Lectures on the History of Modern Philosophy*, 132 (Bowie translation).
2. To express the totality of human questioning by the three traditional loci of
*metaphysica specialis*...

coincidence of modernity and dualism, and I would like to retain them with full force.

Second, my theme: the defining modern dualism of disciplinary distinction, theology, and philosophy. There are various ways to speak of the distinction of philosophy and theology. I am *not* speaking of (as was noted in the previous chapter) the "theology" intrinsic to philosophy, the last and most important stage of divine science or metaphysics (as in Aristotle), *nor* am I speaking of the "theology" of silent "hymn" before the nameless One, realizing the goal of mystical union toward which all philosophy aspires (as in late Antique Neoplatonism). I am speaking, rather, of theology and philosophy in the modern sense, as distinct and irreducible manners of knowing, "sciences" in the Latin or German senses (*scientiae* or *Wissenschaften*). The fundamental question to ask in respect to this dualism is whether it is an aberration or valid development. We could even ask whether the dualism, which, like every conceptual development, *does* have a historical determination (and in this case a very clear one), is still appropriate today, whether it is revisable, and to what degree. We could ask, in other words, if this historically determined distinction is permanent and necessary for Christian thinking, or if we should move beyond it. My thinking about these questions will manifest itself below. I am tempted to propose that the modern distinction of theology and philosophy is not appropriate for Christian thinking outside of the sphere of Christendom—that is, a universal Christian horizon, which includes a self-evident account of the real in light of the Trinity and Incarnation, of Creation and Recreation through Last Judgment—a horizon within which it first emerged, but which today is anything but the normative grammar it once was (and the question whether it was appropriate then, albeit perhaps necessary in highly specific and indeed, idiosyncratic socio-historical circumstances, is altogether different from the question of its theoretical necessity or permanence). "Christendom" as a domain of basic intelligibility providing a universal "grammar," as a "horizon" or "episteme," is perhaps—perhaps—the place within which a distinction can be intelligible and functional. Outside of this domain the distinction devolves into a dualism; outside of this domain we are in modernity. That today we live in a historical situation closer to that of the Fathers of the first three centuries of the Church, before the Edict of Milan (313), seems to me to be more than obvious. It is equally obvious that Christian intellectuals of this period explicitly argued as philosophers for the philosophical character of Christianity; viz., that Christianity is the best way of life lived according to the *lógos*, that Christianity proposes the most satisfying and compelling account of the humanity of man, the worldliness of the world and the divinity of God, and their interrelation. Ought we to think the same way? In what follows I will assume the classical Christian vantage point.

We will proceed through a patient explication of a surprising statement found in the *oeuvre* of 19th-century German philosopher Friedrich Schelling, *not* for the sake of fidelity to Schelling and his thought, but for the sake of fidelity *to that which* Schelling sought to think—a seeking to think, which, whatever the limitations and aberrations of his thinking, shows that his was, in fact, a philosophy. With this observation, that there was something peculiarly philosophical about his philosophy, I begin.

## Explication

In his 1836 *Munich Lectures* (On the History of Modern Philosophy), Schelling remarks that the question by which any philosophy must be judged is whether, simply, it "is found to be in agreement or conflict with the common consciousness [*Bewusstsein*] of humanity." In the first place, Schelling's remark is obvious, an observation tending towards the banal: of course philosophy is judged by its "relation to the common consciousness of humanity," because the elucidation and expression of the latter is its defining task. The question that matters is that of what is at stake in this elucidation or expression. In other words, what is the *content* of this "common consciousness of humanity" in the light of which we must judge the value of any philosophy? What is common to every human consciousness; what defines it as such, making it *human*, in Schelling's view? What matters, Schelling immediately specifies in a luminous phrase, is ultimately the "way in which a philosophy

explains the Most High."[3] The picture of God suggested or proposed by any philosophy is the very measure of that philosophy.
The "explanation" of God is, according to Schelling, the essential
work of philosophy. Why? Because God, the "Most High"—that is,
*the One God*, common to human consciousness, defining it as
such—is universal, present (and whether concealed or disclosed,
equally present) in any philosophy, or else that thinking, whatever it
is, is simply *not* philosophy.[4] Philosophy's aspiration, for Schelling
as much as for the ancients, is *to find and to articulate and to embody*
the universally true, that which defines the humanity of man. (By
"universally true" I mean, in the first place, that which is universally
human, the definitive for us, and therefore by "that which defines
the humanity of man" I mean that fundamental aspiration for the
universally true, the truth as such, through which we can come to
an essential understanding of ourselves, since *we are the beings who
seek this understanding of the truth*; the truth as such is our truth.)
Philosophy is predicated on the possibility of reaching this ultimately true and of participating in it, which becomes the fulfillment
of the aspiration that makes man what he is. This is what I take
Aristotle to mean when he opens his *Metaphysics* with the famous
words, "By nature all men desire to know."[5]

For Schelling as much as for Aristotle, philosophy culminates in,
to use Aristotle's terms, the "most universal" or "first" philosophy,
and therefore the "most divine science," which he terms, following
Plato, "theology," the highest, defining human aspiration that culminates in the vision and imitation of God.[6] Plato already said that
the highest aim of philosophy is "to become like God, as far as that

---

3. SW X, 132; Fr. 141–42. See Courtine's discussion of this passage: "La Critique
schellingienne de l'ontotheologie," *La Question de Dieu selon Aristote et Hegel*, ed.
Thomas De Koninck et al. (Paris: Presses universitaires de France, 1991), 229–30.

4. See, for example, Thomas Aquinas, ST 1, 6, resp.

5. *Metaphysics* I (A), 1, 980a, 1.

6. *Metaphysics* I (A), 2, 983a, 1–10; VI (E) 1026a, 19. Plato was first, it appears, to
use the term "theology," and he does so in book 2 of the *Republic*, 379a. For Plato it
was a matter of "correct speech" about the gods, a concern that develops out of a
critique of the portrayal of the divine by the myths.

is possible."[7] This classical conception of the philosophical enter-prise, determinative of its aim and scope from its beginnings, can be more acutely summarized by noting that philosophy takes upon itself the fundamental human aspiration for "salvation" (inherited from the myths) and claims for itself the unique possibility of actu-ally accomplishing it (in contradistinction to the myths). In Plato's terms this was articulated as the work of "escaping from the earth to the dwelling of the gods as quickly as we can."[8] This pursuit of the divine is the highest human truth. One lives *most humanly*, for Plato or Aristotle (or Plotinus), when one lives *most divinely*. Philosophy's quest for the universally true, the accomplishment of the humanity of man, is realized only by reaching a wholly theological terminus: it is the god, the most divine God, says philosophy, the One God, the Origin and End of all things, that is, the "First Cause,"[9] that, by being known, actualizes, completes, or fulfills the humanity of man. God and relation to God is the most human truth.

By this quotation with which I open this chapter, Schelling shows himself in fundamental continuity with this deepest center of the Western philosophical tradition.[10] So far I have gathered that God is the common consciousness of humanity, the universal truth of man, and therefore the greatest aspiration of philosophy, and that we there-fore must judge philosophy by its capacity, says Schelling, to "explain" God. Philosophy in its classical sense is most deeply concerned with the point of convergence of three terms: (1) humanity, (2) universal-ity, and (3) God. The answer to the question, what is man? is found in the quest for the universal truth that is identified with God. What pre-cisely does Schelling mean here by this "explanation of the Most High"? Let us address the latter term of this phrase first:

(a) Why does Schelling use this term in particular? By "Most High" he seems to refer to the name by which men called on God *before* the revelation of his covenant name to Moses, the exclusive

7. Plato, *Theaetetus*, 176a–b.
8. Ibid.
9. Thomas Aquinas, ST I, 44, 1, resp.; Proclus, *Elements of Theology*, prop. 12.
10. And, in fact, this center is the most proper point of orientation and open-ness to non-Western and non-Christian philosophical traditions: see David Bentley Hart's *The Experience of God: Being, Consciousness, Bliss*.

covenant name with the people Israel (although it continues to be used subsequently as well even within the covenant). Melchizedek, for example, the King of Salem, was "priest of the Most High God" (*El Elyon/ho Theós ho Upsistos*) to whom Abraham tithes in his sojourn, and *El Elyon* is the name by which Abraham subsequently makes an oath to the King of Sodom.[11] *Elyon*, "Most High," is a universal name of the One Creator God in the Ancient Near East, like *El* and *Elohim* (the generic "God" and "*the* God" in a superlative plural, respectively), tied, in Genesis at least, to the common covenant between God and creation in which human beings play of course a representational or priestly role, fulfilling their normative function as the "crown" of creation, utilizing the image of God, being invested with divine authority to "rule" under the Creator's higher Lordship, and mediating his purposes in and throughout the realm of creation. Hence Melchizedek's blessing of Abraham and Abraham's testimony before the King of Sodom both use the full title, "God Most High, Maker of Heaven and Earth": "God Most High" is the one Creator God. We can therefore follow the Hellenistic Jewish philosophers and the Fathers of the Church (and implicitly Schelling here) by seeing the proto-monotheism of the greatest philosophers of Greece, adumbrated above, playing a prophetic role among the pagans in preparation for the Gospel—the Gospel which ultimately brings the covenant God to all the nations, reconciling the "exclusivism" of the Old Covenant with its own implicit universalism (for which the covenant God of Israel is precisely the God of all). It is the Creator, above all gods, who is the Lord of both reason and revelation, the elusive aspiration of mythical and philosophical thought, and the gracious Lord of the covenant, who reveals himself "personally" in the historical itinerary of Israel.

One major mode of philosophical "purification" of myth resulted in the *interpretation* of the plenitude of divinities in the Greek pantheon as various facets of manifestation or aspects of the single, transcendent, divine reality.[12] This was expressed precisely in the

---

11. Gen 14:18–22.
12. See N. Belayche, "*Hypsistos*. Une voie de l'exaltation des dieux dans le polythéisme gréco-romaine," *Archiv für Religionsgeschichte* 7:34–5.

"cult" of the *theós hypsistos*, God Most High, flourishing through-out the ancient Mediterranean until at least the fourth century. And in fact this was the term by which Paul and Silas were named by the female slave in Philippi possessed by a fortune-telling spirit: "These men are servants of the Most High God (*tou theóu tou hypsistou*), who are telling you the way to be saved!" (Acts 16:17). In the fifth century, Cyril of Alexandria[13] called the worshipers of the *theós hypsistos* in Alexandria "god-fearers" (*theosebeis*), identifying them with the group by the same name found in the book of Acts[14] and in Josephus, pagans who participated to a limited degree in the syna-gogues of Jewish diaspora, from whom the majority of the earliest Christian converts seem to have come.[15] One historian and exegete, Richard Bauckham, has suggested that *theós hypsistos* became the proper gentile term for the God of Israel, appropriate for gentiles to use when speaking of the covenant God and for Jews to use when speaking to gentiles.[16]

Here we must therefore disagree with Pascal. The "Most High" can clearly be interpreted as the God of the philosophers, of "enlightened" paganism, *and* of the very God of Abraham, Isaac, and Jacob, a universal name of God—and this on biblical grounds.[17] The ancient name "Most High" that predates the revela-tion of the covenant Name in Ex 3:14 is not of course the greatest revelation of God, which belongs to the covenant mediated by Moses and then ultimately by Jesus Christ, but it is nevertheless a

13. *De adoratione in Spiritu et Veritate*, 3.92 (PG 68, 281 C).

14. Acts 13:16.

15. For a summary of the above, with references, see Stephen Mitchell, "Theos Hypsistos," *Encyclopedia of Ancient History*, 1st ed., Roger S. Bagnall et al. (eds.) (London: Blackwell, 2013), 66–98.

16. Richard Bauckham, "The 'Most High' God and the Nature of Early Jewish Monotheism" in *Jesus and the God of Israel* (Grand Rapids, MI: Eerdmans, 2009), 107–26. See also Joseph Ratzinger's comments in *Truth and Tolerance* (San Fran-cisco: Ignatius Press, 2004), 149–54, which wholly agree with what I put forward here.

17. Though "personally" that is, by special divine initiative, known to the latter, and "impersonally," that is, through the interpretation of the intelligibility of the knowable universe, known to the former, and hence by a "special" and "natural" revelation, respectively, to use a classical distinction that should remain in force.

"proper name" of God, a name by which the Creator is addressed and to which he responds (which is shown by its function before the covenant with Abraham, which comes about in the following chapter, Gen 15, and subsequent to it, in later biblical literature: Deut 32:8; Ps 97:9, etc.).

Can we say therefore, following the logic of Schelling's use that I am beginning to explicate, that "philosophy" should best be understood as an authentic manner of praying, as a "theology," as the intellectual transposition of cult, the "interiorization" of sacrifice, and therefore the accomplishment of the essence of religion? It does propose itself this way from Plato onwards, and if we are happy to consider Christianity in the Patristic manner, in fact *the* "philosophy," then we can answer this question in the affirmative. And although he only has negative things to say about "philosophy,"[18] or traditions of "human wisdom,"[19] St. Paul only does so in order to highlight all the more forcefully the "wisdom of God" in the "foolishness of the Cross," identifying, as Clement of Alexandria will do subsequently, that for which philosophy aspires with "Christ Jesus who has become for us wisdom from God."[20] That is, St. Paul in his own powerful way is making precisely the argument that can readily be gathered from the Fathers: that Christianity is the "true philosophy," and the proper conversation or debating partners with Christians are those who claim to think, to speak, and to act "according to reason," the philosophers.

By the use of this name "Most High," a name that is found in biblical literature and among Greek philosophical traditions, Schelling repeats a movement of transformative openness to the biblical revelation from within philosophy that is familiar, even basic to Christianity. One sees this way of conceiving of Christianity dominating the thinking of the Fathers of the Church, both Latin and Greek, from the first Apologists in the early 2nd century until the early 5th

18. Col 2:8.
19. 1 Cor 1:24, 25, 30.
20. 1 Cor. 1:18. See Clement of Alexandria, *Stromata* I, 18, 90: "The true philosophy is the one transmitted to us by the Son."

century (St. Augustine), who conceived of Christianity itself as the "true philosophy," and conceived of themselves, as Christian thinkers, primarily as philosophers.[21] It is not insignificant that the earliest and most formative era of Christian self-understanding, the first layer of interpretation of the apostolic teachings, understood itself in this way. A division of "philosophy," on the one hand, and "theology" on the other, was not in sight. These thinkers actually preferred the term "philosophy" to describe what they were doing. Why? Because for them Christianity was a matter of right reason, of discovering and inhabiting the truth, *the* universal human truth. And the fact that this very truth sought for by the greatest philosophers, appeared "in the flesh," "in the fullness of time," "in these last days" for our salvation, meant only that the true lover of wisdom should embrace this fact as of the "highest" (indeed) philosophical significance. A mere recognition of truth about the divinity dispersed in a veiled but powerful manner throughout the pagan world, and the impossibility of reaching the definitive truth of God apart from Christ—both already recognized by St. Paul and in fact fundamental to his thinking, the St. Paul who makes no distinction between theology and philosophy, the St. Paul who is concerned, however, with "wisdom"![22]—was *not* enough to justify a concrete division of discourses, philosophy and theology. More on this in a moment...

(b) With this we may now properly approach the first term of Schelling's phrase: The work of "*explanation* of the Most High" that is the specific task of philosophy. In the language of Schelling's philosophy, this work is, precisely, the "presentation of the Absolute." What does Schelling mean by this? Here we are dealing with a technical term of Schelling's thought and of German Idealism more generally. In the first place the Absolute's "presentation" is its manifestation in thought and to consciousness. It is the showing forth of

---

21. From St. Justin Martyr's *First Apology* to St. Augustine's *City of God*. Balthasar summarizes the normative view: "The Fathers gave the name of 'philosophy' to a Christian life lived in consistent praxis in the world." "Philosophy, Christianity, Monasticism," *Explorations in Theology II*, 333–34.

22. Rom 1:19–22; 1 Cor 1–2.

the posited and assumed unitary structure of reality lying behind our intellectual awareness which arises through the distinction between subject and object, but which presumes and seeks the inaccessible unified "ground" that ever transcends it. The Absolute for the later Schelling (the Schelling with whom we are dealing in 1836) is the Living God, the divine Personality, in whom all the dualisms by which human consciousness perceives and knows, are united. This God is the ground that reason seeks; and it is (for Schelling as for Kant) a restless seeking beyond the boundaries of finitude that defines reason (*Vernunft*) itself; the Hidden Absolute is reason's origin and end, but one which reason cannot tragically reach because this ground is a hyper-rational abyss into which reason is born, by which it is always rendered mute in awe. Nevertheless, the intuition of this ground is present to reason in its every act; reason comes to itself within this abyss of being, and it itself is always broken open by this excess of being over reason. The "representations" of reason, the images it constructs, are the means *through which* it intuits the ever-transcendent ground whose immediate-transcendent presence makes it what it is. The Absolute is too close to reason, as it were, for reason to focus on it; reason can only awaken to itself as reason through being divided from its origin in the Absolute—the fact of its own being always precedes and exceeds reason. Now we reach the point of this repetition of Schelling's conceptual apparatus.

Crucially developing Kant's account of the antinomies of reason, Schelling proposes that the ideal task of representation, the perfect squaring or transposition of our images constructed by reason in its response to the Absolute with the Absolute itself, is *impossible*: reason always exhausts itself in *antinomies*, in contradicting theses that are both rationally valid on their own terms. And the reconciliation of these contradictory theses that reason requires is fundamentally beyond the reach of reason and can only be intuited *through* the very contradictions themselves. Like Nicholas Cusanus's coincidence of opposites, the mind *must* posit the connection of the dots but it cannot *see* how this works. Philosophy thereby always fails in the pursuit of its defining *telos*: it ends up by expressing itself in contradictory theses that it must hold as equally true. For Kant of course these antinomies require the thoroughgoing critique of reason made possible by the dogmatic distinction between unknowable objective reality (noumena) and the knowable order of experience (phenomena).[23] Yet for Schelling, who recovers (however problematically, but that is a question for another time) the original "problematic telos of philosophy,"[24] this failure is actually the beginning of wisdom. The divine can only be given *divinely*, that is, by a grasping that cannot grasp the conditions of the very grasping by which it is received. For religious consciousness, this "ungrasping" becomes the principle of self-understanding (to be human is to be capable of the unknowable) and therefore the paradigm of all knowledge and experience. If Kant defined reason as such through an interrogation of the strict limits intrinsic to human knowing, Schelling understood from this that the "ground" of reason, a question at the heart of reason, is not intrinsic to reason, but always exceeds it, and hence the rationally knowable is not known in advance of the act of knowledge itself. In other words, the limits or conditions of knowledge and our account of reason itself (and ultimately of human being) can only be derived from out of an account of what is given to be known, the concrete data of human existence ensconced in the history of civilizations (and most acutely and deeply in religion), which we restrict out of any *a priori* fidelity to some account of the possibly knowable or occurable only to the peril of our account of reason itself.[25]

I confess freely that we here begin to depart from Schelling's philosophy, even his late philosophy (since Schelling always equated the "positivity" of revelation with a possible transparency to knowledge, a metaphysical *a priori* which took the form of an esoteric divine "becoming" from unconsciousness to consciousness through the history of humanity, culminating in his own philosophical religion), but I submit that by taking my leave precisely here I am being wholly faithful to his most crucial philosophical intuitions regard-

23. Immanuel Kant, *Critique of Pure Reason*, A406/B433–A567/B595 ("The Antinomy of Pure Reason").
24. This phrase comes from Husserl, whose late fragment "Denial of Scientific Philosophy" I invoke precisely here.
25. See Miklos Vetö, *De Kant à Schelling: Les deux voies d'Idéalisme allemande I-II* (Grenoble: Millon, 1998–2000).

ing the divine and philosophy as such.[26] These intuitions have been articulated before: the "antinomy of pure reason" is a dead-end unless, as Russian philosopher Pavel Florensky, highly influenced by Schelling, asserted, making of it a fundamental principle, and which his disciple Sergei Bulgakov essentially systematized into a methodology, we make the recognition of this antinomical structure the *defining* expression of human reason, and in fact evidence of its successful encounter with transcendence, crystallized like nowhere else in the antinomies of dogma. The Russian thinkers saw—much like Chesterton—antinomy (or paradox) as the hallmark of Christian thinking, antinomies which are again and again crystallized in the fundamental dogmas of Christianity. Revelation in itself is expressed rationally only antinomically; because the hyper-rational expresses itself in a way that exceeds the categories of distinction by which reason normatively grasps truth. Divine truth, the Truth as such, is "grasped" in an ungrasping way, therefore with a properly religious attitude, through the respect of the inhabitation of the divine truth in its human expression as antinomies, or in the language of Kierkegaard, Chesterton, and de Lubac, in "paradox."[27] I will only refer to one of these authors, to Chesterton's *Orthodoxy* here, allowing it to stand for the entire manner of thinking that I invoke: Christianity is a matter of "combining furious opposites . . . keeping them both and keeping them furious." For Chesterton (like Florensky), this fracturing intensification of rationality in encounter with the revealed Absolute (which I termed logos$_2$ in a previous chapter) was proof of the truth of Christianity, since our experience of ourselves in the world before God is always expressing itself in contradictions, and by inhabiting the pathos of this contradictory character of experience we glimpse the wonder-

26. In this way his thinking anticipates certain breakthroughs in contemporary French phenomenology, to which I am indebted. See, for example, Jean-Luc Marion's characterization of the relation of philosophy and theology in "On the Foundation of the Distinction of Philosophy and Theology," *Budhi* 13. 1–3 (2009).

27. And today by John Milbank, as we discovered above: a thinker whose brilliance always exceeds itself, if I can put it that way, and whose writing is marked by a breathless astonishment at what he is saying; his thought exceeds the (in his case) restrictive norms of academic scholarship.

ful truth. Only paradox is worthy of God, and therefore of man;
only antinomy, the expression of the excess of reason, is worthy of
reason itself. "If you can comprehend it," said St. Augustine, "it is
not God."[28] And now we can add: if you can comprehend the comprehension of it, it is not reason either.

## Conclusion

Does this paradoxicality of what is and this antinomical structure of
intelligibility have any upshot for the way we conceive the relation
of theology and philosophy? I begin to answer this final question
(all that is possible here) by returning once again to Schelling's
phrase. What can I say but that Christian faith in particular places a
specific and acute burden on the philosopher: his thought must be
in agreement with nothing less than the very revelation of God.

Our first observation should be (a) that this requirement of
"agreement" was paradoxically the condition by which philosophy
and theology (in the sense that we understand them today) became
distinguished at the beginning of the modern era, when, after the
rediscovery of Aristotle, the veracity of the philosophy of *the* Philosopher came into conflict with the established truths of Christian
faith and therefore (b) that we are *not* required to articulate this
agreement in the manner in which they had to do it in their day.[29]
At the foundation of the University there is a working compromise,
and it is signified by the establishment of two faculties, Arts and
Theology. The limitation of this new and necessary compromise
was acutely felt: only the Master of the Sacred Page could do both
philosophy and theology, and he was expected to. The Master of
Arts, the philosopher, however, was *only* allowed to do philosophy,
which took the form of the exposition of certain authoritative texts,
mirroring the exposition of certain authoritative texts, Holy Scripture, which was the central business of the academic theologian.
The Master of Arts' exposition of the Philosopher had strict limits,

28. Augustine, Sermon 52, 16.
29. Unless of course we are "Neo-Scholastic," and we think that the teachings of
Aristotle are exclusively normative for our accounts of reality and intelligibility…

but, nevertheless, what it defined, viz., "natural reason," actually performed a displacement of the theological: reason no longer needed revelation but possessed its own self-sufficiency. Here we see the "conflict of the faculties" emerge in the heart of Christendom. Philosophy came to possess a relative but established autonomy over the essence of the humanly knowable, resting on the authority of Aristotle over this domain.[30] Theology hands over the rational as such in order to retain its own autonomous sphere, revelation. Reason thereby conceives of itself as *outside* the religious horizon, governed by specific conditions, becoming atemporal, *abstracted* from the horizon of sacred history, with its beginning in the creation of the heavens and earth, and its end in a destiny of fulfillment disclosed in principle albeit in a pre-rational (and therefore) densely hyper-rational "mythic" form—but a form that uniquely forms the definitive context of reason as *historical* (history itself as *factum* ["the made"] as the mythic ground of reason). The eschatological ordering of reason that defined the Christian thinking of the Fathers comes to an end in the late Middle Ages, and out of this is born the distinction between philosophy and theology as we understand these terms today. We witness here therefore the original parting of the ways between reason on the one hand, and revelation on the other, which takes this specific form at the extreme: reason becomes "de-eschatologized" and revelation is posited as wholly extrinsic to the domain of natural human reason. The "secular" (in the modern sense) is born out of the de-eschatologization of reason, a freezing of rationality into an abstract de-historicized mode (as if Aristotle's enactment of reason is an absolute representation of reason itself).

Now what must we say if Schelling's recovery of the classical philosophical enterprise is correct? The "place" that his philosophy has for God must be faithful to the "presentation" of the Most High as he reveals himself. We presume that God reveals himself in a history, a history in which we discern a *lógos*. Now, to reach some truth, even some universally valid expression of one truth or

---

30. For the essential elaboration of the view I articulate here see Jean-Yves Lacoste, *From Theology to Theological Thinking*, trans. W. Chris Hackett (Charlottesville, VA: University of Virginia Press, 2014).

another, reason does not have to take account of this fact. (It is true that human beings are finite; it is true that the world is an all-embracing horizon that never comes to direct experience; it is true that God is one, that God is all-powerful, that God is the origin and end of all things, etc.) This is surely banal. A "distinction" (at this level) of philosophy and theology is not in question. Yet to reach the truth of itself, its own defining truth, reason (and hence philosophy) *must* take account of this fact that God reveals himself: God reveals himself rationally, by a revelation which "expands" the rational itself and which must therefore be taken into account in any universal, that is, philosophical, account of reason, any philosophical account of itself as philosophy. God reveals himself as the truth of reason: the revealed God, the Word or Logos of God, is therefore the highest *philosophical* aspiration.

A fundamental assumption of Christian faith is that when God reveals himself he does so truly and definitively in Jesus Christ. Jesus, the Jewish prophet from Nazareth, the miracle worker, the Messiah of Israel, who suffered, died, was buried, rose, and ascended to "the right hand of the Father," who will return in divine glory to judge "all flesh," before whom every knee will bow, who will banish death and all evil, who will oversee the renewal and glorification of creation in a world without end and in a reign without end, is God's total revelation, in whom, says the Apostle, dwells nothing less than "all the fullness of the divinity."[31] After Christ, God the Father has "nothing left to say," as St. John of the Cross puts it in the *Ascent of Mt Carmel*, and this brief litany abstracted from the core Christian belief makes it easy to see why Christians might assume this.[32] I can summarize what I mean therefore when I say "the God of revelation" by taking the words of revelation itself and determine their reference as God, the "living God," and oppose this God to the gods that humanity constructs for itself, "idols," also called by the prophets "dead gods" and "not gods."[33] Philosophy's task, when it

31. Col 2:9.
32. St. John of the Cross, *Ascent of Mt Carmel*, II, 22. See Rémi Brague's remarkable treatment of this passage in *On the God of the Christians*, trans. Paul Seaton (South Bend, IN: St. Augustine's Press, 2013), 74–115.
33. See Jer 10.

sets out to determine finally what it itself is, if my clarification of Schelling is correct, is to think the living God, the God of faith, the God of theology, and nothing less. *If here we reach or surpass the limits of the distinction between philosophy and theology, then we can only acknowledge this with a sense of wonder.* We do not ourselves have to be Pascalian—or Lutheran for that matter—to note that philosophy—that is, "philosophy" *in the modern sense*, conceived as distinguished from theology by virtue of possessing a unique object, reason itself, which it can then hand over to theology in order that then, and only then, theology may apply it to its specific object, revelation—has not even raised itself to this task of *thinking the living God* (which is a thinking that would be the result of a loving…). This is because modern philosophy *is* the "death of God"; it is predicated on the death of God, and the accomplishment of this death is its sole task. As such it would be the death of philosophy. Why is this reciprocal death the case? Philosophy in this modern sense *must* kill God, that is, make God an inert and lifeless object, an idol in the religious sense, in order to be able to know God on its own terms, on the terms that it determines in advance by which God can be known, through which God can have access to *our* rationality.

Only by killing God, separating the idea of God from the living God and equating this static, impotent God with *the* God, can philosophy carve out for itself a domain separate from the theological and the eschatological horizon that it gives us. It is specifically under the regime of this separation that Pascal's distinction remains in force, precisely as a *philosophical* protest, emerging out of the fundamental philosophical desire to think and love the truth itself, even, and especially, *the* Divine Truth, the truth that is the Living God. Its foundational move at self-establishment therefore already contains within itself the death of philosophy. For philosophy here leaves to theology—now conceived for the first time as distinct from philosophy, defined over-against philosophy—the real world, the world of concrete reality, of events and of life. Paradoxically, therefore, the abstraction from existence for the sake of comprehending a frozen, and dead, absolute, makes the basic task of philosophy impossible. Philosophy—again, modern philosophy—from the beginning is only a contemplation of the possible; it is concerned only with abstractions and the relations of these abstractions with one another. It is an anti-philosophy, a wolf in sheep's clothing. Philosophy is merely "thinking about thinking," an advanced determination of the limits of reason, and refuses to acknowledge the limits implied by this separation of itself from life for the sake of its own illusory auto-foundation. Philosophy, again, in the modern sense as "not-theology," as the science of reason as such, which is necessarily an abstraction, is, by this its foundational move, *from the beginning* cut off from what it seeks, the real, that which is as it is in itself. And that which philosophy wants to think above all, that which is most really real, most true, most eminently good and beautiful, *most divine*, is *a priori* that which is *most impossible* for philosophy to think under the conditions that define it in modernity. In killing God, philosophy killed itself.

But is there a place for philosophy, as distinct from theology, in the Christian representation of God? Or can philosophy only really be theology in the end given the Christian radicalization of the philosophical vocation, which draws the thinker into the orbit of belief, of relation and trust in the Living God, a life from which one abstracts at his peril? Until the modern period Christians thought this way. Philosophy and theology were simply equated by St. Augustine (for whom, as we have seen, the true lover of wisdom is the lover of God, thereby making the Christian the true philosopher, full stop),[34] and they were "restlessly" transposed upon one another (by virtue of the strange teleology of the human mind towards God) by St. Thomas.[35] At the end of wisdom we must at least consider this much: revelation brings to completion the aspirations of the philosophers, making their philosophy *more acutely philosophical*, just as it analogously brings to completion the prophetic aspirations of the ancient people Israel, bearers of the Name and Word of the Living God. In saying this, I am not *necessarily* denying a distinction between theology and philosophy, but only

34. *City of God*, VIII.
35. *Summa theologiae* 1,1,1. See the previous chapter. That is to say: eschatology thoroughly determined the shape of the thinking of these two central pre-modern Christian thinkers and their conception of reason itself.

saying that I do not exactly know where and how to draw the line between them, always whether I am doing one, the other, or both at once, and hence, *if* I am truly engaged in one or the other, or, especially, *if I am asking the question about the philosophical as such*, why I ought to care all that much about the distinction at all.

# III

# APOCALYPSE

*D*emus Deum aliquid posse quod nos fateamur investigare non posse*: "Let us allow God to be capable of something that we must admit we are incapable of scrutinizing" (St. Augustine, Ep. 137, 2, 8). The paradoxical relation of Christian intelligence to the mythic horizon of revelation points to the incontrovertible fact that the goal of philosophy can only be eschatologically realized and hence only understood with the end in mind. Myth and theology lead us here, or rather, liberate us from the lesser myth of an autonomous, merely immanent reason for the sake of a vision that can be lived in the body, in history; a vision that radically founds a truly this-worldly reason, founded on a common Good that through its unconditioned excess over the here and now, as its end, gives it density and direction: the resurrection of the dead for a final judgment.

I do not want to be afraid of the paradox. The conceptuality of a "temporal separation of beginning and end" introduced at the end of the key above must here be reintroduced and deepened. This defining separation or opening within Reality is of course a miracle, a supreme impossibility as expressed in the doctrine of creation *ex nihilo* (and which is a dogma, like the others, that can only be contemplatively, experientially understood). But eschatology, which is inseparable from the logic of creation, and is in fact of one seamless piece with it, reveals that this separation between Beginning and End has a *specific intelligibility* that must be provided under the heading of this third key to a Philosophy in Word and Name now to be sketched out. This key has two main features: it has a contingent or unfolding character and a partially realized character. The first feature depends on the second.

Traditional, cosmic divine kingship in Israel is undone by exile. It had uncertain and tenuous beginnings anyway. Only God was properly King, but like the request of the People made at the foot of the mountain before Moses, to mediate between them and the terrible and dangerous YHWH whose presence was too frightening,[1] or like the granting to men of the capacity to write a certification of divorce to a wife that displeases them, the request for the king was another accommodation to the limitations of the people. It was due to that particularly human malady, "hardness of heart."[2] Yet this tenuous beginning, like the unique conception of God in Israel reflected in the absence of any material image on the throne in the temple, allowed kingship (in theory!) to survive in Israel after the exile. There developed Messianic traditions that awaited the return of the true heir to David's throne, an ultimate world ruler, an anointed *Pantokrator* who would be like God's instrument, his right hand, in the conquest of the nations.

In Christianity kingship took on even vaster dimensions: Christ was conceived already in the earliest strain of Jewish Christianity as pre-existing the creation, as present with God like Wisdom and Word and Spirit. In St. Paul, for example, he was understood as the "one through whom and for whom all things exist." But despite its resurrection, the death of kingship through exile was a certain death of the royal wisdom matrix in Israel as well. Intellectually speaking it was (to be curt) the "problem of evil," unjust human suffering—the success of the unrighteous, the persecution of the just—that brought wisdom to its crisis point, and converted it to something new, something untamed: apocalyptic. Suffering and injustice were always central to the wisdom traditions of the Ancient Near East; this locale was not distinct in this regard.

Yet wisdom was intensified, perhaps, in Israel, inasmuch as her God was more and more radically conceived as the matchless Creator, and the exile, the subservience, of the people of this God to the peoples that defined injustice and idolatry, was conceived as suffering *par excellence*. The radically recalcitrant interpretation of exile as divine judgment, and the tenacious grasping on to faith in God's ultimate fidelity, God's "justification" of the covenant—because of his love, alone, his faithfulness—led to the interpretation of the "problem of evil" (evil: that black cancer running rampant like a

1. See Ex 20:19.
2. Said Christ: Matt 19:8.

plague through the generations of humanity) as the introspective problem of self-evil: exile was God's just judgment. God's people, his chosen medicine for the healing of the world, are themselves infected, eaten up by the same malicious cancer. In this context wisdom—the solution to the problem of evil—could only be discerned by a divine gift because it could only be enacted by the God whose power could bring about not only a restoration of Israel, but an installation in her of a "new heart" of flesh that could love God and neighbor as human existence requires as well as the transfiguration of the entire world from the starting point of the final installment of God's presence in the midst of his people. God's justice and his aim, tied together, demanded that he purify his world of all evil and bring about the cosmic restoration, of which the temporal and political restoration of Israel anticipated by the prophets was, as it were, a microcosmic center and (somehow) the instrumental means of his reign.

The Apocalypse of St. John makes the reign *with* Christ a central feature of biblical apocalyptic: "To him who overcomes I will grant to sit with me on my throne, as I also overcame and sat down with my Father on his throne."[3] I would ultimately argue—though not here—that there is a similar secret sense in the apocalyptic letters of St. Paul as there is in the Apocalypse of St. John: the angelic mediation of the former dispensation, under which stood Israel along with the nations, has come to its goal in the death and resurrection of Jesus, which has (somehow...) brought their reign to an end. (The difference between Israel's divine polity and that of the nations is only that Israel is covenanted with the true God, whereas the nations are covenanted with gods, idols, submitted to the lordship of malicious powers that ultimately control them, which their injustice and lawlessness only expresses.) This angelological-cosmopoliticography can only be understood in the mythic horizon, which purports to communicate at the level of human (earthly) intelligence truths about the (heavenly) realities that fundamentally

3. Apoc 3:21.

transcend it. This opposition of kingdoms, the Creator's and that of the false gods, behind the political history of Israel's interaction with the nations is a feature of biblical apocalyptic that can only be demythologized at the expense of the whole. What to do with that is not my concern, besides accepting it—with the understanding that myth is precisely the first language of humanity, the first language of revelation, the only language in which the presumably unfathomably vast and variegated levels and modes of "angelic" realities that transcend the thinnest outer crust of being that humans inhabit can be dimly perceived.

In a dense and difficult passage at the center of his Letter to the Galatians (2:15–4:9), Paul places the Mosaic covenant in its cosmic and temporal context. It pertains to a particular age, he says, the pre-eschatological age, the age before Christ, who inaugurates the inbreaking of the final reign of God, the reign of charity and justice, which is the final end of the Law of Moses. Christ's task on earth was the prophetic announcement and initial enactment of this imminent kingdom (centered on the announcement of the forthcoming destruction of the second Temple, tied to the former age). He symbolically enacts this inbreaking in various prophetic actions such as healings, parables, cursing the fig tree, etc., and above all in his death at the hands of those representing all human power of the former age, and in his resurrection, which destroys personified death, the true lord of the age, the power by which humans were relegated to slavery to the undying powers. Christ's covenant administration is marked by a refiguring of the entire cosmic order: assuming the throne of David, there is Jesus, son of Mary, a man, the Son of Man, who administers the divine reign in heaven and on earth, re-tying these separated realms together. And yet, bizarrely, the "present evil age" continues (Gal 1:4)—due it seems to God's merciful, and to a Christian humbling, awe-inspiring response to the rejection of the Messiah by the majority of Israel (see Rom 9–11) even as the "new age," the Messianic age, has begun to flow.

The Law, for Paul, pertains to the era of angelic ministration of the divine reign: "it was promulgated by angels at the hand of a mediator."[4] The mediator is Moses. This is contrasted with the "covenant of promise," which refers to the Abrahamic covenant with God, on the one hand, but more importantly, to the covenant of Christ, which is the way that God brings to fulfillment the promises to Abraham ("through your seed all the nations shall be blessed"). In relation to this promise to the children of Abraham, the people Israel, the Mosaic covenant was a "custodian." The covenant with Christ abrogates the Law, since entrustment of oneself to the divine promises (after the model of Abraham himself) is what brings one into the covenant community where there is "neither Jew nor Greek. . . . All are one."[5]

But already in the figure of Moses the human mediatorship of the divine covenant is present: Moses is not a god, or god-like, he is a man. The proximity and fluidity of God and King that marked the divine political institutions of the surrounding nations is different: Moses is the friend of God, but he is a creature. Moses knows God's Name, but it is "too wonderful" to grasp and remains wholly elusive in being given; he sees God's face, but only in the form of hearing God's name and seeing his backside as God passes by. To know God he too must follow behind him, just as Peter must cease being a "stumbling block" and "get behind" Jesus on his march to crucifixion, to death at the hands of the (pseudo-divine) powers of the world through the instrumentalization of human political powers that are in their grip, in Jerusalem.[6] From the Christian point of view this particular demythologization of angelic cosmology, correlate to the demythologization of cosmic kingship, is a result again of this ancient Jewish view of the sole Kingship of God.

This perspective becomes even clearer when we turn to Paul's use of the term *ta stoicheia tou kosmou* at the climax of this section of Galatians under analysis, in 4:3, and then 4:9. Continuing the argument of the intermediary, temporary and safeguarding character of the Law, between Abraham and Christ, Paul continues the analogy of an heir awaiting young adulthood when he is recognized as a cit-

---

4. Gal 3:19.
5. Gal 3:28.
6. See Matt 16:21–28.

izen who can own property: "I mean that as long as the heir is not of age, he is no different from a slave, although he is the owner of everything, but he is under the administration of guardians and administrators until the date set by his father. In the same way we also, when we were not of age, were enslaved to the elementary powers of the world."[7] Here Paul seems to make no distinction between Jew and Gentile. "We" is written by a Jew to a mixed Jewish and Gentile audience. If anything the passage demands to be read as a Jew speaking to fellow Jews: the Law is a part—albeit the capstone, the centerpiece, the glory—of the age that has been eclipsed with the advent of its "last things";[8] with the dawning of the age to come, the Law is like "flesh" that must die in order to be raised.[9] But Paul is speaking here against the background of his statement standing at the apex of the argument in 3:28 ("neither Jew nor Greek . . . you are all one in Christ Jesus"), of which the remarks in 4:1–9 are a simple explication. The event that has brought about the "culmination of the ages," the resurrection of the Messiah, reveals that the Law and the pagan religions belong to the same epoch, the one determined by an angelic economy. Both belong to the fundamental powers of the world: pagan idolatry is pure enslavement to these powers; the Law is certainly not, but it was intended as a pathway for Israel through that "evil age," that she may come to term; it was a protection, a tutor, a custodian. And yet it became, for Paul, judgment, exposing the root of human sin all the more fully (as he argues in Rom 3:20, 7:7–8) and even given for the sake of increasing transgression (as he argues here in Gal 3:19–22) so "that God may have mercy on all" (Rom 11:32), that is, extend the covenant to all humanity in fulfillment of the promise made to Abraham. The Law does not "bring life" or "justification"; only the "faith" (fidelity, entrustment to the promise) of Abraham does that, which is what is required of the Christian believer, just as it has always been required of the people of God.

The reading of *ta stoicheia tou kosmou* given here therefore

---

7. Gal. 4:1–2.
8. See 1 Cor 10:11; Eph 1:21.
9. See Gal 3:1–14.

encompasses all of the classical positions of interpretation of this passage: (1) the elements of the world are the celestial beings that rule over the pagan nations, and the entire earth, through the ubiquity of death; (2) the Law of Moses—that pure expression of the divine goodness, bearing the covenant people out of Egypt to the establishment of the nation in the Land of Promise, through the tragedies and terrors of exile and proto-restoration in the Land, but still, exiled even in their re-enfranchisement, all the way, through the silence of the prophets to the advent of the Christ—is still under the reign of death: it looks for, awaits the resurrection, and the definitive Passover of God in Christ's resurrection-ascension and the cosmic exodus from "bondage to decay" to liberation in the "New Heavens and New Earth"; (3) finally, Paul is referring as well to human "religious principles" as such before Christ: the Law of Moses, God's great gift to his beloved people, is perverted by human nature just as the nations have perverted God's revelation in nature (the burden of Rom 2–3:19). From the vantage of the Gospels the proof of this judgment (which parallels but exceeds the Babylonian exile, as the *telos* does to a stage preceding it) is that the Temple and the Jerusalem monarchy had become themselves only a manifestation of the root issue. Before Christ every human institution (the shadow side of angelic "political" order in the cosmos, mythically speaking) stands under judgment. Likewise, the pagans sink into the chaos of rebellion before the Creator, trading their innate knowledge for ignorance. "All have been delivered over to disobedience, so that God may have mercy on all."[10]

In the context of his argument in the Letter to the Romans, this mercy on all over-against the sin of all takes an initial form in the *ekklesia*, which follows upon the covenant order of Moses, just as Moses followed on and elaborated, inherited, the "religion" of the Patriarchs. More radical than the merciful divine multiplication of strictures surrounding his Presence amidst the people in response to the Golden Calf episode, the opening of the covenant to the Gentiles is, for the Apostle to the Gentiles, a *result* of Israel's disobedience: "Just as you once disobeyed God but have now received mercy

10. Rom 11:32.

because of their disobedience, so they have now disobeyed in order that, by virtue of the mercy shown you, they too may receive mercy."[11] This reversal of fates in no way eclipses or sets aside God's love for his chosen people but in the end will only bring it to completion: "In respect to the gospel they are enemies on your account; but in respect to election, they are beloved because of the patriarchs. For the gifts and call of God are irrevocable."[12] And yet Israel suffers judgment through exile. With privilege comes not only responsibility but a heightened degree of justice, in order that God shows "no partiality."[13] For the reconstituted community *in* Christ the same is true: "judgment begins with the household of God."[14]

This mystery of God's undying fidelity to Israel is a decisive feature of the *mustērion*, the plan of God that requires true "wisdom" (contrasted implicitly here with being "wise in your own estimation," which does not reach the discernment of the mystery) in order to be perceived: "I do not want you to be unaware of the mystery, brothers, so that you will not become wise in your own estimation: a hardening has come upon Israel in part, until the full number of Gentiles comes in, and thus all Israel will be saved."[15] Our discussion finally discovers its biblical anchor precisely here, as it is expressed by St. Paul in the subsequent verses after the apostle's disclosure of the mystery:

> Oh the depths and riches and wisdom and the knowledge of God!
>     How inscrutable are his judgments and how unsearchable his ways!
> "For who has known the mind of the Lord
>     or who has been his counsellor?"
> "Or who has given him anything that he may be repaid?"
> For from him and through him and for him are all things. To him be glory forever.
>     Amen.[16]

11. Rom 11:30–31.
12. Rom 11:28–29.
13. Rom 2:11; Acts 10:34.
14. 1 Pet 4:17.
15. Rom 11:25–26.
16. Rom 11:33–36.

This "wonder" is the beginning of theology. It sets aside self-inter-est, and fuses the will of the seeker with the divine purpose alone, in order for the divine glory to be seen.

It is worth recalling here the great evil harbored in the heart of Western civilization against the Beloved People, and which reached an unspeakable dénouement *anno Domini* 1941. The transcendent powers of evil are real, and the human order is paired with or coun-terparted to them—perhaps these malevolent spiritual forces even co-"emerge" as quasi-distinct powers in heaven's regions *through* human freedom on earth (from one perspective: causality must be stranger and stranger beyond the dimensions of our material matrix)—but like bizarre psychological disorders that spawn quasi-independent centers of personality, human persons become subject to them, and may still become their instruments today. There is no contradiction between subjection to hidden maleficent powers and freedom in human action.

In Daniel 7 (a central source of Pauline apocalyptic) the Son of Man figure brings the lordship over the earth *to* God as he receives it. As the great, royal representative of Israel he makes the total act of obe-dience to the Creator: Kingship is God's alone. The author of the remarkable Book of Daniel requires of its readers the same wisdom of which the book's hero partook. Daniel sought this wisdom through prayer, as one central element of fidelity to the covenant of the God whose promises seem smothered by the might of worldly powers and their gods. To understand the book, the reader has to be "in the know." The parables of Jesus partake substantially of this very genre.[17] They are, from this vantage, versions of apocalyptic. Understanding has to be imparted from someone (like an angelic being or a human prophet privy to the secret, the *mustērion* of the heavenly court). The "Son of God," the political title "borrowed" from Egypt and Rome, is *a* son of man. As *the* Son of Man, the greatest act of his reign, its primary and final action, is to give the Kingdom of the world to God, who alone deserves it. God's reign

17. See Luke 8:10.

comes, *finally*, on earth through the Son of Man as it exists already in the heavenly council, although it is, hidden, deeply at times, behind the events of the world. The Anointed of Israel brings it about: this is accomplished eschatologically when his human reign becomes wholly transparent to the divine reign itself, present now in principle (through his death and resurrection, his ascension and royal installment above the angelic beings), but fully accomplished at the end of the ages. Here I locate the logic of St. Paul's obscure, mythic claim that at the end, Christ "will hand the kingdom to his God and Father, when he has destroyed every authority and power. For he must reign until he has put all his enemies under his feet," including, finally, death, the "last enemy."[18] The King in Israel is first and finally God: "When everything is subjected to him, then the Son himself will be subjected to the one who subjected every-thing to him, so that God may be all in all."

We have reached, out of the depth of myth, its transfiguration through wisdom, and already anticipated in the deepening enigma within wisdom, the third term of my governing typology, apoca-lypse, the great, final revelation of the divine wisdom itself, by which alone evil is destroyed, justice is realized for the poor, judg-ment is finally, definitively doled out on the mountainous pile of shit dropped on human history through the injustices enacted by human rulers and the hidden powers of which they are, finally, the puppets. And the whole creation is liberated to enjoy its goodness: God becomes King.[19]

On the Christian reading, the demise of kingship, the central and nearly ubiquitous political institution from the Neolithic revolution to the Industrial revolution, or from the roots of the Archaic age to

18. 1 Cor 15:24–28.

19. I am indebted to Louis Bouyer for this expression: see *Le Fils éternel* (Paris: Cerf, 1974). It has recently become the central theme of the "biblical theology" of N. T. Wright: *How God Became King: The Forgotten Story of the Gospels* (NY: Harper-One, 2012). These are clearly independent attestations to a radical theme of the Christian Scriptures that has been mostly overlooked by modern scholarship yet taken for granted by pre-modern understandings of the world, archaic or axial.

the Modern period, has its clear origins in the core stories of the People Israel. And it has its *end* in the post-resurrection *ascension* of Jesus, Son of Mary, the Messiah of Israel, to the throne of his father David (the archetypal king for the prophetic literature of Israel) where he sits "at the right hand of the Father."

The three keys to a Philosophy in Word and Name are the property of the One who alone may bear them; they open the door of understanding to his Eternal Reign: the Beginning and End, the Firstborn from the dead, through whom all things were made and for whom all things were made, the perfect *Eikon* of the Father, the King of the kings of the earth, the Last Judge, the Word of God, the Crucified, the Lamb of slaughter, the Son of God. In his apocalypse all the stories of the peoples of the world are his "by right," just as are all the riches of the kings of the earth, of human history, with its unfathomably rich trove of civilizations past and future: they will be brought before him in the great political homage of the world at its unfathomable emancipation from the smothering straightjacket of evil: after death comes resurrection. And these keys are given to lambs, who likewise will sit with him on the Father's throne to judge angel and man.

# STUDY 5

WORD: Eschatologicity, Conditionlessness
NAME: Jean-Luc Marion, Jean-Yves Lacoste
STYLE: Disquisition
MATTER: On the Philosophy and Phenomenology of
Revelation

"The first chapter in philosophical approach should consist in the free examination of some ultimate notions as they occur naturally in daily life."—Whitehead, *Modes of Thought*

IS THERE A PHILOSOPHY OF REVELATION? This question, once posed, raises essential questions about the nature of philosophy itself, about its limits, purpose, and meaning, and it even elevates them to the highest pitch. A thesis presents itself with force: the question of revelation is therefore, as far as philosophy is concerned, *the most philosophical question possible.*

Yet this observation only opens the door to answering the question, which presumably requires a demonstration of the logic and meaning of the thesis. The common sense approach, which I desire to take here, proposes that whether or not philosophy is an *adequate* mode of approach to the data of revelation, it is evidently possible even if it fails, since posing the question raises such fundamentally philosophical questions: if it turns out that philosophy only ever corrupts or distorts (or whatever) the traditional "object" of theology and faith, then the "Philosophy of Revelation" (PR) is at least important to philosophy in its difference from theology.

The bare logic of what follows can be mapped in two simple steps: (1) a discussion of what Christianity means by "the reality of revelation," from which the validity of the PR can be understood, followed by (2) an introduction of two conditions that revelation would seem to demand of any PR: first, the "eschatologicity" of revelation and second, the "conditionlessness" of revelation. These two conditions explicate the basic features of PR in its most influential contemporary form, French phenomenology. I will elaborate this tradition, which I term Philosophy and Phenomenology of Revelation (PPR), with reference to its two central figures, Jean-Yves Lacoste and Jean-Luc Marion. With them, the thesis named above breaks open onto a new plane. The reader may take the approach represented by this statement as simultaneously the proposal of a lens of interpretation for understanding Lacoste and Marion, an expression of the significance of their "school" of thought within the history of philosophy, and as an indication of the proper direction for philosophical work in their wake.

## The "Reality of Revelation"

"With the reality of revelation, Christianity stands or falls."[1] This is a self-evident statement; initially I allow it to stand without comment. For with it we have a starting point for a path of questioning. At this inaugural point of orientation I have to confess that there is not yet any differentiation between the philosophical and theological. What is given alone matters, and as such, gives rise to thought. There is only "the Christian," his reason and its validity, deriving from what presents itself to be thought.[2] I bracket labels (philosophy, theology) therefore as not (yet?) directly important. It is not impossible that here, at a kind of absolute beginning, one is doing both at once, or at least doing that which can, even for valid though not absolute reasons (since it is a distinction with a clear, circum-

1. Herman Bavinck, *The Philosophy of Revelation: The Stone Lectures for 1908–1909, Princeton Theological Seminary* (New York: Longmans, Green and Co, 1909).

2. See Hans Urs von Balthasar, *The Glory of the Lord*, vol. 5: *The Realm of Metaphysics in the Modern Age*, trans. Oliver Davies, et al. (San Francisco: Ignatius, 1991), 646–56. And see also Lacoste's discussion of this text in the third lecture of *From Theology to Theological Thinking*.

scribed history in Western thought), be divided out later into distinct realms of thought. And I cannot rule this out *a priori*. Perhaps we could even get theologians and philosophers to agree on a general intellectual principle: what matters more than the distinction is the questioning itself and the challenge of what is given to be thought.

Opening up the quotation to comment, we should first ask: what is "the *reality* of revelation" that Bavinck says wholly determines Christianity? Fundamentally such a statement surely means that if what Christianity claims about revelation is not true, then Christianity is not true. Christianity depends on and lives from a word that comes from God the Creator, the "King" and "Father" of Israel, "the LORD," the Master of the covenant and God of creation. A lot could be said here that is surely "theological." I only make the partial though fundamental observation that—and whether I am speaking as a theologian or a philosopher God alone knows—for Christianity revelation *is* a word, a *lógos*, which, while being a word cast onto the vast, chaotic sea of human words and their history, is at the same time unique, absolute, the "word of God," *lógos tou theou* (only secondarily is it "about" a word, an explication of the divine word). "Religion" says Jean-Luc Marion,

> attains its highest figure only when it becomes established by and as a revelation, where an authority that is transcendent to experience nevertheless manifests itself experientially. Such an experience, effectively beyond (and outside of) the conditions of possibility of experience, is affirmed by words . . . rightly accessible to everyone.

"Revelation" therefore, he continues, "speaks universally, yet without this word being able to ground itself in reason within the limits of the world."[3] This *lógos* is the divine word: the *lógos-theos*, identified with the man, Jesus of Nazareth, is the universal *lógos*, "sent" from the common *Archê*, the origin or "beginning" of everything,

3. Jean-Luc Marion, "The Possible and Revelation," *The Visible and the Revealed*, 2.

whom he called "Father" and taught his followers to call the same.[4] Christianity stands or falls (to continue with the grammar of this classical linguistic universe) on this identification of the *lógos* of faith, the "word of salvation," with the *lógos* of all things, the original, divine mediation of their common intelligibility, that which ultimately makes that which is a unity, a "creation"—the *lógos* "through whom all things were made."[5] This latter *lógos*, the *lógos tou kosmou*, was the object of Greek philosophical inquiry in late Antiquity; and a fundamental task of early Christian thought with its formative encounter with its Greco-Roman milieu was to argue for the conviction that the cosmic *lógos* studied by the greatest philosophers among the pagans (e.g., the "Platonic writings" for St. Augustine)[6] is the very *lógos* who "became flesh and tabernacled among us," though now understood to have been disclosed through reasoned reflection on the world in a shadowy, elusive manner: the ultimate unity of the *lógos* of the world, the principle of all intelligibility, the *lógos* sent from the Father who reveals, for St. Paul and early Christian proclamation, the "manifold wisdom of God," the Master of the covenant who is still the God of creation.[7] The consensus Christian view in Latin and Greek from Justin Martyr to Augustine in fact, following the lead of St. Paul and the Epistle of St. James,[8] is that Christianity is first a matter of (a *revealed*) wisdom, and as such it proposes itself as the "true philosophy."[9]

4. Here I follow Augustine of Hippo's identification of the "Beginning" with God the Father. See *Unfinished Literal Commentary on Genesis* 3:6: "The beginning without beginning only the Father is; and that is why we believe that all things come from one beginning. The Son is however the beginning in such a way that he is coming from the Father." *Saint Augustine on Genesis*, trans. Edmund Hill, O.P. (Hyde Park, NY: New City Press, 2006), 117.

5. See Bavinck, *The Philosophy of Revelation*, 27–28.

6. *Confessions*, Book VII.

7. Eph 3:10.

8. See for example Origen's remarkable statement in the preface to *De principiis*, paragraph 3: "Zealous study of the apostles, enacted by the 'lover of wisdom,' is a preparation for the true wisdom that is only a gift of the Holy Spirit"; and St. Augustine, *De Trinitate* 14.4.15: "Worship is the highest act of the philosopher."

9. See again Clement of Alexandria, *Stromateis*, I, 18, 90: "The true philosophy is the one brought to us by the Son."

Here I have taken the previous study's conclusions as our starting point. Now we may pass, with reason, to a clarifying determination of my thesis and apply a label to the specific question that will continue to hold our attention: is there a PR? Our question is not whether there "was" one, since we could, again with reason, take "PR" as a name for Christianity itself, with the total way of life that Christianity proposed, as was the case, for example, for the school of Christian thought and practice in Alexandria to which Origen belonged, as much as, later in the Latin world, for St. Augustine himself: in his own mind he is a philosopher (and is not the justification of itself before the pagan intellectual class a fundamental motivation of Patristic thinking?), who reasons from and through a revealed wisdom—and is therefore all the more philosophical as the revealed wisdom is all the more wise, since it is divine.[10] There is a seamless tradition from Pythagoras (who coined the term "philosophy") and Plato (who coined the term "theology")—both of whom identified wisdom with the divinity that is its source no less strongly than the Christians—to Clement of Alexandria and Augustine. Instead, our question is more difficult: it concerns the veracity of the words "philosophy" and "revelation" when brought together today, the power by which they may or may not grip us: does revelation matter to humanity *as such*? It proposes itself as being the absolute matter for us. And if it proposes itself as mattering in this way, which the original Christian conviction of the unity of the *lógos*—a conviction grounded in its universal (and eschatological) soteriology—made an enduring justification, then it remains indeed a philosophical question—one worthy of the definite article.

## Little History of a Modern Meta-Philosophy

Is there, therefore, a PR? The point we have now reached in the inquiry highlights the obvious: we first have to know *what* we are looking for. The ancient and Socratic paradox of fore-understanding within every question indicates among other things that to

---

10. As he states classically in the eighth book of *City of God*.

begin to know what we are looking for is to find ourselves at least a little down the road of actually *attempting* to find it.

Let us pause here in order to ask another, simpler question than what my subtitle affords: Has the "PR" ever been attempted? A moment at the university library affirms it. At least three texts, from the nineteenth and twentieth centuries, have dared to take the name.[11] In the first place, I speak, of course, of Schelling's late and unfinished project, *Philosophie der Offenbarung*, which I will have occasion to introduce below. A false start for this project is found in the work of a Schelling devotee, B. H. Blasche: *Philosophie der Offenbarung als Grundlage und Bedingung einer höhern Ausbildung der Theologie* (1829).[12] Blasche, who seems to be the first to use the term "Philosophie der Offenbarung," was an adherent of Schelling's system of identity (for which the self-conscious subject is the product of the *Selbstoffenbarung*, the revelation of being to itself, which is exhaustively what being is: the real is the revealing ideal and the ideal is the real revealed to itself, etc.).[13] And he intensified its explication as a religious pantheism. In this book he distinguishes between the philosophical concept of revelation, marked by universality, and the theological concept, delimited and particular. The concept of revelation intrinsic to theology can therefore only be properly ("scientifically") understood by a philosophical explication of the concept that liberates it from the narrowing limitations of the theological conception, which is always merely empirical. This distinction between the empirical and ideal anticipates (inasmuch as it performs an analogous disciplinary organization)

---

11. A fourth text, now from the twenty-first century, should also be noted: Peter Koslowski's *Philosophien der Offenbarung: Antiker Gnostizismus, Franz von Baader, Schelling* (Paderborn: Ferdinand Schöningh, 2001). Koslowski shows how the PR, rooted in the traditions of *gnōsis* in late antiquity (heterodox *and* orthodox) resurfaces post-Enlightenment as a third tradition of intellection beside philosophy and theology. In a broader treatment of the PR, Koslowski's research would have to be thoroughly taken into account.

12. Carl Glaeser Verlag, 1829.

13. This concept is of course assumed into theological reflection on the continent in its persistent attempt in the mid-twentieth century to define revelation in a way that overcomes the limits of the mainly epistemological account that crystalized in the Catholicism of the First Vatican Council.

Heidegger's influential statement in the Marburg essay "Phänomenologie und Theo-logie" (1927), which relegates theology to the status of a "science" of the ontic domain alone, whereas philosophy is universal and foundational for every science because its proper subject is the ontological.[14] The Kierkegaard of the *Fragments* and their *Postscript* trades, of course, on the eclipse of this defining sort of modern distinction with the idea of the "Absolute in history."[15] Kierkegaard's decision would serve as a crucial turning point in any narrative history of the PR and PPR.

There is also a lesser-known work by the Dutch theologian, Herman Bavinck, from which we have already heard above. Developed out of a lecture course given at Princeton in 1908–1909, it is concerned with showing the relevance of revelation to every "sphere" of human life touched by knowledge, a relevance that is articulated through the coordination of a "PR": "positive" revelation, answering the innate sense of "religion" (which remains, without a disclosure of the divine will coming from beyond the order of the world in an absolute way, stuck in one or another version of "monism," inclusive or exclusive of the divine), draws the mind beyond the entire order of the world to its source, exposing a transcendent personal will at the origin, and from the perspective of this elevation of the intellect through the will into vast reaches that exceed it, the intellect undertakes training allowing it to see all of the worldly, human spheres in which it is engaged in new light.[16] In Bavinck this opening of "natural" religion by "special" revelation (or divine "essence" by divine "personality," as we will see below) is an apologetic exercise in implicit dialogue with Hegelian idealism, for it shows how the existential and intellectual conundrums that disturb modern thought are answered by revelation: in order not to wallow in contradictions, the antinomy of freedom and absolute depen-

14. Heidegger, *Phenomenology and Theology, Pathmarks*, trans. James G. Hart and John C. Moraldo (Cambridge: Cambridge University Press, 1998).

15. Søren Kierkegaard, *Concluding Unscientific Postscript*, ed. Alastair Hannay (Cambridge: Cambridge University Press, 2009), 485: "The historical is that the god, the eternal, has come about at a definite moment in time as a particular human being."

16. See above.

dence at the base of self-consciousness points inchoately to the hidden God above the order of the world and the human duty to worship him. The task of "PR" is to "correlate" this "special revelation" of God's will to the "natural revelation" within self-consciousness, the revelation of the divinity, the world, and the self arising from faith's acceptance of the Christian *Heilsgeschichte* that philosophical reflection comes to discover as its ultimate condition.

Reflecting on the existence of these "primary texts" that form (for good or ill) the backstory to any contemporary PR, we could ask about the conditions of their development in the history of ideas and propose that modern philosophy could be very well defined by—or at least is fundamentally marked by—the "creation" of this manner of meta-philosophy ("discipline" is too strong a word), inasmuch as it has become a requisite way of bringing to its end the founding disciplinary distinction of philosophy and theology. But beyond that, along the path from the ancient to the modern, something happened for us all in Königsberg: no longer do any realities that have been principally affirmed to exist independently of human experience have any compelling rationality about them in a possible independence; "metaphysics," which turns on the affirmation of this independence as a founding principle of intellectual practice, is thereby called into question and the transcendent realities of revelation and of religious belief, finally completely separated from philosophy, are necessarily and *a priori* unknowable and impossible.[17] The PR—in Schelling and Bavinck to be sure—is a response to this intellectual predicament.

Again, I take the long view that the end of an epoch affords. The earlier history of philosophy is instructive and should not be forgotten: Porphyry's lost *Philosophy from Oracles*, a powerful critique of Christianity's fundamental intellectual proposal as seen by a pagan philosopher at the height of late Antiquity, is at least analogous to

---

17. See Schelling's comments in Lectures Two and Three of the *PR* in *The Grounding of Positive Philosophy: The Berlin Lectures*, trans. Bruce Matthews (NY: SUNY, 2007), 110: "Ever since that great movement initiated by Kant, it has been a question not of this or that philosophy, but rather . . . of philosophy itself." This text will be referenced subsequently in this study simply by "Lecture 1," etc.

what we have after Kant. According to Porphyry (in Augustine's presentation of him…) the Christian self-identification as *the* universal
way of salvation is contradicted by its own particularity, an isolation
to a historical and marginal fragment of reality over against all others. Whereas Porphyry agrees with the Christian assumption that a
universal path of salvation is the supreme goal and primary task of
philosophical inquiry, the Christian claim is based on a fallacy that
contradicts the basic character of the tradition of philosophical
intelligence, which turns on a clear and infallible distinction
between the universal (and divine) and the particular (and mortal).
The universal path, for Porphyry, is only *possibly* found through a
learned integration of all the "oracles" of the various religio-intellec-
tual traditions of far Antiquity (Egypt, Babylonia, the Greek Mysteries, etc.) into a single program for the ascent of the soul to the
divine.[18] The spirit of our age, if it agrees with anyone, agrees with
Porphyry.

In light of this virtually defining philosophical debate of Late
Antiquity we can see the full range of Schelling's conviction about
the fundamental challenge of Kant to traditional metaphysics and
make it an expression of *a*, and perhaps *the*, perennial challenge for
Christianity. As Kierkegaard expressed it (whom we may dare, given
what we have already heard from him, to call a philosopher of revelation and thereby both elucidate the character of the meta-philosophy itself and signal a separation of the wheat and chaff in Schelling
for which many readers surely already are strongly impatient), the
entrance of the Absolute into historical becoming, "impossibly"
remaining the Absolute while "becoming" simultaneously a thing of
this world, introduces "the absolutely different" into the heart of
*human* rationality and creates the terrible ecstasy of rationality's
"crucifixion."[19]

Surely since German Idealism, "revelation" has become an impor-

18. Excerpts and extensive comments are to be found in Augustine's *City of God*
(see esp. Bk 10, 23–32). For a scholarly reconstruction of the text, see John O'Meara,
*Porphyry's "Philosophy from Oracles" in Augustine* (Paris: Etudes augustiniennes,
1959) and also his "'Philosophy from Oracles' in Eusebius of Caesarea and Augustine's
Cassiciacum Dialogues," *Recherches augustiniennes et patristiques* 6 (1969), 105–38.

19. See *Philosophical Fragments*, 55.

tant *philosophical* term in its own right. A "PR" (orthodox or otherwise, it does not matter here) is at least wholly implied by Kant, by Hegel, Schelling, Kierkegaard, and then Rosenzweig, as well as by Lacoste, Marion, and Michel Henry, among others today: from Hegel on, revelation is a philosophical master-concept.[20] It is not of immediate concern whether or not the first treatise in the history of philosophy to be entitled "metaphysics" by its author, that of Francisco Suárez, counts as or contains a PR, or, even more fundamentally, whether, on the one hand, the possibility of the PR only arrives with the late medieval distinction between philosophy and theology, and hence out of the ingenious division of labor that the 13th-century university devised as a way to handle the rediscovery of Aristotle, or, on the other hand, whether the conditions are to be traced back to the univocal conception of Being in Scotus or the capacity of the intellect to represent to itself the totality of being in a concept in Henry of Ghent, that is, to the new beginning of metaphysics as a "transcendental science":[21] no genealogy will be offered here. What I have said above is enough to affirm that not everything that emerges in the wake of modern metaphysics, though indebted to it, accomplishes its very enactment. This enactment can be elaborated, quite strictly, as a threefold process of erasure, collapse, and nihilation: that is, (1) the erasure of transcend*ent* reality through its collapse into (2) transcendent*al* conditions spelled out in advance of the itemization of the whole sphere of intelligibility for (3) human experience conceived merely as a temporal movement of transcend*ing* that is in itself absolute.

---

20. See Jean-François Courtine, "Phenomenology and Hermeneutics of Religion," trans. Jeffrey Kosky, in Dominique Janicaud, et al., *Phenomenology and the "Theological Turn"* (NY: Fordham University Press), 121–26: "[I]n Hegel and Schelling, the key concepts of all philosophy of religion (phenomenon, manifestation, revelation), concepts that phenomenological reflection is obliged to pass through, are determined in contrasting ways" (124–25).

21. The gauge of Ghent's "modernity" is found in the unique structure of his *Summa theologica*: it begins, not with a direct treatment of God, but with the question of the possibility of human knowledge. The transcendental turn is medieval. See Olivier Boulnois, *Être et représentation* (Paris: Presses Universitaires de France, 1999).

Though the explicit moments of the PR from Blasche to Bavinck, from 1829 to 1907, have been (it would not be difficult to show) entangled with intellectual trends and attitudes that thinkers like Marion and Lacoste would like to name with names provided by Nietzsche and Heidegger (death of God, nihilism, metaphysics, technological enframing), the PR that along with them I am driven to explicate from out of the plane of a nihilation, demands to be, *inasmuch as revelation is its matter*, proposed as a twofold path: (1) of "overcoming [the onto-theological tradition of] metaphysics" (OTTM),[22] enduring through the era of nihilism, and anticipating the "thinking" tied to a [non-]experience of the coming God, as well as (2) of calling into question any rigid distinction between philosophical and theological disciplines in this ultimate case in order to advance the very task at hand. Name (1) of the path expresses the Heideggerian parameters of PPR of Marion and Lacoste. Name (2) of the path expresses precisely what is shared by Marion and Lacoste's positions "after" Heidegger, which is analogous to Heidegger's own position vis-à-vis Nietzsche.

To explain some crucial dimensions of this twofold path, I remind myself of my working definition of revelation outlined above: the *lógos* of the Living God, the speech of the Almighty, Lord of the Covenant, Creator of all. Revelation partakes of an intelligibility that is absolute, as the word of the Absolute, and as such, is terrifyingly free. Mortal: Know thyself. The concepts of novelty, impossibility, and others to come (my own meta-concepts, eschatologicity and unconditionality: both already broached along the course we have taken) have been slowly congealing around it.

Proposition (1) can be expressed in this way: if the *lógos* sent by the Father is ultimately, because firstly, the very *lógos* of the world as creation, then the world's *lógos* is subject to all the qualifications and intensifications provided by "negative theology":[23] the doctrine

---

22. To avoid misunderstanding in the use of the term.

23. The Christological expressions of divine wisdom at the apogee of the Pauline reflection (the philosophical "hymns" of Ephesians, Colossians) are authoritative witnesses here.

of creation *ex nihilo* is brought into play, which is a "contemplative" doctrine, an intellectual practice of seeing experience *before the possible*, thinking the world in light of the pre-possibility or impossibility of its being. As I said before, this is the basis of classical Christian (and Jewish and Muslim) philosophy. The revelation of God in Christianity shows that God transcends the totality of the cosmos in an absolute way, existing in excess of the distinctions basic to our knowledge of the world, albeit, alas, only knowable by way of them, which God is *not*. God, the form of ultimate intelligibility, and through his *lógos*, the final paradigm of all intelligibility whatsoever, is more than merely absolutely free *from* this world, but is also therefore absolutely free *for* it. It is a higher freedom that we contemplate. The intelligibility of creation is based on its connection with the Creator, who creates "through" his word, his *lógos*. Though unnecessary, without (sufficient) reason and *ohne warum*, the creation is freely given itself and finds its intelligibility inscribed in this freely bestowed word. To look to God in philosophy is therefore not to answer the philosophical question in advance, but rather—at least this is the case that revelation makes—to enter into the most profoundly open way of posing it: the horizon of absolute love is greater, is *more absolute*, than the horizon of nothing at all. To reprise a word of the mystics: the love that gives being is a fertile nothing. Why is this word appropriate here? Because the thinkable as unknowable Principle is a *Néant par excess*.[24] But not only so. It is also because of the ancient ("axial") breakthrough to the idea of the One as *beyond* multiplicity (the One does not exist) and as the unity *of* multiplicity (the One exists).[25] God as Principle is understood as the interval of bliss across which thought arrives to itself in the contemplation of the Divinity in relation to which the world has "no dual existence" (*ad-vaita*)—as expressed (this is a monumental but

24. See Stanislas Breton, *Du principe. Essai sur l'organisation du pensable* (Paris: Aubier, 1971).

25. See Jean Wahl's commentary on the first two theses of Plato's *Parmenides* in *Étude sur le Parménide de Platon* (Paris: F. Redier, 1926), an interpretation summarized in his *Traité de Métaphysique* II.9.3 (Paris: Payot, 1953), 642–49.

not large claim) in the classical theistic philosophies of the Abrahamic and Indian traditions.[26]

I turn in support to Indian philosophy. The word of the mystics is above all appropriate in the PR because the idea of God as Principle is only the point where intellectual "adoration" awakens to *bhakti*: the "way of devotion" carries the philosopher's way onto new vistas of *terra incognita*. Is the shudder it experiences at the edge of this vista the first tremor of its annihilation or its divinization? Only if it refuses to come to an end, to close the questioning, will it ever find out. The intellectual practice of the Divine Principle as creative Nothing (as *Brahman*, impersonal absolute) reaches its terminus in a desert of emptiness that is an unimaginably greater "nihilism" than that of the absolute finitude of Heidegger. Unfathomably more radically, in the qualification of non-dualism represented by Ramanuja, this desert is the spiritual locale where the soul, completely naked, shorn of every created support, finally arrives before the personal Lord, who, in his eternal Idea, loves the creature with the very love that constitutes the divine essence that, in its unity, founds the possibility of multiplicity. In Christianity this is called the divine tri-hypostatic bliss.[27] "For I am the base supporting Brahman..." says Krishna, the incarnate Vishnu, God Almighty.[28]

Here I think the wisdom of a classical programmatic distinction emerges as important, that between *de Deo Uno* and *de Deo Trino*:

26. See David Bentley Hart, *The Experience of God: Being, Consciousness, Bliss* (New Haven, CT: Yale University Press, 2013), and the indications in David Burrell, *Towards a Jewish-Christian-Muslim Theology* (Chichester, UK: Wiley-Blackwell, 2011), and Sarah Grant, *Towards an Alternative Theology: Confessions of a Non-Dualist Christian* (South Bend, IN: Notre Dame Press, [1989] 2002).

27. See St. John of the Cross, *Living Flame of Love*, 4.1–17.

28. *Bhagavad Gita*, xiv. 27. In the *Gita*, says R.C. Zaehner, no longer is "liberation" (*mokṣa*) sufficient: "It is no longer regarded as the ultimate goal. Total detachment from the world is still rigorously insisted on, for this brings one to Nirvana of Brahman, but this is not enough" (Zaehner, "Introduction," *Hindu Scriptures*, trans. R.C. Zaehner [NY: Dent and Sons, 1966], xvii). The deeper word for which

the essence, the unity, of the One God is known (as Unknown) by the great monotheistic ("Axial") philosophies East and West; it is the tri-hypostatic enjoyment of the Essence that is unique to the Christian revelation (though Personality's "transcendence" of the essence is shared among Indian and Semitic spiritual attitudes, as just witnessed). A constructive PR will enact here a new, expanded calibration for a *summa cum gentilium.*[29] From this new vista granted by this point of conjunction between Eastern and Western philosophy, I propose a summary of the import of Schelling's later thought (which I will now discuss): *higher than possibility stands personality.*

If Kant denied that "God could ever become the principle of science" since God can only be an idea, the "highest idea," the "end" of reason that reason can only strive toward without ever reaching (a "regulative" as opposed to "constitutive" idea),[30] then Schelling wants to elucidate, in a new way that is appropriate after Kant's "destruction" of Scholastic metaphysics, the "principles that hold human life together" of which the source, centerpiece, and crown is found in religion, viz., revelation:[31] "[A]ll real religion can only relate to a real God, and indeed to him only as the lord of reality and . . . a being that is not this can never become the object of religion."[32] The capacity *to think this that is contained in religion* is the first and last measure of a PR, and, says Schelling elsewhere, of any

---

the entire Upaniṣadic philosophy is a preparation is "Attach thy mind to Me" (*Bhagavad Gita*, vii.1). Compare Bavinck: "Revelation is the disclosure of the *mustē-rion tou theou.* What neither nature nor history, neither mind nor heart, neither science nor art, can teach us, it makes known to us—the fixed unalterable *will* of God . . . a will at variance with well-nigh the whole appearance of things. This will is the secret of revelation" (*Philosophy of Revelation*, 25). And the 10th-century Zoroastrian text, *Shkand-Gumanik Vichar* 10.37: "It is not enough to know only that [God] exists, but one must know his nature and his will" (ed. P. J. de Menasce, O.P., Fribourg, 1945, 117).

29. I take Thomas Aquinas, of course, as the reference point: *Summa contra gentiles* 1.3.2.

30. Schelling, Lecture 2, 120–21.

31. Schelling, Lecture 1, 95.

32. Ibid., 121.

philosophy whatsoever.[33] For Kant, however, the God of religion, the lord of reality, is strictly unknowable (in a this-worldly and banal sense of the term). Schelling's judgment: "real religion is . . . negated," and philosophy fails its task.[34] In Kant, God is and *can only be*, merely, the "end" of reason, which reason must presuppose, but at the same time necessarily knowing nothing of the "real being" of God. God can *never* appear, can never be God, and can never be, consequently, the "beginning," the "constitutive principle" of reason. Hence, as Schelling's logic goes, *only* the lord of reality, the Living God, can, paradoxically, be the "end" *and* "beginning," the Living Idea most immanent (as it were) to our reason and "science" (*Wissenschaft*)—according to which what we reason about is *unvordenklich*—"unanticipated"—ever-greater than our reasoning, and as such, initiates and guides our reasoning, expanding and transforming it. Revelation, for Schelling, reveals God as the end and beginning, and therefore as the *living heart* of all true metaphysics, beyond the tradition of Scholasticism, which for him achieves its consummation in Kant. A return to revelation, to "real religion," alone allows philosophy to realize its end and aim of the elucidation of the *total mystery* of human experience. In this, Schelling agrees with Thomas Aquinas, for whom "the last end is the first principle of being."[35] Christ, the *lógos tou theou*, "Alpha and Omega" (Apoc 1:8)—the unity of intelligibility as such in God who reveals himself in history—is the meaning of the "overcoming" of the OTTM for the PR.[36] The eschatology of reason is an eschatology *from the beginning* and not as a Kingdom that can never come because it has never made its historical appearance, which, for Christianity, is a "kenotic" appearance: the disclosure of the truth of

33. As we have discussed in a previous study, above. *Lectures on the History of Modern Philosophy*, trans. Andrew Bowie (Cambridge: Cambridge University Press, 1994), 132.

34. Ibid.

35. *Summa Theologiae* I-II 2.5 ad 3.

36. The "messianism" of Jacques Derrida, governed as it is by the absolute structure of *différance* (a quasi-transcendental rule governing reason) that allows no exceptions—even (especially) God's revelation (*Offenbarung*), inseparable from revealability (*Offenbarkeit*), which from this vantage must be seen as an extension

the "nothing" of the divine essence by way of a self-showing of divine tri-hypostatic personality, a revelation in the flesh of history, under its conditions, but as a *sign* of their overcoming (in a particularly philosophical way: the way of "union").[37]

With the introduction of the logic of the *eschaton*, therefore, we find a (historical) principle of intelligibility coming from revelation. Such a logic supersedes the transcendental logic of modern OTTM.

Proposition (2) is perhaps clearer, though it is drawn directly from the above and serves as a summary result of our disquisition so far.

If, for Heidegger, Nietzsche anticipates the way out of nihilism precisely by bringing to its consummation the era of the OTTM with his discovery and apotheosis of the will-to-power, a concept that unveils the hidden truth of the tradition, for Marion and Lacoste, Heidegger represents the very "moment" before which the definitive turn of tomorrow may take place, inasmuch as he names the essential—"nihilism":[38] for Marion this particular overcoming

of Heidegger's "metaphysical" (again, expressed in the modern sense) ontological difference, would fall under the same criticism outlined above. See Jacques Derrida, "Faith and Knowledge," *Acts of Religion*, ed. Gil Anidjar (London: Routledge, 2001), 46–47. As far as this correlation is the case (and no farther) we can apply Marion's proposal of the God of revelation in excess of Being—and of its iron law, the "ontological difference"—to be also a passage outside of the text of Derrida. See Jean-Luc Marion, *God without Being*, 2nd ed., trans. Thomas Carlson (Chicago: University of Chicago Press, 2012), 235: "the onto-theo-logical frame of the ontological difference . . . itself thought in a metaphysical manner. . . ."

37. In *Experience and the Absolute*, Jean-Yves Lacoste uses the term "symbol" (defined as "the redistribution of the field of experience"; see esp. §§6–10) to designate what I mean here by "sign" (following a common trope of the set of authoritative ecclesial documents from the Second Vatican Council: see *Gaudium et spes* §39: "On this earth the kingdom is already present in sign, when the Lord comes it will reach its completion.").

38. See Martin Heidegger, *Nietzsche*, vol. 1: *The Will to Power as Art*, trans. David Farrell Krell (NY: HarperCollins, 1979), 4: "If in Nietzsche's thinking the prior tradition of Western thought is gathered and completed in a decisive respect, then the confrontation with Nietzsche becomes one with all Western thought hitherto." Marion: "Today, when nihilism marks our age. . ." *The Erotic Phenomenon*, trans. Stephen E. Lewis (Chicago: University of Chicago Press, 2007), 18.

involves a return to Husserl and an interpretation and elaboration of the latter's most basic insights as a truly post-metaphysical, post-transcendental manner of proceeding;[39] for Lacoste this involves an advancement of the concept of "thinking" through a profound conscription of Heidegger's own analysis and answer to the problematic of Western thought, life, and culture;[40] for both Lacoste and Marion this involves a recovery and advancement of a pre-Scholastic and Patristic model of the fidelity of human intelligence to its end—which requires, beyond Heidegger, an erasure of the disciplinary distinction of the theological and philosophical inasmuch as it short-circuits reason's response to the intelligibility of the Living God.[41] As we will see, for Marion the paradigmatic character of the disclosed intelligibility of the divine for human rationality demands an elucidation of the concept of "revelation" that promises to "save" the unity of reason. For Lacoste, by contrast, the question of the concept of revelation does not enter the task of "re-blending thought and praise":[42] but I will treat these here as two complementary ways of inhabiting the same path.

In both Marion and Lacoste the PPR calls into question any rigid distinction between philosophy and theology, since, if revelation can become an object of philosophy, even if only as the final test for philosophy's own self-reflection, then philosophy and theology are

39. See Marion: "Phenomenology opens the way of . . . leaving metaphysics to itself," *Being Given*, trans. Jeffrey Kosky (Stanford, CA: Stanford University Press, 2002), 4.

40. Lacoste, *From Theology to Theological Thinking*, lecture 3, 63–90.

41. An end of reason disclosed *ephapax* in "the revelation of Jesus Christ" (Gal 1:12, Apoc 1:1). Such a profound revision of the philosophical claims a Christian pedigree and separates itself from the account of a "separated" philosophical account of reason, which, according to such a genealogy, is only—to speak apocalyptically—a particularly terrible face of a monster (nihilism) arisen from the chaotic sea of *a* modernity, a medieval course taken and come to dominate European thought and culture. Marion, "On the Foundation of the Distinction between Theology and Philosophy," *Philosophy, Religions and Transcendence*, ed. Philippe Capelle-Dumont (Manila: Atelone University Press, 2010), 47–76; Lacoste, *La Phenomenalité de Dieu* (Paris: Cerf, 2008), 9–11.

42. Marion, "Faith and Reason," *The Visible and the Revealed*, trans. Crina Gschwandtner et al. (NY: Fordham University Press, 2008), 145–54; Lacoste, *From Theology to Theological Thinking*, 79.

revealed to be, at times and at worst, *a priori* categorizations that delimit the scope of revelation (and reason) before it is given. According to Schelling, the PR is "a question of the meaning of philosophy itself."[43] What counts in both case (1) and (2), in the overcoming of metaphysics and the calling into question of disciplinary distinctions, is that revelation is considered in itself and from itself, on the terms by which it presents itself—that is, phenomenologically; and it presents itself as a matter fundamental to humanity, and therefore of primary importance to thought of the human kind, concerned with the Unknown Essence of the One or with the Tri-hypostatic excess that is the ultimate key to the enigma of ourselves. I can now clarify a hypothesis of the PR: the conceptual distinction between essence and person basic to Trinitarian theology may make intelligible the far subsequent disciplinary distinction between theology and philosophy.[44]

Such propositions are laid out in the form of theses at the beginning, neither to be proven, nor as the object of direct argument. They are instead pledges or promises that the PPR may or may not be finally able to fill in our day, but that are intrinsic to its proposal to us—of a philosophy for which revelation is the central matter.

The justification of the PR, then, can be summarized by the following syllogism:

(1) Philosophy is the human "science" *par excellence* inasmuch as it endeavors to articulate or grasp at least something of the essential, of the truth, of the meaning of the human as such; yet the humanity of the human is the most enigmatic of questions.[45]

(2) Revelation is the revelation of humanity to itself precisely because it is the revelation of God, *humanity's* Alpha and Omega. The revelation of God, the living God, the Lord of Being, is the key that, in unlocking itself, unlocks the mystery of humanity as well. Therefore:

43. Schelling, Lecture Two, 110.
44. This is a vista that will have to be made the theme of another text.
45. "Thus, far from man and his endeavors making the world comprehensible, it is man himself that is the most incomprehensible. . . . It is precisely man that drives me to the final desperate question: Why is there anything at all? Why is there not nothing?" (Schelling, Lecture 1, 94).

(3) the PR is the greatest intensification of the philosophical questioning, and necessary for philosophy; its task is philosophy's fundamental achievement.

The modern individual discipline or set of disciplines—"philosophy" and "theology"—has *typically*, if also crudely, understood philosophy as dealing with reason, alone, that is, reason within the horizon of the world, whereas "revelation" is the domain of theology, and theology alone, for theology, again, is defined as the *science* that takes its method from revelation as an "object" (and is therefore somehow not, or no longer, philosophical...). But this observation about the theoretical conditions of the modern distinction between "philosophy" and "theology" only shows the historical conditions for the possibility of writing something called a "PR" (even if such an activity, as in the case of Schelling and Bavinck, is a means toward *transgressing* the academic and disciplinary distinction and showing its theoretical limitations), not its present possibility or meaning. To the latter we must commit ourselves in the following introduction of two proposed conditions that revelation would require of any philosophy of it.

## Two Conditions of the PR
## First Condition: The *Eschatologicity* of Thinking Revelation

Perhaps the reader is as shocked as I am about what has been uncovered of PR so far. I would like to distill what seem to be two basic conditions for its deployment, firstly, with analysis of PR in a post-idealist interpreter, Franz Rosenzweig (but in dialogue with explicit practitioners, Schelling and Bavinck), and secondly, with analysis of the contemporary *telos* of PR, the PPR (continuing my generalized presentation of Marion and Lacoste).

Starting with an introduction to the modern history of the idea of revelation in (1) its ecclesial and (2) philosophical receptions. (1) It is strange, but nevertheless ought to be observed, that revelation becomes a direct theme for *philosophical* reflection only in the modern criticism of it (and *subsequently* a theme for *theological* reflection on its heels).[46] It bears recalling that the concept of "revelation" is in fact a latecomer in theology, having for the first time received direct treatment at a conciliar level at the First Vatican Council (1869–1870) in the four terse paragraphs of the third chapter of *Dei Filius*. Not until the Second Vatican Council (1962–1965) did revelation become the theme of a document in its own right (*Dei Verbum*), mostly in order to reorient the frankly epistemological and propositional character of Vatican I's treatment. The other modern council, the Council of Trent (1545–1563), only used the word once, without any interest in the concept as such. Vatican I seems to have thought of revelation (which it never explicitly defines) primarily as a content of ideas *about* God and God's relation to all things, as *revelata*, the content of communicated knowledge. For Vatican II by contrast, revelation is *revelatio* proper, an activity of God in the first place, yet with (peculiar) intelligible content: the "showing forth" and "self-communication" of (a) God and (b) "the eternal decisions of his will regarding the salvation of men" (§6). This double form of "showing forth" is enacted through the "realization" of God's hidden "plan" for the salvation of the world. It is disclosed, specifically, "through words and deeds" of God, which possess, further, an "inner unity": deeds that guide history to this end (the fulfilment of the plan, or mystery), and words, God's self-interpretation of his deeds (taking concrete form in, the text later says, Scripture and tradition, together "one sacred deposit of the word of God, committed to the Church," §10) that "proclaim and clarify the mystery contained" in the actions. The play of divine words and deeds in history simply describes the character of the two parts of the content of revelation, God's self-communication and the communication of his will. These two dimensions are finally unified in Christ, "who is both the mediator of revelation and its fullness" (§2), since in him the divine union with humanity is accomplished, a union that is in itself the consummation of the Creator's plan, which is none other

---

46. For the following lines see especially Jean-Yves Lacoste's article, "Révélation," *Dictionnaire critique de théologie*, 3rd ed, ed. Jean-Yves Lacoste (Paris: Presses Universitaires de France, 2007), 1215–22.

than the complete self-communication of God to man and man to God (a description of what in Christology is termed the "hypostatic union" of divine and human natures in the one identified as Jesus of Nazareth). Hence as far as the intellectual content of revelation goes, *Dei Verbum* uses the words that the earlier *Dei Filius* applied to the trans-historical "supernatural end of man" in relation to the historical revelation itself, describing the self-communication as participation in "divine treasures which totally transcend the understanding of the human mind" (§6; cp. *Dei Filius* III.2). For Vatican II, the words and deeds of God bring within the horizon of history the supernatural end itself. Revelation transgresses the conditions of history, not by destroying or overcoming them, but by performing the impossible, using them to communicate trans-historical truth. This discloses the destiny of the entire created order for life in God, and manifests the final meaning of the enigma of history itself, its aim and purpose. The "epistemological interpretation of revelation" (to use Marion's language in the first of his Gifford Lectures)[47] is wholly muted here and yet the intelligibility becomes more dramatic, more difficult, and more profound.

*Dei Verbum* is partially indebted to the Pauline language of the "revelation of the mystery," *apocalypsis tou mysteriou*, which is the startling unveiling of the plan for the end of history in its middle (in the crucifixion and resurrection of Jesus) that serves as God's final self-"justification" (*dikaiosunē*), which was the Christian answer to the basic question of Judaism of Paul's day (at least in Paul's understanding): how is God going to bring to completion the promises found in the election of Israel when the entire vocation of Israel seems to have failed (along with humanity in general) and to have fallen under God's judgment (*apocalypsis dikaiokrisias tou theou*)?[48] How will God remain faithful to the election of Israel and accomplish his universal intention in it for the salvation of the world? For

---

47. Jean-Luc Marion, "Givenness and Revelation," *The* 2014 *Gifford Lecture Series*, Lecture 1: "The Aporia of Revelation: The Epistemological Interpretation," https://www.youtube.com/playlist?list=PLZg7vx6J9ioJJCoce_ltuHDFH5K9w-ed5. Accessed September 11, 2015.

48. See Rom 2:1–5 and chs. 9–11.

St. Paul, in his most intellectually ambitious—one can say (why not?) most "philosophical"—letter (Romans), "revelation" is the Creator's answer to this problem, *the* basic problem of human history. The *philosophia tou apocalypsis* involves the explication of the intelligibility of the words and deeds of God, an examination of the conditions of revelation, the discernment of the "wisdom of God" under the appearance of the "foolishness of man." According to Harry Austryn Wolfson (*The Philosophy of the Church Fathers 1*, 1970), PR (though he doesn't use the term) is the construction of the intellectual scaffolding required to understand revelation, developed out of the intellectual horizon, the cultural instantiation of the "world," the cultural milieu within which one lives and thinks.[49] PR, on this view, provides a hermeneutic of revelation, no more and no less, through the generation of doxological practices (what Christians used to call "prayer") that give rise, finally, to concepts and theories with the aim of affording understanding of the divine self-showing and self-communication, which at their terminus return to consummate doxologically in an intellectual immersion in the words and deeds of God. This biblical and Pauline explication is the *common root* of the modern ecclesial and philosophical explications. There is therefore one PR even if it assumes two (one should say, impoverished) modes in the modern period ("sacred theology" and "natural theology [of philosophy]"). It is worth noting that the gap between these two modes closes in the PPR of Marion and Lacoste. We will return to this.

(2) Overlapping the modern development in the ecclesial sphere is a philosophical passage that begins with Fichte and Kant and runs to Schelling, Rosenzweig, and ultimately Marion and Lacoste.

In a manner similar to early Schelling's disciple Blasche thirty years later, the young Fichte in his *Attempt at a Critique of All Revelation* (1792) argues that God can reveal himself only within the strict limits of the moral law, or rather, the moral law itself *is* the universal content of revelation, which is already capable of being fully known apart from any special revelation. Fichte's task to "pro-

---

49. H. A. Wolfson, *The Philosophy of the Church Fathers*, vol. 1: *Faith, Trinity, Incarnation*, 3rd ed. (Cambridge, MA: Harvard University Press, 1970).

nounce judgment" on revelation from the philosophical point of view, that is, according to "*a priori* principles," is accomplished specifically by "abstracting completely from anything particular that might be possible in a given revelation; indeed, it will even ignore the question of whether any revelation is given, in order generally to establish principles valid for every revelation."[50] Published the following year, Kant's *Religion within the Limits of Reason Alone* (1793) hardly needs comment: an "experiment" in what can only be called moral esotericism, which sets as its task the "unification" of the "Biblical theologian" with the "philosophical theologian" (the rightful task, he says, of a "philosophical researcher of religion") by means of separating revelation from that which is historical in it, thereby "leading back" the data of "revelation" to the "pure rational system of religion," showing, *de facto*, the intellectual coincidence of practical reason and positive revelation, and *de jure*, the latter's utter redundancy (except for the simple-minded, who need an external authority, which motivates by fear, to guide them).[51]

As we have seen, Schelling attempted, explicitly, a *positive* PR. His posthumously published lecture series, *Philosophie der Offenbarung* is erected on the failure of speculative Idealism to grasp the divine through rational deduction ("negative philosophy") and rather takes as its starting point precisely that first matter that is given to think, the condition of thought that thought cannot ground: here there is not only Being, the very fact of existence, but the *Herr des Seins*, the "Lord of Being" who gives himself to thought within historical existence and as the disruptor of every conceptualization: the "abyss of reason."[52] I drew analogy with the Vishishta Advaita Vedanta, the "nondualism of the differentiated" above. Here, as

50. *Attempt at a Critique of All Revelation*, §1, Introduction, 16, trans. Garrett Green (NY: Cambridge University Press, 2012), 7.

51. See Kant's preface to the first and second editions for this reference (33–39 and 40–41 of the Cambridge edition, trans. Allen Wood and George Di Giovanni [NY: Cambridge University Press, 1999]). Compare Aristotle's similar attitude in *Metaphysics* XII.8.

52. In his first chapter Bavinck notes, and I repeat it here, that Hamann said somewhere that speculative rationalism has forgotten that God is a genius *who does not ask us* whether we find his word rational or irrational.

there, the soul, *rationally* experiencing a union of identity, uncovering the ultimate ground of reality, before which reason becomes speechless, its light refigured as "dazzling darkness," awakens, in its volitional and empirical experience of radical facticity, to an irreducible encounter with the Absolute that is necessary for reason, but incomprehensible.[53]

Franz Rosenzweig is perhaps the greatest student of Schelling's thought; he continues the quest for a philosophical appropriation of revelation that does not reduce revelation to the scope of human thought, and, as his little essay "The New Thinking" (1925) shows, he is perhaps more aware than Schelling of the limits of an approach that still attends to revelation with, as it were, a "haughty" conception of reason: in Schelling revelation is reduced to the content of a speculative *gnōsis*; reason plumbs the depths of the divine without remainder inasmuch as the divine is thoroughly laid bare through the outworking of the world process. For Rosenzweig by contrast, human language, the medium of revelation, is ever immersed within a mythic-symbolic horizon that only reveals the shadow of God inasmuch as language itself is the transposition of the unassimilability of God, of man, and of the world, which are all "absolute," strictly unknowable. Revelation is not a grasp of God by reason, but the disclosure of an infinite alterity, beyond the double alterity of man and the world, first, narratively (into the pagan past), then ritually (into the Judeo-Christian future), since it is through the experience of man in the world that God is given. Rosenzweig refuses Schelling's claim for philosophy to speak a greater word of God than what revelation gives in the irreducible mode of symbol, simply, in the first place, by refusing the demarcation, and then, hierarchical arrangement, of theology and philosophy. In this way Rosenzweig opens up a "new thinking," which is an

53. See Josef Sudbrack, *Trunken vom hell-lichten Dunkel des Absoluten: Dionysius der Areopagite und die Poesie der Gotteserfahrung* (Einsiedeln: Johannes Verlag, 2001). Sudbrack opposes Buber and Levinas in particular to Hegel's idea of true infinity, which, desirous of overcoming the contrast between God and the world of "bad infinity," collapses the opposition of alterity into a mysticism of identification, wherein the infinite [freedom] alone is real. Schelling would be to Hegel as Ramanuja is to Sankara.

authentic recovery of ancient ways of thought for which the theological and philosophical are inseparable if not indistinct.[54] For this tradition, what matters to philosophy is the "absolute empiricism" for which the Absolute becomes possible for us—not whether it is possible, but how it happens when it happens.[55] Knowledge as knowledge of the whole is impossible—but through experience of this impossibility in the fragmentariness of experience as linguistic beings, the immense positivity of God presses into our world. This is revelation; it demands a "new thinking."

"Man's understanding," Rosenzweig therefore says with reference to "the Pharisees of the Talmud and Saints of the Church," "reaches as far as his doings."[56] I delay the explication of this remarkable aphorism until the end of this study.

The PR, then, will only be based on the conviction that the eschatological orientation of thought, its orientation to the "coming" or "appearing" of God, is oriented to the future by means of the past, by revelatory events of the future in the past, beachheads, epiphanies of the eschatological future that form the narrative of sacred history and its transformation from within by breakthroughs of the natural, hierophanic character of mythic experience. And the inquiry into the meaning of revelation *for* philosophy, the complete rethinking of thought by revelation, is precisely the place, as the historical constellation of thinkers gathered here (Schelling, Rosenzweig, and Heidegger, above) shows, that the PR begins. The isolation, in fact, of revelation to a history, to a fragment of history come and gone, reducing God to a past moment which did not bring the history of the world to its direct end, is the path by which the *specific* universality of revelation can emerge.[57]

This observation now made recalls the significance of Bavinck's "theological" PR. As Bavinck expresses it: "Revelation, while having

54. Franz Rosenzweig, "The New Thinking," *Philosophical and Theological Writings*, trans. Paul W. Franks and Michael Morgan (Indianapolis, IN: Hackett, 2000), 109–39.

55. Ibid., 138; cp. 122.

56. Ibid., 110.

57. At the same time it creates the possibility of the atheism we know today, important for a PR, but I will bracket that here.

its center in the Person of Christ, in its periphery extends to the uttermost ends of creation. It does not stand isolated in nature and history, does not resemble an island in the ocean, nor a drop of oil upon water. With the whole of nature, with the whole of history, with the whole of humanity, with the family and society, with science and art, it is intimately connected."[58] Christianity is "based on revelation"—a revelation that "transcends reason" to the extent that reason could never discover these truths, the ultimate realities, on its own. Yet this "contradiction of reason" by revelation hides within a greater continuity that can only be disclosed in the distance, the gap, the interval opened up within the finite horizon of the world by revelation and which is only resolved eschatologically. Revelation reveals the beginning in the end. It is this connection and distance that the PR wants to understand: God, "the first principle and last end" of all things. The first principle is given as promised to come: this eschatological belief articulates the essential regarding the human predicament and its task, to think the impossible, to find anew and traverse its believability, that a thing of this world is— provisionally but determinatively, eschatologically—the absolute measure of it.

We must think this thought under the sign of the provisional in order to attest with fidelity to the definitive. How?

## Second Condition: The *Conditionlessness* of Thinking Revelation

This leads us to a final observation from the history of philosophy, specifically from the most recent history, in relation to which Lacoste himself is a key witness. Here the distinction between philosophy and theology is certainly put in brackets, or at the very least found unstable and unidentifiable. And such is finally the importance of contemporary *phenomenology* in particular for the PR: for phenomenology does not decide *a priori* about its content; it is by

---

58. Bavinck, *The Philosophy of Revelation*, 27.

definition, as remarkably hard-won battles of the last generation have shown us, open to *anything* that can appear, and here the articulation of what is possible only comes *after* the event of appearing,[59] which makes possible what Marion calls, as far as God is concerned, the "impossible": God always transgresses the formal conditions for his appearing which we cannot help but throw in the way before God and his coming.[60] As Lacoste says, "phenomenology is without limits," even the limits that differentiate the philosophical and the theological, or, if you like, the natural and the supernatural—for phenomenology, in its return to what is given, "brackets every limit."[61]

What is given, therefore, gives its own conditions, and this giving is an integral part of the phenomenon itself—in philosophy as much as theology, in revelation, and all else. And here, in the PPR, we find the shared principle of intelligibility to philosophy and theology, and the condition for the distinction between them. The distinction turns on that which revelation first introduced: that between what is revealed and what is not, the revealed and the non-revealed. And what about the principle of their unity? The PR is not theology. Nevertheless, it is concerned with the theological, primarily the contribution of revelation to intelligibility as such: revelation gives to rationality its greatest test and is at the same time its unsurpassable paradigm. It is both of these because in order to be thought, it requires a radical *expansion* of the domain of rationality.[62] If Anselm's "definition" of God has any merit, then this is

59. See the late László Tengelyi's article, "New Phenomenology in France" (*The Southern Journal of Philosophy*, 50.2 [2012], 295–303), which is a précis of his landmark study (with H.-D. Gondek), *Neue Phänomenologie in Frankreich* (Berlin: Suhrkamp, 2011). Here Tengelyi articulates the major outlines that set apart the "third form of phenomenology," after Husserl's, founded on transcendental constitution, and then Heidegger's hermeneutical thinking. For this "third form," the phenomenon as such is of central concern, and is understood as the *event* of spontaneous constitution, in relation to which the phenomenon can only be understood as self-establishing.

60. *Certitudes négatives* (Paris: Grasset and Fasquelle, 2010), ch. 2.

61. Lacoste, *La phénoménalité de Dieu* (Paris: Cerf, 2008), 9–11.

62. See Jean-Luc Marion, *Certitudes négatives* §31, "Eloge du paradoxe," 309–18.

precisely what it tells us: as "that than which nothing greater can be thought," God can be thought, but he can only be thought in a way that transcends thought. Intellection turns to love, and finds that love knows, and that knowing is love or knows nothing.[63] Put in terms relevant to what I am saying here, revelation is intelligible, but its contribution to intelligibility as such turns on its impossibility, its *difference* from every other intelligible and kind of intelligibility. This difference, however, does not *isolate* God from everything else; rather it shows the *relevance* of God to everything given —not understood as "giver" in the first place, but as paradigm. Revelation gives the greatest possible expansion to the rational that is possible by *proposing itself* as the paradigm, or, if you like, *absolute* case of the rational itself.[64] It is this expansion of the intelligible offered, even demanded, by revelation that the PPR attempts to understand.

We learn the important lesson here from phenomenology that the PR cannot be what is normally practiced under the banner of the "philosophy of religion," nor especially "philosophical theology"—what Lacoste calls that "hideous compromise"—at least insofar as these academic disciplines approach the phenomenon of revelation from a realm that does not consider itself finally, and therefore firstly, wholly conditioned by revelation itself, that is, by the limitless, the frontier where the impossible reigns. This reign is marked by an expansion of the intelligible—of rationality itself—by virtue of its appearing as *most intelligible*. Revelation is the revelation of the paradigm of intelligibility that cannot be superseded, for it reveals itself as ever-greater, as ever-more intelligible. By its appearing then, it refigures all possible appearing, and by this refiguring of appearance as such, it refigures intelligibility and human rationality.

Now we are right to ask a difficult question: what is the mode of access to this frontier? According to Marion, it is charity. With this

63. St. Augustine, *Confessions* 7.10.18: "He who knows the truth knows that [uncreated] light, and he who knows the light knows eternity. Charity knows it."
64. See Jean-Luc Marion's programmatic sketch, "On the Foundation of the Distinction between Theology and Philosophy."

Lacoste agrees: God is known through being loved.[65] The first thing we must remember about knowledge of God is that

> to know someone is to love someone and to love someone is to let oneself be—to give oneself to be—mastered by another.[66]

"But by worship of love addressed to Me alone/Can I be known and seen/In such a form as I really am: [So can my lovers] enter into Me" (*Bhagavad Gita* xi.54). The PPR consummates in *bhakti*. This second aphorism towards a PR bears a poverty of expression that seems unavoidable. Here we could appeal to the conceptual apparatuses of a Pascal or al-Ghazali in order to express the "higher" knowledge of intuitive contact with another that transcends us through the pathway of the "heart." I will settle for Thomas Aquinas, so that I am not misunderstood: "Love . . . even in this life tends primarily to God and from him passes on to other things; according to this, charity loves God directly but other things through the mediation of God. In knowledge, however, the converse is true, since we know God through other things, either as cause through effects or by way of eminence or negation."[67] The "reasons of the heart" appear within rationality under the form of incompleteness or even contradiction. Because they undergird rationality as a principle, they manifest a higher rationality that can only be grasped in partial and mutually irreconcilable ways without the "key" of love, which "approaches nearer to God" than reason.[68] But in this way the reasons of the heart express the mode of access to the divine frontier of reason which is nothing less than an "affront" to reason, its "stumbling-block," its contradiction—and through this, its radical refigurement. Love saves reason, as it does

---

65. See his essay translated as "On Knowing God through Loving Him," *Christianity and Secular Reason*, ed. Jeffrey Bloechl (South Bend, IN: Notre Dame University Press, 2012), 127–51.

66. Marion: "Knowing signifies loving and love cannot be divided" ("Faith and Reason," 154); Lacoste: "In God . . . we are powerless to discern anything but a pure act of love. . ." ("On Knowing God through Loving Him," 133).

67. *Summa theologiae* II-II q. 27 a. 4 resp.

68. Ibid., I-II q. 26 a. 3 ad 4.

everything else (or, alternatively, nothing at all). Because, when approaching revelation on its own terms, revelation reveals that there is nothing—*finally*, eschatologically—outside of its domain, then reason itself is no contradiction to this rule. To the contrary. Not only does what is given to be thought, and the way it is given, tell us what thinking ultimately is, but in the case of the divine at least, and in the deepest way, the knowledge emerges from love, a love that binds the lover to the beloved. In the case of God love is absolute, and therefore the love by which he can be known is, in return, without limits in what it may require of us. Only love may demand infinite devotion, absolute *bhakti*. The PR must be frank about what is at stake for the human in knowing *God*, who either can be known or cannot, and if he can, by way of his initiative in revelation, then such knowledge, by its limitlessness, will require the human to pursue it without placing on it in advance *any conditions* that God must first respect—the human takes even these *from what God gives when he gives himself*. If there is no possible place in our philosophy for this radicality implied for philosophy by revelation, then we have to ask whether what we are calling philosophy today is philosophical enough. (How well do we comprehend St. Augustine's equation of the love of wisdom with the love of God?) Or, alternatively, we must ask whether Christian belief, as a "way of life," is truly dead with the advent of this age's nihilism. And whether, therefore, on the one hand, we must be content to finish with ourselves, as we understand ourselves in ourselves as a terminus shorn of any possible "transcendent ground," or, on the other hand by contrast, continue by seeing the PPR as reaching the point of a new beginning: one may choose. "One could receive," says Marion in debate with Jean-Luc Nancy, "the 'deconstruction of Christianity' as the introduction to what is finally appropriate to term Christianity."[69] The radical affirmation of the ontological difference, to the point of its mystical erasure in the creative Nothing, opens onto the vista of the essential.

---

69. See Marion and Nancy, "Débat," *Dieu en tant que Dieu*, ed. Philippe Capelle-Dumont (Paris: Cerf, 2010), 278–79.

## Final Unity

Returning to the historical situation of the PR, we could say that, on the one hand, the history of philosophy as modern academic discipline can be seen as an attempt to *erase* completely the *possibility* of the PR. In this path, philosophy is united with theology in its rejection of the PR as a possibility. Philosophy deals with (natural) reason, which becomes reason as such, the only reason accessible to reason; theology deals with (supernatural) revelation: two disciplines no longer in "competition" through a division of labor. If the data of revelation are off-limits to philosophy, then both discourses are fully secure in their own domains. In fact a hermetically sealed *duplex ordo* (even if one side finally becomes wholly absorbed by the other, as in a "vitalism," or, alternatively, rejected altogether, as in a "materialism") is the way to stabilize and control, to mark off territory in advance that creates the respective fields of inquiry. On the other hand, the history of philosophy could be seen, as it certainly was by Heidegger (and for whom a "methodological a-theism," a silence of "difficult proximity" of philosopher to God was the best response), as a sustained attempt to *appropriate* revelation for itself, as it were, to domesticate transcendence, to circumscribe the divine with the rule of possibility in order to guarantee mastery of its intelligibility, a procedure that requires reducing the divine to an abstract principle at the service of rationality. But here, in this circumscription, the halo disappears; God is lost—the idol remains.[70] This vantage, expressed *at its maximum*, sees revelation as wholly open to the gaze of human reason; revelation, and therefore God, is fully exhaustible. At its minimum, this vantage sees religious revelation as a less sophisticated form of the truth. Hegel is the apogee of this kind of approach. Yet what we hold in each hand here are two sides of the same coin (as we already find in Hegel): the domestication of transcendence becomes the means of its erasure, just as the absolute bifurcation of the discourses domesticates transcendence by relegating revelation to a pure domain that we have

---

70. The great tree of Schelling falls by the action of such a little axe as well.

circumscribed by the rational force of our own categories. Permit me to quote the theologian's PR again here:

> The philosophy of revelation, just like that of history, art, and the rest, must take its start from its object, from revelation. Even its idea cannot be construed *a priori*. There is but one alternative: either there is no revelation, and then all speculation is idle; or else there comes to us out of history such a revelation, shining by its own light; and then it tells us, not only what its content is, but also how it comes into existence. The philosophy of revelation does not so much make this fit in with its system as rather so broadens itself that it can embrace revelation too in itself. And doing this, it brings to light the divine wisdom which lies concealed in it.[71]

And the PR of the philosopher says very much the same:

> There is no one among those who know what they are talking about when it comes to revelation that would think that [revelation] is necessarily something to be understood *a priori*. On the contrary, everything that the philosophy of revelation knows to say about revelation, it is content to say only after revelation has occurred.[72]

In the case of intellectual domestication, which dominates our general, unreflective philosophical attitude today, the PR is impossible, since it would only be understood as an enactment of the "transcendental attitude," of the "metaphysics" that annihilates God and instrumentalizes Being. We are warned: the PR must allow revelation its own intrinsic intelligibility and give to theology, and in the first place to religious faith, the proper honor of *knowing* what it is talking about when it investigates the content of faith. The PR is, in other words, not about articulating what is *really* the case behind religious belief and its history. This is the precise point where the PPR must part ways with Schelling, for he eclipses the content of dogma and makes it the main point of another narrative that philosophy alone can grasp: the exhaustive unfolding of God in historical becoming, for example (history as the Trinitarian revelation of

---

71. Bavinck, *The Philosophy of Revelation*, 26.

72. Schelling, *Philosophy of Revelation*, Lecture 24 (*Philosophie de la révélation*, vol. 3, 31).

God to himself). The PR concerns itself with the "positivity" of revelation, and the impact that revelation has for philosophy. Philosophy's task in the PR is not the way of the Upaniṣads or of the Hellenes of Late Antiquity, to allegorize the myth, to find the words and rituals from the ancient dawn as archetypes for states of soul, to abstract the eternal human truth from its mythical expression; it is not "demythologization" and does not "allegorize," however subtly, the theological… The "Axial Age" accomplishment is only a backdrop for PR. The harsh first principle of eschatologicity—viz., that the very historicity of our history derives from an encounter of finitude with the living infinitude beyond the order of finite contrasts, but through them and by (non-)contrast with it as a whole—refuses in advance this facile way. "For a God," says Schelling, "who is merely an idea of reason does not allow an actual religion, or much less, an actual revelation to be conceived."[73] The PR takes revelation, and even its authoritative interpretations from within the religious, cultic domain, as a given. It is not a *gnōsis* in the classical sense: the PR refuses the distinction between esoteric and exoteric levels of revelation, for which the latter is the domain of theology and the former is the domain of revelation's "philosophy" that somehow pierces to the core of reality that religion, as non-speculative practice for the uninitiated, cannot.[74] Either of these methodological dualisms would be only conditions that attempt to domesticate the divine and to accomplish human mastery over it. It is precisely by giving oneself to be by receiving one's being wholly from the other, thereby entering into the inner path of charity, by "letting be" the religious domain as expressive bearer of revelation, that the PR proposes itself as overcoming OTTM—and it does so to the degree that it gives revelation the scope that its intelligibility intrinsically demands. In this perspective, the PR is an attempt to take part in such an overcoming that revelation proposes (or it is not revelation at all).

It is this sense of "the reality of revelation" that the PPR wants to

---

73. *The Philosophy of Revelation,* lecture 7, 188 (*Sämmtliche Werke* II/3, 141).

74. See Jean Borella, *Christ the Original Mystery* (Brooklyn, NY: Angelico Press, 2018), 55–88.

understand, and understanding, to enact. In light of this enactment, and as an explication of it, I quote Schelling one last time, and return to the quotation from Rosenzweig, left unexplicated above. In the second lecture from the *Philosophy of Revelation*, he responds "for the last time!" to the misguided "pretense" of some critics who consider that the undertaking of a "philosophy of revelation" is "a religious one" and think that he "wants simply to establish religion in the old sense—particularly positive religion—and so on..." By these words and the self-blinding attitude they express, says Schelling, these critics "believe themselves to have already sufficiently discredited *this* aspiration"[75] of the PR, namely, "to become aware in a new way of the principles that hold life together,"[76] or, let *us* say, gathering the threads dropped above, the peculiar "overcoming" of metaphysics as nihilism by revelation as first *and* last. Schelling's response to this godless and therefore unphilosophical accusation resounds like a refrain through his first lectures: The PR is not a matter of "establishing" religion "in the old sense" but is nevertheless "a very serious question ... it is a question of the meaning of philosophy itself."

What I have called the overcoming of OTTM by reference to the conditions for any PR, we can also call the salvation of philosophy by revelation. Even if revelation is too much for philosophy, whether this is philosophy as it is, or as we take it to be, or even as whatever it may possibly become in the shadow of revelation—and whether it is finally, *eschatologically*, too much or not, God alone knows—does not negate the salvation of philosophy, but rather, enacts it. Hence Rosenzweig:

> Man's understanding reaches as far as his doings—apparently, to the honor of mankind. . . .[77]

It is tempting to see this remarkable aphorism as the crown of the PR. Rosenzweig introduces this thought in his essay, "The New Thinking," discussed above, with these words: "What the Pharisees

---

75. Schelling, Lecture Two, 110. Emphasis in original.
76. Ibid., Lecture One, 95.
77. "The New Thinking," 110.

of the Talmud and the Saints of the Church always knew deserves to be understood."[78] This deserves reflection.

The God of the philosophers, on the one hand, and of Abraham, Isaac, and Jacob, on the other, may very well be the same God in the end, if, as revelation's eschatologicity requires, the covenant God is the Lord of all, including being and metaphysics. The test and criterion of this final unity is whether the philosopher as thinker, as philosopher, can be or become a saint, one whose word and deed aspire together in a philosophical life to be one in the truth of God.

Though it is not clarified as an intellectual concept until the recent present (a clarification that is continuing), revelation—I mentioned this above—is an idea with the highest possible pedigree in Christianity. "Revelation" is the disclosure of the *mustērion tou theou*—the "mystery of God"—the *apocalypsis*—"revelation/disclosure/unveiling"—of the world's last and therefore first truth. Its "reality," though "kenotically" hidden in history as a sign of history's eschatological meaning, is of course taken for granted by religious faith as its content and reason for being. The question regarding how it is given and how it is lived, its intelligibility, marked by *eschatologicity*, given as promised, and by the *conditionlessness* of love, however, is the question of the PR, particularly in its present phenomenological form.

78. Ibid.

# STUDY 6

WORD: *Jñāna. Scientia. Gnōsis.* Knowledge

NAME: Thomas Aquinas, Sankara

STYLE: Preparatory Note

MATTER: On the Concept of Knowledge within a
Shared Metaphysics Between Advaitic and Trinitarian
Philosophy

"For what does the soul more strongly desire than truth? For what
ought it to have a greedy appetite, with which to wish that there be a
more healthy palate for judging the things that are true, unless it be
to eat and drink wisdom, righteousness, truth, eternity?"[1]

FIRST THOMAS (A), then Sankara (B)—condensed to a level
of purity, and subsequently a Comment (C) that introduces
Augustine's conception of revelation as "drawing" or "allure-
ment," for the sake of clarifying a conception of "knowledge" in the
thinkers with which we are dealing. (A) attempts an analogy with
St. Paul, (B) a comparison with the results of that (with a little help
from Plotinus), and (C) illuminates Augustine by St. Paul, again, for
the sake of its stated end, above.

A. *Thomas.* For Thomas Aquinas "theological" knowledge (*scientia*)
is the replete divine self-knowledge, given to the creature in relative
form. This relative form has two modes: that of the *beati* and that of
the *viatores.* The *blessed* share in God's self-knowledge in a maximal

---

1. St. Augustine, *Tractates on John* 26 (6:41–59), 5.

way, through the vision of God; the *wayfarers* share in God's self-knowledge through the given form of revelation, Holy Scripture, of which the Church is the organ of its distillation into the given principles of reasoning in its dogma.

A previous chapter has demonstrated that, for the wayfarer, knowledge of God takes two forms according to Thomas: "suffering divine things" and "intellectual learning." Both are called "wisdom": the former is complete wisdom because it joins right action and knowledge, whereas the wisdom of learning may be true, but is nevertheless incomplete, for it can exist without the corresponding habit of virtue that conforms one to the known (which is realized by grace manifest in the mode of faith).

This knowledge, *scientia divina*, is God's possession, fully coterminous with his tri-hypostatic Self. To participate in it, by God's mercy, is, paradoxically, to realize the created intellectual creature's "naturally supernatural" end or purpose. It is called the "beatific vision," or the "knowledge of God's essence," and is realized by the new "creation" of an identity of the mind with the divine nature as the site for the fullest share in the divine self-knowledge, which is nothing else but love. The Eastern Church calls this sharing in the divine nature "theosis," although there is a difference: they forge in their classical period a distinction between essence and energies/names, whereas in the West the "transcendence" of the divine essence over creaturely knowledge is a matter of the limits intrinsic to the nature of the creature itself. (Although this essence/energies distinction is paradoxically qualified by some thinkers influenced by the onomatodoxy tradition: these names/energies *are* the divine nature, although the divine nature *is not* these names/energies: the energies, although distinct, manifest the divine essence itself.)[2]


Perhaps I can give this concept of knowledge in St. Thomas a technical significance by offering it a name: *gnōsis*. By *gnōsis* I do not mean the "heterodox" modalities of Christianity for which *gnōsis* is the

---

2. See Study 1, above.

knowledge of the self's divine character comprehended *within* the mythic milieu of a fall of divinity into matter identified with the creation of the world, which is tantamount to salvation (and which, I believe, shares a family resemblance with Indian Vedanta *only superficially*). Rather, I mean *gnōsis* found first in the LXX but in the technical sense developed by Paul, to which Irenaeus in the second century and Clement of Alexandria in the third century remain committed: a charismatic gift from above by means of which the intelligence may assent to, and grow in understanding of, the eschatological mysteries revealed in Christ. Or in even more brutal shorthand: "knowledge by anticipation of ultimate realities" that have invaded history disclosing enigmatically its *telos*.[3] These invading eschatological realities are the ultimate truth of the believer's "life," "hidden with Christ in God"—to use the startling expression from Ephesians—partially but principally disclosed in the events surrounding Jesus of Nazareth's life and death. One reaches this highest truth of the self and of the world by sharing in this knowledge, *gnōsis*. The character, content, and conditions of this *gnōsis*—resembling only nominally, on the one hand, the various movements coengendered with what became orthodox or imperial Christianity collected by modern scholars under the banner "Gnosticism," and, at the same time, on a completely different page from them—will have to be explicated with any sufficiency elsewhere. Yet, a pathway will be indicated first by the juxtaposition of Sankara and then a triangulation with Augustine's conception of revelation and Thomas's own, so stringently digested here. I can only repeat the question:

Do we in fact have an explication of this Pauline sense of *gnōsis* as the very characterization of the principles of *sacra doctrina* in St. Thomas? The Eastern Fathers called *theologia* the knowledge of God in Godself (i.e., as separate from the world). And they contrasted it with the *oikonomia* (God's activity *ad extra* in creation and salvation), which is nevertheless the only source for any theological knowledge properly so-called. *Theologia* is the condition for right knowledge of the *oikonomia*, for it is the *theologia* that the *oikono-*

---

3. See Louis Bouyer, "Gnosis," *Journal of Theological Studies* 4 (1953), 188–203.

*mia* reveals. Compare St. Thomas, for whom a share in this theological knowledge enjoyed by God, *scientia divina*, is the very condition
and content of theology, *sacra doctrina*; it is a gift of God to the
human mind, as a condition for its salvation. It may be explored
"academically," (ostensibly) as a preparation for one's greater
immersion in the experience or suffering of the divine things in
liturgical and sacramental life of the Christian faith, which is the
"material" passage the wayfarer must take in order to ascend to
God. (In this way Thomas bears considerable resemblance to one of
his most important sources, Pseudo-Dionysius the Areopagite...)[4]

I begin to see an answer to this question in the acknowledgment
that, for Thomas, as for St. Paul (I think), the knowledge with
which the wayfarer deals is therefore a secondary or derived form,
suffering a necessary transposition from God's boundless self-
knowledge to that of a finite share in it, in the form of the present
"order of things," of which, for both Thomas and the New Testament author, the incarnate form is Holy Scripture (something similar can be said for Sankara vis-à-vis the Upaniṣads; see below). In
contemporary terms we may extrapolate and express the scope of
this necessary transition as one determined by the ontological-
hermeneutical conditions of our finitude, which, though ultimately
relative, are, for us, absolute: we are powerless before death, which
surrounds and permeates our fragile, embodied condition. And so,
for example, the "last things" are disclosed in the modality of
bizarre, terrible mythic images, which is as close as we can get to
them (according to God, at least) under the conditions of history.
Our vampire-like abstractions, drained of life, parasitically living
off the lifeblood of the fleshy images, are necessary for our wayfarer
activity of intellectually making sense of these hieroglyphs, but concept and theory are, nevertheless, condemned (in themselves) to a
kind of immortal death-state. They are *of this world* as much as our
sacred stories, symbols, and images on which they feed.

Secondly, for Thomas, Holy Scripture is the Mind of God made
flesh, and its singular *skopós* is Christ, the incarnate Word *par excel-*

---

4. Again, I summarize the essential conclusions articulated above.

*lence*, who brings historical existence to a "head" and serves, finally, as the principle of the accomplished return of all things to God. The knowledge imparted through the medium of Scripture (of which the hermeneutical organ is the Church's core confession) is finally God's self-knowledge, coincident with God himself in eternity. But this Knowledge of God is like the silent, permanent accompaniment to the "economic" knowledge of salvation: "the end must first *be known* (*praecognitum*) by men who are to direct their thoughts and actions to the end."[5] This "end" is God, who makes himself known. Similarly for St. Paul, Christ is the Mind of God searched out by the Spirit given to the truly wise, whose gift is the capacity to discern through the lens of the Prophets the ultimate, final, "eschatological" meaning of the death and resurrection of the People Israel's "Anointed One," and to give material voice to this "knowledge" through the words of these prophets themselves. This knowledge, however, is permanently undergirded by that of which it is the expression: the *knowledge of love*, of being loved by God and knowing God in that love: "At present I know partially; then I shall know fully, as I am fully known" (*epignōsomai kathōs kai epegnōsthēn*).[6] This "knowledge of love" (*agapē, caritas*), for St. Paul, like the prophets, is inseparable from the image of the "knowledge" pertaining to sexual consummation: an intertwining, and exchange of interiorities, in the dark.

B. *Sankara*. The Christian concept of theological knowledge, the highest wisdom, wherein one has a "taste" for divine things, a proximity, proclivity, and interiorization *to* and *of* them, is classically explained in the Christian intellectual tradition by means of Platonic exemplarism: the truth of all things, both wholly independent of them, unchanging without them, *and* the deepest truth within them, is coincident with God's idea of them (the Father's idea in the *eikón* of the Son) and his will to love them (in the Spirit), which *is*

---

5. *Summa theologiae* I-II q.1 a.1 resp.
6. 1 Cor 13:12.

their being. This view is clearly present behind St. Thomas's view of the divine self-knowledge as principle and object for our properly theological knowledge. How different are things in Sankara and his world of Upaniṣadic wisdom?

Sankara accepts a traditional threefold distinction of *pramāṇa*, means of knowledge: sense perception and inferential reasoning (for the world of our experience) and "revelation" (authoritative testimony of the sages) for knowledge of things beyond this world. It is this third kind of knowledge that provides *jñāna*, metaphysical knowledge, which is the nature of the Self, *Ātman*, identical with *Brahman*, ultimate reality. *Ātman-Brahman* is autonomous of the means of knowledge; it is "self-evident" and "self-established."[7] Hence one accomplishes *mokṣa*, release from conditioned existence, through no action; action is tied to the undoing or negation of the mistaking of relative existence for reality, whereas the metaphysical knowledge of *Ātman-Brahman* is *identical* with its unconditioned being. It "comes automatically"; "no effort is necessary": "In the Upaniṣads nothing is spoken of as a means of attainment of the highest end of man except the knowledge of the identity of the self and Brahman."[8]

Against this background I will limit the purview of my comments mostly to I.iv.10 of his commentary on the *Brihadaranyaka Upaniṣad*. For Sankara the single object, the *skopós* of the Upaniṣads, is to dispel darkness and communicate the truth—these being coincident with one another: the removal of ignorance *is* the revelation of the truth, which is the impartation of the highest knowledge. This highest knowledge is the knowledge of Brahman, in other words, the identification of one's deepest truth, the Self, with Brahman, the ultimate, conditionless reality. This knowledge is the removal of every limitation, every relative means by which we know and act within the world, for the world is defined by the limi-

7. I am indebted for this manner of expressing the matter to Sengaku Mayeda, in his introductory essay to Sankara's *Upadesasahasri* (*Thousand Teachings*) (Tokyo: University of Tokyo Press, 1979), 46–47.

8. *Brihadaranyaka Upaniṣad with the Commentary of Sankara*, I.iv.7 (Mahavananda trans., 91).

tations through which we know it: the world is illusory, only relatively real. When ignorance is removed through knowledge, the world itself is removed, since the "cause" of the world of relative existence, including the gods who rule it and the highest god through whom it subsists as its manifestation, is ignorance.

To have this knowledge is to transcend the entire ritual order of worship and sacrifice, which only pertains to relative existence; and it is also to transcend, at least in principle, the cosmic law to which the gods themselves are subservient, and hence the body itself: at death the one enlightened by this knowledge is no longer subject to the order of transmigration based on the law of just cause and effect that perfectly doles out fate across lifetimes.

This knowledge is the "eternal vision" of an object seen that is identical to the seeing itself: it therefore "must be eternal," says Sankara. This seeing the sight by which we see is the goal and content of liberating knowledge: "I am Brahman"—this world in which I see by means of differentiation and comparison, and consequently see myself as a separated self over-against the world, as an actor within it, is only the veiling of the conditionless reality that alone is real. In that one reality "the vision itself is [the Self's] nature"; it is consciousness without limitation: "self-effulgent light."

For Sankara the impartation of knowledge is concerned with avoiding evil and gaining the good: the highest good is "liberation" from relative existence and it is imparted through the knowledge of Brahman. This knowledge, in itself, is contentless, it seems to me, for it is, positively, the untying of the knots of ignorance that compose the order of our experience. For us, as separated souls in the form of "historical" existence (i.e., spanning birth and death in the world), the knowledge of Brahman has ontological *content*: not only, for example, knowledge of the order of the gods as a cascading manifestation of the Unmanifest from the single point of Brahman manifest as cosmic intelligence or "world soul," Hiranyagarbha, but also of the "vision" of ontological monism that is itself passed on from teacher to disciple as a metaphysical "thesis," a philosophical proposition: "Atman is Brahman." The world must be woven in a particular way for its unweaving, through the "neti neti" series of negations, to reach its end, the knowledge that is like a breakthrough of the Unmanifest, as when the light of a lamp dispels darkness or like the shattering of a clay pot. Said another way, the world of relative existence possesses an inherent intelligibility; the philosopher or seeker may gain knowledge of this relative existence and "save the appearances"—but only in order to discard them *as* appearances, for the sake of the ultimate reality that alone is real, and is the sole goal. At the same time, knowledge of Brahman makes possible right knowledge of everything else, for one understands it in its essential character as relative. Furthermore, this knowledge of Brahman is remembered or recovered: one may almost say in counterpoint to the Platonic Good "beyond being," that Knowledge, *jñāna*, precedes what is.

For Sankara, much like the Platonic "One"—wholly absent and utterly simple, though pervasively present through every multiple element composing subjective experience—Brahman is wholly other to the order of contrasts by which knowledge is subjectively had in our lower, worldly selves. Insofar as things are, they are "one," they experience a unity that distinguishes them from other things, says Plotinus; and insofar as the relative world is relative to that which alone really is, it itself is, says Sankara. But when the rope is no longer seen as a snake, when the world is not mistaken, as if out of the corner of our eye, for substantial reality, not seen as worthwhile in its normative ends (wife, son, wealth, recognition), then "desire to know"—to quote Aristotle—may reach its goal.[9] Sankara quotes here the *Muṇḍaka Upaniṣad*, "Om is the bow, the soul is the arrow, and Brahman is the target."[10]

Hence for Sankara, the Upaniṣadic texts communicate the simple, transcendent, incommunicable truth, *by means of* a teacher who possesses the knowledge itself. This communication of a "positive" hermeneutic principle for the right understanding of texts alone may guide the aspirant to the truth. Hence one may proceed

9. "All men by nature desire knowledge" begins Aristotle's *Metaphysics* (Bk A 980a). We may say something analogously programmatic here in Sankara.

10. *Brihadaranyaka Upaniṣad* with Sankara's Commentary I.iv.10 (Madhavananda translation, 151), quoting *Muṇḍaka Upaniṣad* II.ii.4.

to this knowledge of the truth by learning what the Upaniṣads teach—the identity of Self and Brahman, the uselessness of the rites, the wiliness of the gods in hiding this truth, the unmanifest character of Brahman, etc.—but only when the aspirant understands this third person description of reality in the Upaniṣads to be in actuality a "second-person" address to himself, only when he discovers Knowledge, not as another thing to be known in the set of knowable things, but as a comportment of reality to itself which he himself *is*, then he can understand the character of this utterly simple knowledge, *through* the manifold complexity of experience and reasoning by letting go of which he first awakens to it: the communication of positive "metaphysical" knowledge is even itself only "negation" of relative knowledge.

Let it not be lost on us that these two modalities of knowledge, Unmanifest and Manifest, the knowledge of un-qualification (if I can say that) and qualified knowledge of the unqualified, draws analogy to Thomas's distinction between God's absolute self-knowledge (and that of the *beati* who enjoy his presence), and ours "here below" accessed through faith as the principles of its reasoning. For Thomas, unlike Sankara of course, this saving knowledge, or knowledge of salvation, is a gift from God, who freely gives it, but *like* Sankara, this knowledge is the communication of our essential nature: in Thomas's Christian terminology, we are created to behold God. This is our final end. Another difference is the twofold character of this knowledge within the horizon of "historical" (or relative) existence for Thomas (following Augustine): the two modes of wisdom, theoretical, unaccompanied by a habituation to its object, and virtue-wisdom, which "knows" in a "personal" way the One Origin and End of the universe discerned rationally through the revelation of nature. It is the latter mode, wherein intellectual knowledge is grounded in God's prior action of grace, that awakens the soul to its final end which is, for Thomas as we have seen, the "highest wisdom." This wisdom is communicated by God as a relative share in his absolute, unqualified self-knowledge. Its historical form is faith, but its basis is love, which already "knows" God, experiencing that saving knowledge of the *beati*, anticipatorily, "here below."

May we say that, from the Christian vantage point within the knowledge of faith, the truth of Sankara's position is the knowledge of "essence"—that is, of the non-dual truth that "God + world" does not add anything to "God"? This knowledge is indeed sacred, and if it must therefore be brought within Christian self-understanding (according to the primary theological rule of *chrēsis*), it, like every sacred and blessed "fragment" of divinity we find, will have to be carefully transposed into the new idiom of Christian tradition. Only then will the truth of Hinduism shine its proper light *for Christians*, illuminating more brightly the dazzling light of the Empty Cave where dead (Divine-)Humanity once lay, cold and silent.

A question arises: may this non-dualism that Christianity finds more completely within itself through the light of Advaita be strangely intensified in the Christian context which asserts the complete coincidence of "essence" with "person" in God? For Trinitarian reflection the Unmanifest and Manifest are One; the way of "neti neti" becomes a condition for a higher knowledge through which the soul is eternally expanded or "stretched" in the infinite passage into the divine mystery of "love" to which there is no behind or beyond. Again, this is a Christian idea, not a Hindu one. But this intensification is indebted to the Hindu difference, and the hospitality of Christianity to it. A reverse debt may or may not ever be the case. Does the next stage of indebtedness come from an encounter with the Bhagavad-Gītā and Ramanuja, through which, I imagine, the understanding of the Trinitarian character of God will be intensified by juxtaposition with the limitless goodness of the Almighty revealed by the incarnate Krishna, who is "known" in the highest manner through being loved?

C. *Comment.* I have attempted to draw some reflective, close parallels between knowledge in Thomas Aquinas and Sankara, in Classical Latin theology and the Advaita Vedanta of the Hindu and Christian traditions. The aim of this comparative theology in the briefest compass is (as always) to understand oneself. One knows that when understanding the other, one's self-understanding is forever changed. The Christian must go farther and say that to understand the Christian *res* he needs the gift of the other's light, he *must* make "right use" (*orthé chrēsis*) of the truth he finds in "external" milieux, for that is precisely what Christian thinking is.

The comment I would like to make as a conclusion will draw more formally into the comparison with what in Christianity is called revelation, *apocalypsis, revelatio.* We have already glimpsed its importance to "knowledge," *gnōsis,* in the Pauline literature, as well as, by (tentative) extension, to St. Thomas Aquinas. This occurs in the latter through his conjunctive disjunction between creaturely and divine modes of knowledge, wherein, again, creaturely knowledge of God *is* God's self-knowledge. I would like to add here as a sort of *coda,* or better, *envoi,* to that discussion that this knowledge is only the properly human, intellectual extension of the *acknowledgment,* at the basis of Christian mysticism, that God knows himself through the medium of the world in the same way that he knows himself "internally." It is this word, "acknowledgment," that will become a central feature of my exposition here.

St. Paul, I would argue, is the intellectual systematizer, as it were, of the apocalyptic literature traditions of late second Temple Judaism he inherited. According to him (as we have observed) *apocalypsis* is the disclosure, or better, unveiling, of the *mustērion tou theou,* the Creator's eschatological act to bring about his original purpose for the world, "hidden" in the creation from its "beginning." It is to this purpose that the entire history of this world attests, centered on the election of the People Israel in Abraham, but broken open, as intended, from its heart for the internalization of the Gentiles into this one, restored people of God, composed of all peoples.[11] Revelation is the event before which one without "wisdom" remains ignorant. He cannot *interpret* the *apocalypsis* of the divine wisdom without this charismatic gift. It appears as "foolishness" (*mória*) to the "learned of this age"—whose knowledge is of a different order

---

11. See Eph 2:11–21. I take Ephesians to be at the least a "Pauline" text. This is uncontroversial. Here it summarizes very well arguments he makes in other letters, Rom 9–11, or the entirety of Galatians, for example.

from the divine wisdom, namely, what we might call "book learn-ing," the accumulation of information, knowledge "about," which astoundingly (but in the Creator's plan) has missed the ultimate disclosure of the truth that it seeks.[12] Thomas's (Augustinian) dis-tinction between higher and lower modes of wisdom (and perhaps the one in play in Sankara between knowledge through study and the Knowledge that accompanies it) may bear analogy to this dis-tinction in St. Paul, as well as to the conception of *avidyā*, "igno-rance" in the Upaniṣads, wherein right knowledge of the world may miss the one thing essential:[13] the highest human wisdom becomes ignorance or foolishness when what is passing is taken as lasting. This mistake is a result, in both the Indian and Christian contexts, of misapplied affection—worshiping the creature instead of the Creator in St. Paul's language (Rom 1:18–32) or "enjoying" what is only worth being "used," in Augustine's language.[14] In both cases, likewise, *knowledge* of the divine truth is present, but is covered over, either through suppression (in the Pauline reading) or through superimposition (in the Advaitin's reading).

The Creator gives the gift of wisdom, which is the basis, therefore, for the "understanding" of the *apocalypsis*. This basis of understand-ing is not "knowledge" in the objective sense with specified con-tent—in the first place; rather, it is a *recognition* that what is *present* in the event is truth. It is an *insight*, out of which unfolds the whole universe: Christ was "slain" as the sacrificial lamb of the world's Pass-over, "from the foundation of the world" (Rev 13:8).[15] Wisdom per-sonified is present with God at the beginning. Wisdom is what Pilate

12. See I Cor 1–2.
13. See *Chandogya Upaniṣad* 7,1,2: the sage Naridya is learned in every possible kind of science but finds himself ignorant of Brahman.
14. *De Doctrina Christiana* Bk. 1.
15. Christ's own "election" (I Pet 1:20) but also therefore that of the church (Rom 8:29; Eph 1:4), which pre-exists in Christ as the end of the work of creation itself, achieved by the Father "through" the Son (Jn 1:3; Col 1:16; etc.). Attestation in multiple traditions points to the fact that the phrase "foundations of the world" is a technical term in Christianity, with parallels in Rabbinic Judaism's understanding of the Torah, pre-existing in heaven as the blueprint at the basis of the world. The background is the Temple itself, which is a small-scale reproduction of the creation,

did not have with Christ standing before him, to whom he posed the question "What is truth?" (Jn 18:38). The "knowledge of revelation" is therefore first the knowledge of the *mustērion*, "mystery": the mystery is not dispelled, but "known," recognized as *the* truth of the world. It is *acknowledged*; one *becomes conscious* of it: this new state of awareness of the all-determining truth of the event of divine action—in the death and resurrection of the Son as a parallel to the original creation event, somehow completing it—is the *revelatio*; it is a gift of knowledge, at the basis of wisdom, a precondition for one's maturation in understanding or interpretation of it. "Book knowledge" does not know in the manner appropriate to the object; one must love what one knows in order truly to know it. In this love the knowledge "happens upon" the knower: the model, I think, is St. Paul's encounter on the road to Damascus:[16] he is blinded; the event has no immediate content; it cannot be comprehended; there is simply a call to obey; over time, and through fidelity to the event, the immense truth of it unfolds, first through the mediation of another (Ananias, "a disciple in Damascus") who imparts the charismatic gift of knowledge through which the "things like scales fell from his eyes"—and then continues to unfold over the course of his lifetime as the legacy of his letters attests. This *acknowledgment* is like the knowledge of the child learning to read: the accumulation of ideas and rules regarding the identity of letters and sounds, of grammar, syntax, etc., somehow, magically, leaps to a higher level that transcends the mere accumulation of parts. Suddenly the child is reading, or playing the piano, or hitting the baseball. One does not know the mechanics or grammar but simply is in them. St. Augustine elaborates this knowledge of revelation in another way.

In a profound comment on John 6:44 (*No one can come to me unless the Father who sent me draws him*), St. Augustine says that revelation

of earth, heaven, and the heaven of heavens, which, as a totality, is a reflection of an uncreated reality, the Temple in which God dwells in unapproachable light—into which, according to Hebrews, the resurrected Christ has entered, "behind the veil," serving as an "anchor for our souls" (6:19).

16. See Acts 9:1–19.

in the Christian sense is an activity of "attraction":[17] "The Father draws to the Son those who believe in the Son, because they consider that God is his Father." Those who believe in the perfect unity of Father and Son, who discern the Uncreated gaze in the human face of Jesus, are drawn "to" Christ "by" the Father. To explicate this, St. Augustine refers to the case of a man in love: "that one feels what I say," he says; similarly, someone traveling in the wilderness, tired, thirsty, and panting for rest: "give such, and he knows what I say." By contrast, "the cold and indifferent do not understand what I say." The one who does not acknowledge the Father as the One who sent the Son in love, who does not see the Son as One in the Father's love, is not "drawn to" the Son: here there is no revelation in the Christian sense. Thus far in his explication St. Augustine has not himself used the term "revelation": he has used the word "knowledge," as we have seen, the peculiar kind of knowledge found in the attraction of awoken desire, in "love" and "longing." But the climax of his explication is found when he turns to Peter's "confession" of Jesus as "Son of God" in response to the Lord's pointed question: "But you, who do *you* say that I am?" (Matt 16:5, emphasis mine). Peter responds: "You are Christ, the Son of the Living God." St. Augustine observes: "See that he was drawn, and drawn by the Father." To make the confession like Peter, which for St. Augustine captures the essence of the basic Christian confession itself, is to be drawn by the Father. This is remarkable enough, but he focuses even more on Jesus's affirmation of Peter's confession of faith: "Blessed are you, Simon Barjonas, for flesh and blood has not *revealed* it to you, but my Father who is in heaven" (Matt 16:6–7, emphasis mine). And here St. Augustine provides the enchanting definition: "This revealing is itself the drawing." As the previous study argued, this is the most transparent definition of the term revelation, and perhaps its most complete conceptualization, until the modern period, where it becomes (extremely belatedly) a central theological concept.[18] To explicate it

17. *Tractates on John*, 26 (6:41–59), 2–5.
18. See Jean-Luc Marion's development of this conception as a response to the "epistemological concept of revelation" that has dominated modern thought since the late medieval period in *Givenness and Revelation*.

further Augustine offers analogies from common experience: "You hold out a green twig to a sheep and you draw it. Nuts are shown to a child, and he is attracted; he is drawn by what he runs to, drawn by loving it, drawn without hurt to the body, drawn by a cord of the heart. If, then," he continues, "these things, which among earthly delights and pleasures *are shown to them that love them*, draw them . . . does not Christ, revealed by the Father, draw?" (emphasis mine). "Are shown to them that love them": the showing of Christ to us, who is the love of the Father in the flesh, in human flesh, is the self-revelation of the Father, which takes the shape of the attraction to him in our love. In being drawn to Christ, in falling in love with him, the Father reveals himself to us—to the degree, in fact, that we love Christ. Revelation is the "attraction" at the basis of this love; it is a matter of *eros*, self-interested love, lack seeking fulfillment, thirst seeking to be slaked, but an *eros* transfigured by "agapē," charity: the one who truly loves another loves him for his own sake, desiring only his good, and in the case of human love of God, desiring his will to the point of the *nirvāṇa*, "blowing out," of one's own individual will, ecstatically dissolving it in God's will, where it becomes one with the all-consuming fire of infinite love—in this union, through the awakening that comes in the recognition of being loved in the divine way, finds itself again, *to be* love.

With Augustine, Thomas, Paul, we move in a wholly different intellectual universe than that of Sankara. Yet all witness to a startling aspiration that understands the highest knowledge to be knowledge of the Unconditioned. All affirm a religious vision that demands an eclipse of the elemental powers, the gods, the cosmos that they order, and of the rule by which they order it (sacrificial system and moral law), relation to which is fundamentally reordered. And for both the Vedantin and the Christians this knowledge, or at least the *jñānapatha*, "path of knowledge," assumes the conditioned form of authoritative texts—the Christian Bible or Vedic literature (especially the Upaniṣads). I have focused in particular on the notion of awareness or acknowledgment as the content of the highest knowledge, *gnōsis*, implied within Augustine's concept of revelation as "drawing," the awakening of desire by the perceived presence of the Desirable. If the Christians perceive this knowledge as a union of love by which the relative world itself is finally integrated into the *mokṣa* of God's own *ānanda*, the Advaitin sees only the world's relativity, its unsubstantiality in relation to the Ultimate. That difference is massive, but no difference is absolute—except the difference by which God is one with the world. And the knowledge that identically forms God's being and the foundation of the cosmos may be a point of metaphysical agreement between Thomas and Sankara, which now emerges to me as a condition for a grateful Christian reception of the gifts of India into its storehouses that, when ground, kneaded, baked, and offered, through the intellectual practice of "right use," may nourish the followers of Christ.

# Closing Sketch:
# A Final Classification

THERE IS A VERY BRIEF but disarmingly beautiful text taking up about eight pages of the fourth volume of the *Philokalia*, a famous set of writings on prayer by spiritual masters of the Eastern Church between the fourth and fifteenth centuries, collected in the eighteenth century by Sts. Nikodemos of the Holy Mountain of Athos and Makarios of Corinth and initially published in 1782. It is entitled *The Three Methods of Prayer* and is traditionally ascribed to St. Symeon the New Theologian (949–1022).[1] In this closing sketch I would like to recapitulate the threefold classification that has from the first ordered this proposal about the three keys to a Philosophy in Word and Name by proposing a brief commentary on and interpretation of this text.

In the leading sketch I proposed a rather traditional evolutionary or progressive account of human religion by inlaying the eschatological religion, the Christian elaboration of the Revealed Religion, the religion of Abraham to John the Baptist, within the wider context of cosmic religion at the basis of archaic agrarian societies. Out of this context the Revealed Religion was drawn, by its prophets; and through them, the Call of God was made known. That brief, self-reflective account sought simply to propose the barest contours that revelation demands of Christian intelligence in order to provide a simple framework for the subsequent explication of the three key words of a Philosophy in Word and Name for which this sketch-book, with its studies, hopes to be of some use. Now in a closing

---

1. *The Philokalia*, trans. G.E.H. Palmer, Philip Sherrard, and Kallistos Ware, vols. 1–4 (London: Faber and Faber, 1979–1994). *The Three Methods of Prayers*, vol. 4, 67–75.

sketch I want to wrap the three words in their native dress, namely, address to God, prayer. Just as there is no philosophy without concepts and theory, so there is no theology without prayer. As I have said before, one cannot comprehend a Philosophy in Word and Name without exploiting its proximity to the practice of religion that is the "site" where the basic, motivating questions of every philosophy are most deeply disclosed. The words of this sketchbook are of course no exception. If the first classification system with which I began elaborated a rough sketch of the basic contours of the three keys—I can finally be explicit—with myth corresponding to the cosmic religious background, with wisdom corresponding to the descent of the divine into the human milieu in the form of a Presence at the heart of Revealed Religion, and finally with the eschatological intensification of that form through an *unveiling* of that Presence in the face of Jesus of Nazareth, then now I want to propose another classification within religious practice, that corresponds to three methods of prayer.

Saint Symeon was the champion of direct experience of God in the form of a divine unfading light at the basis of the self, reached through deep prayer. The divine light seems to be quite literally both sensory and suprasensory, or rather, equally neither; it is experienced as equally transcending both the physical senses and the interior, spiritual senses, precisely as their common root. One's tapping into this transcendently immanent root awakens the sleeping spiritual senses, and the path of sanctification defining the Christian life is a matter of calibrating these two sensory orders, the physical and the spiritual, through an ever-deepening unification with this source and end. These two "lower" dimensions of the human person, the twofold expression of my totality, as a physical and spiritual being, are not opposed to one another essentially, although, in worldly experience, they are in fact opposed in an, as it were, established sense. Yet the hesychast tradition of which Saint Symeon is a major figure is articulated precisely through the proposal of a metaphysic of analogical correspondence, of (as it were) "magical" sympathy, between these universes.

# Closing Sketch: A Final Classification

In order to explain this metaphysic, I need to recall an experiment initiated in another place, my book *Eclipse of World*.[2] There several thinkers from Boehme to Newman to the "objective idealisms" of Schelling and Peirce are called on in order to practice an intellectual experiment of a "Vedic" metaphysic of hidden sympathies between worlds, visible and invisible. The present world, our physical cosmos, was considered as the external crust of unfathomed depths and dramas, of layers upon layers of ever-denser and profound spiritual reality, properly, intellectually understood, as in Pico's Renaissance recovery of Christian "right use" of late Neoplatonic thought, as symbolically presentifying those vast worlds of which it is an echo.

The practice of sanctification, Christian likening to God, in the domain of prayer is a matter of reaching, activating, and developing these real but hidden points of contact, doorways to be opened between every level of reality, within the created order, cosmic on the one hand and anthropomorphic on the other, and then (ultimately), between the creaturely cosmo-anthropomorphic totality and the Uncreated God, which serves as the foundation or key that opens pathways between the lower orders of cosmos and humanity. If the human, as a being of mixed spiritual and physical properties, recapitulates the entire cosmic order in its physical and spiritual dimensions, then God (as Origin and End, as first and final Cause) is equally, immediately present at every level, both to humanity and to the cosmos. One "activates" (so to speak) this divine key through the prayer of "quiet," *hésychia*, which encompasses the practice of forming this key within oneself and the use of the key to access one's ownmost truth (an activity that is *both* divine and human, *therefore* truly sanctifying). This prayer therefore is both a physical and a spiritual activity; it involves both the domain of symbols, of informed matter, and the domain of intelligence, extrapolated from that domain to reach, by negation, the divine darkness. In the creaturely world, breath (in the human) and wind (in the cosmos) correspond to the divine Spirit. The inhaled breath is a vehicle, therefore, of the Spirit.

2. *Eclipse of World* is a set of spiritual exercises undertaken between the poles of *orthodoxia* and *orthé chrēsis*, "right belief" and "right use" in the Christian tradition.

Similarly, the heart is a vehicle of the intellect. They correspond to one another; they are realities that share a kinship, a likeness, an affinity. Again, that which wholly transcends the order of matter and spirit and, thereby, interpenetrates it at every part, God himself, *is* the key to the unification of self, fragmented and disordered by sin, and of self with cosmos through the calibration of these correspondences.

In this highly (I would say) Vedic vision of the world, God renders himself present through the invocation of his revealed human *Name*, Jesus, sought and loved in faith. One properly uses this key, therefore, *through* aspiration for union with God, who transcends the cosmo-anthropomorphic totality in both fundamental directions—those of intensity (spiritual interiority) and of immensity (cosmic exteriority).[3] The inhaled breath, as breathed in longing for Jesus, carries the intellect toward the heart and into it, reintegrating the human self dispersed and disordered by sin. Intellect and heart are not necessarily opposed, though they are distinct. Just as, on the level of the symbol, the heart is the shared vital root of both the brain and the bowels, so also is the intellect the shared spiritual root of both the discursive reason and the emotions. To find God in the cosmos, to see the world as what it is in reality—a kaleidoscopic vision of God—one must enter into oneself to find the common, integrating root of oneself and the cosmos. By joining intellectual vigilance (*nepsis*) to the heart's yearning (*eros*), the hesychast finds that common root of world and self in God, and experiences *theória* (contact with the Uncreated). The inexhaustible principle of intelligibility within the divine life, the Word or Son, is also the source and principle of the creation, of cosmos and self. The Incarnation of Christ into the world is—as truly, an incarnation—at the same time an incarnation into the depths of the human totality. When Jesus is called on and found in the depths of the heart, the cosmos discloses its hidden glory; one descends into oneself and spiritually enters *at*

3. For this distinction see Jacques-Albert Cuttat's "An Essay on the Prayer of Jesus," appended to his brief treatise *The Encounter of Religions: A Dialogue Between the West and the Orient*, trans. Pierre de Fontnouvelle with Evis McGrew (NY/Paris: Desclée, 1960), 85–159.

*the same time* into the world. The experience of the "prayer of the heart" is one of a coincidence of opposites, where enstatic interiority meets with, reveals its identity with ecstatic transcendence.

## Opening the Treatise

"There are," Saint Symeon begins in this brief treatise under our examination, "three methods of prayer and attentiveness by which the soul is either uplifted or cast down."[4] I want to make two points immediately: (1) the author is not concerned to reject two methods while proposing the correct one, which a superficial reading of the text, focusing on his criticisms of the first two methods, might possibly lead one to think. His second line puts forth his thesis: "Whoever employs these methods at the right time is uplifted, but whoever employs them foolishly and at the wrong time is cast down." If there are three separate methods of prayer, that is only because they are in fact three moments of the prayerful life, the ascent to God, which can be undertaken separately. But rightly ordered, placed in the proper sequence, these separated methods form the stages of one unified way of prayer. (2) The key to this small treatise is the distinction between "attentiveness" (or "vigilance") and "prayer" that the author makes in this opening paragraph and repeats throughout the text: "Vigilance and prayer," though linked together properly like the body and soul in a human being, work together—"vigilance first goes ahead like a scout and engages sin in combat. Prayer then follows afterwards, and instantly destroys and exterminates all the evil thoughts with which vigilance has already been battling."[5] One should pay attention then when the author elaborates his theme as "three methods of prayer *and* attentiveness" (emphasis added). It is, in fact, the distinction between attentiveness and prayer that when rightly understood leads to a proper ordering and unification of the methods, making them into a ladder by which one ascends by stages on the way of prayer: "This,

4. *Philokalia* 4, 67.
5. Ibid.

then, is the gate of life and death. If by means of vigilance we keep prayer pure, we make progress; but if we leave prayer unguarded and permit it to be defiled, our efforts are null and void."[6] As I will show you, the first two methods of prayer, undertaken on their own, that is, without the third as their "foundation," will not properly fight the fight of vigilance, which can only be properly, or essentially, fought in the realm of the heart. The work of the third method *is* the labor of attentiveness and vigilance; it is therefore the starting point of true prayer. Let us now follow the author in his elaboration of these three methods. I will first name them, and then sketch the author's description of their distinctive features.

The first method may be called "imaginative prayer"; the second method may be called "intellectual prayer"; and the third method may be called "the prayer of the heart."

## The First Method

The first method is described in a single sentence, and the rest of the section is concerned with describing its significant pathologies. The "distinctive features" of the first method: "When a person stands at prayer, he raises his hands, eyes, and intellect heavenwards, and fills his intellect with divine thoughts, with images of celestial beauty, of the angelic hosts, of the abodes of the righteous. In brief, at the time of prayer he assembles in his intellect all that he has heard from Holy Scripture and so rouses his soul to divine longing as he gazes towards heaven, and sometimes sheds tears."[7] The central problem with this method, the use of images and the experience of mystical phenomena in various forms that correspond to the senses, is that one cannot attain here the necessary emotional state for progress in prayer ("holiness or dispassion"): "Those who adopt this method of prayer have ... been deluded into thinking they see lights with their bodily eyes, smell sweet scents, hear voices and so on."[8] The upshot,

6. Ibid.
7. Ibid., 67–68.
8. Ibid., 68.

the core problem, is the sin *par excellence* of the human heart, "pride": "But when someone prays this way, without him realizing it his heart grows proud and exalted, and he regards what is happening to him as the effect of divine grace." Yet these miraculous phenomena are identified by St. Symeon primarily as the productions of the monk's own imagination or of the deceptions of the devil. He even unfolds a litany of their bitter fruit, which always proves the ultimate source: wandering from the community in states of madness (a result of "possession by demons"), "refusing to accept the counsel of anyone else," which in these kinds of cases is, he notes, "a state of delusion" that lasts "until death" (a result of someone "putting their trust in the devil when he transforms himself into an angel of light"), even, finally, suicide (again, at the instigation of the evil one).[9] The problem, in short, is the disorder of the self, which this method of prayer does nothing to deal with. Although, St. Symeon observes, these terrible pitfalls he mentions are less likely (by contrast to solitaries) to affect a monk who lives in community, nevertheless, he concludes, this monk "will pass his entire life without making any progress," making his entire life's commitment to the monastic life totally fruitless. Undertaking this way of prayer leads "almost inevitably" to "derangement" for solitaries and fruitlessness for coenobites. Yet, almost remarkably, the method of prayer described is not bad in itself; rather, it is not properly conditioned, the self is not rightly prepared: "the good is not good when it is not done in the right way."[10]

## The Second Method

The second method of prayer is described by St. Symeon in the following way: "A person withdraws his intellect from sensory things and concentrates it in himself, guards his senses, and collects his thoughts; and he advances oblivious of the vanities of this world. Sometimes he examines his thoughts, sometimes pays attention to

9. Ibid.
10. Ibid.

the words of the prayer he is addressing to God, and sometimes drags back his thoughts when they have been taken captive; and when he is overcome by passion he forcefully strives to recover himself."[11] By contrast to the first method, this method seeks to order and to temper the passions, to detach them from the world of the senses. The monk is "struggling," engaged in the relentless fight to conquer the flesh, whereas the monk engaged in the first method only deepens his attachments to the world. In a similar way, since in St. Symeon's judgment "a moonlit night is better than a night that is pitch-dark and starless," so also is this method better than the first one.[12] But it is nevertheless harmful: "One who struggles in this way . . . can never be at peace or win the crown of victory. He is like a person fighting at night: he hears the voices of his enemies and is wounded by them, but he cannot see clearly who they are, where they come from and for what purpose they assail him."[13] Like the Pharisees in Matthew's Gospel, he is a blind man leading the blind, though he "imagines he is capable of becoming the shepherd of the sheep." On the one hand, the monk of this method has vanquished some enemies, the enemies of the imagination; he has entered into a higher realm of the self, that of the intellect, by which he endeavors to keep mastery over his passions and to collect his attention on the words of the prayer. He is engaged in intellectual prayer, but he does not succeed in passing through the words to the one he is addressing. The battle in the darkness is the result of an interior darkness, the "darkness of the intellect."[14] "Fighting in this manner," says St. Symeon, the monk "cannot ever escape his noetic enemies, but is worn out by them." His prayer is an exhausting battle to keep his mind detached from the passions and focused on the prayer itself. Like the monk of the first method, the champion of noetic prayer also "falls victim unawares to self-esteem." He proudly "despises and criticizes others for their lack of attentiveness," but his own concentration and attentiveness are based on a fallacy: the intellect in itself

11. Ibid., 68–69.
12. Ibid., 69.
13. Ibid.
14. Ibid.

is not the final or definitive stage where the encounter with God is to be had.[15] By the negations of intellectual prayer one in actuality never transcends the limits of one's own mind.

## The Third Method

St. Symeon begins his discussion of the third method with the acknowledgment of its strangeness, its elusiveness and its scarcity among the community. There are as few who practice it as the virtue of obedience is rare. And as obedience is the foundational virtue of monastic life, so also is this third way the foundation of true prayer. This method is in fact necessarily paired with obedience to a spiritual father, through which one places all of one's cravings and desires, anxieties and "entanglement with this evil world" into the hands of another. Through the practice of absolute obedience, one no longer lives for oneself or desires the good opinion of others; he has no anxiety, and is "dead to every worldly and bodily attachment."[16] With the classical practice of obedience as its context, and from which it is indissociable, the third method deals with the core problem of the second method, the "enslavement of the intellect" to its own products. This third method does not annihilate the intellect itself or its activity, but rather "sets it at liberty" to "wage war with its full strength," which is the important work of examining the thoughts in one's mind, to push them away from consciousness. But that, even that, is not the essential work of prayer—thinking this is the delusion of the second method. Rather, the intellect engages in its war in order for prayer, true prayer, to begin to happen. Mental purification, the silencing of the intellect, is an activity of clearing room "while," simultaneously, "the heart in its purity offers prayers to God."[17] This, he says, "is the beginning of a true life of seclusion"; a proper sequencing, a pathway of prayer is established.

How, then, does this prayer work? St. Symeon describes it first by contrasting it with the former two methods: "The starting-point of

15. Ibid.
16. Ibid.
17. Ibid., 70.

this third method of prayer is not to gaze upwards, to raise one's hands aloft, to concentrate one's thoughts and to call down help from heaven. These, as we said, are the marks of the first form of delusion. Nor does it begin, as the second method does, by keeping guard over the senses with the intellect, while failing to observe the enemies who attack from within." The work of prayer is located below the surface where the first two methods remain. It is located in one's innermost depths, at one's deep core, in the heart. Here St. Symeon deepens his appeal (again) to a renewal of the practice of obedience, which he here describes as doing "everything as if you were in the presence of God." This practice of the divine presence he elaborates as maintaining purity of conscience in three ways: in regards first to God (by always giving him proper worship), second to one's spiritual father (by precise obedience, nothing more), and third to other people and material things (by meticulously following the "golden rule" and by not misusing food, drink or clothing).[18] He describes the method further as "true and unerring attentiveness"—not that the intellect, as in the second method, keeps watch over what in the first method runs rampant and free, the senses and material attachments, but rather that it "keeps watch over the heart while it prays." Prayer is not the proper work of the intellect except where it is *properly* attentive, or rather, *proper attentiveness*. It must be attentive to the right things and in the right place: the intellect "should always be in patrol within the heart."[19] It does the same work it previously did, therefore, but in a new location: "repulsing and expelling all thoughts sown" in the heart "by the enemy." In imitation of those whom Symeon reverently calls "holy fathers," the founders of the monastic way of life, the great elders and teachers of Eastern monasticism, the monk should "abandon all other forms of spiritual labor and concentrate wholly on this one task of guarding the heart." He points to the various names by which these spiritual masters have named it ("stillness of the heart," "attentiveness," "guarding the heart," "watchfulness and rebuttal" or "the investigation of thoughts and guarding the intel-

18. Ibid., 69–70.
19. Ibid., 70–71.

lect," and he lists six renowned authors venerated by the community, as well as a text, *The Paradise of the Fathers*, all of which
likewise teach this method). And he finally refers to Old and New
Testament texts that anchor this practice in holy writ, and especially
the teachings of Jesus.[20]

After demonstrating the continuity of his teaching with a tradition of authorities from Jesus to the founders of monasticism and
the classical texts of this tradition, Symeon yet again elaborates on
the practice of obedience, which here he ties not only to a pure conscience, but also to the necessity of learning from experience and to
complete detachment. Finally St. Symeon is ready to describe the
practice itself: it is, simply speaking, a quest or search, by the intellect, for the "place" of the heart, a descent of the mind into one's
inner self, the heart, the crossing point, the point of union of body
and soul at one's human core. Once the monk has through obedience learned detachment and is free from any anxiety, he is ready to
experience the method. "Sit down," instructs Symeon, "in a quiet
cell, in a corner by yourself. . . . Close the door, and withdraw your
intellect from everything worthless and transient. Rest your beard
on your chest, and focus your physical gaze, together with the whole
of your intellect, upon the centre of your belly or your navel.
Restrain the drawing-in of breath through your nostrils, so as not to
breathe easily, and search inside yourself with your intellect so as to
find the place of the heart, where all the powers of the soul reside."[21]
Through this bodily posture and control of one's breathing one can
direct the intellect towards an exploration of one's interior regions
and find the heart, the seat of affections, the intellect, and the body,
the source and sustaining vitality of our emotional, intellectual, and
physical powers. After reaching a state of "darkness and impenetrable density" and persisting there, one finds "as though miraculously,
an unceasing joy."[22] The inner darkness, vigilantly guarded by the
intellect, is suddenly transformed into light, which fills the place of
the heart. This light newly empowers the intellect to engage in a

20. Ibid., 71–72.
21. Ibid., 72–73.
22. Ibid., 73.

radically simple way in its battle with distractions: distractive thoughts are driven away and annihilated simply by the invocation of the name of Jesus. Here the practice is described as "keeping guard over your intellect and retaining Jesus in your heart." This descent of the intellect into the heart, which is itself now kept guard over by the heart, and thereby, paradoxically, keeps its guard over the heart through the presence of Jesus, who is repeatedly invoked there by calling on his name, can only be taught through experience. "The rest," says St. Symeon, "you will learn for yourself, with God's help." But this appeal to the classic saying that "your cell will teach you everything," only leads to the intervention of an imagined question by the student:

> "*Question*: Why cannot the monk attain perfection by means of the first and second form of keeping guard?"[23]

With the answer we enter into the full teaching of the text on the integration of the methods, which takes up its remaining pages.

## Integration of the Methods

This proper ordering of the methods is articulated by reference to three images: that of a ladder with four rungs, that of the life stages of a person from childhood to old age, and finally that of a building, with a foundation, a structure, and a roof. The first image is taken from St. John Climacus's *Ladder of Divine Ascent* (which has thirty rungs, here condensed to four): first, "curtailing the passions"; second, "practicing psalmody"; third, "perseverance in prayer"; and finally, "undeviating absorption in contemplation." Like Climacus's ladder—the thirty chapters of which were meant to relate to the thirty years of Christ's life—St. Symeon's ladder also corresponds to the life-stages of a human being: the first rung corresponds to childhood; the second to the step from adolescence to youth; the third is the step from youth to manhood; and the fourth is "that of the old man with grey hairs." Both the ladder and the stages of life emphasize the proper sequencing of the practice of prayer: "It is not possi-

---

23. Ibid.

ble for the child to grow up to manhood and to attain old age except by mounting the first rung of the ladder and so climbing to perfection by the four steps in succession."[24] The first three stages of the ladder or of life correspond to three methods of prayer: the first rung, childhood, curtailing the passions, is the work of the third method of prayer, guarding the heart. One makes the greatest progress in initial catharsis by taking on the hesychast discipline, which is like a new or true beginning; even the adept is always a beginner. The practice of psalmody, the second rung, is practicable after the passions have been wholly stilled "through the heart's resistance to them" until they are "laid to rest." This corresponds to the second method of prayer, now thoroughly refigured by the method of the third rung, which is the attentiveness of the intellect through "the invocation of the Lord Jesus" which drives distractive thoughts away from the heart. Here intellectual prayer is described, profoundly, as "inflaming" the intellect with longing "for intimate union with God," which is the precise point where the second method, built out of the third, unfolds into what was originally sought in the first method, imaginative prayer, where the heart's passions seek but without the guardianship of the intellect.[25] Note that Symeon does not explicitly refer to a fourth rung of the ladder. This is because the "fourth rung" is the unification of the three; one only really begins climbing by starting with the prayer of the heart. But reaching the prayer of the heart and the vision of the Uncreated Light means one has already reached the goal. The ladder dissolves into a rope that binds the aspirant to God.

The third image, that of the spiritual life as one of building a house, makes St. Symeon's teaching a little clearer: "We first lay the foundations, then build the house, and finally put on the roof. We must do the same in relation to spiritual matters. First we must lay the spiritual foundation of the house, that is to say, we must watch over the heart and curtail the passions arising from it"—the third method of prayer. "Then we must build the walls of the spiritual house, that is to say, through the second form of attentiveness we

24. Ibid., 74.
25. Ibid.

must repulse the turbulence of the evil spirits that fight us by means of the external senses. . . ." Finally, one must finish the house by putting on the roof, "that is to say, detach ourselves entirely from all things and give ourselves wholly to God."[26] This is what the first method sought, but could never find, since it practiced an ecstatic movement toward God from an external surface of the self; but to move ecstatically towards God, one must move inwardly. The point of *écstasis*, where the soul may meet the divine other, its Beloved, is found only by an enstatic deepening to the point where the encounter of love may happen, in the heart, and where one progresses towards a deepening union with God. Only by entering into the depths of the heart may one truly ascend and it is through the depths of the heart that one passes beyond oneself. Symeon says: "But if without following the sequence of which we have spoke you raise eyes and intellect to heaven in the hope of envisaging noetic realities you will see fantasies rather than the truth. Because your heart is still unpurified, as we have said many times, the first and second methods of attentiveness do not promote our progress. When we build a house we do not put on the roof before laying the foundations. . . ."[27] In our worldly state, the mind follows what the body does; hence the need for the bodily and respiratory practice within the context of spiritual obedience. Once the practice is accomplished where the inordinate power of the body is neutralized through detachment and the mind itself is purified through intellective descent into the heart, the bodily and intellectual domains themselves undergo a transformation, where the divine light encountered in the heart slowly comes to permeate the self, body and soul, through the pathways created by the work of sanctification, the prayer of the heart. This prayer is an end in itself, but it bears surprising fruit: the monk becomes, in the totality of his person, more and more transparent to the Presence he ceaselessly invokes. His entire self becomes this invocation; to the degree that this transparency is realized everything in his world is only a pathway of intensification of the longing for union. He may pray the

26. Ibid., 75.
27. Ibid.

psalms rightly, and look up to heaven, raise his hands, with a pure heart. Here again, the path of progress in prayer is reversed. To have learned what Symeon teaches about the three methods means that his student has initiated the prayer of the heart and has learned to orient his life by it. He still prays in community, sings the psalms at the appointed hours, but he also enters his room, crosses his legs on the floor, rests his chin on his chest, regulates his breathing by the invocation of the Name of Jesus; and he has set off on the interior exploration of his inner regions in search of the heart. He has found the heart and learned to immerse his intellect in its vast sea. And the darkness has been illuminated by the experience of the Divine Light.

In the closing paragraph St. Symeon warns against hastily progressing to the second and first methods (now stages) of prayer: "Thus, if you practice all this in due sequence, completing each at the right time, your heart will first be cleansed . . . you will be able to concentrate wholly on psalmody; you will be able to wage war . . . and you will gaze heavenwards, *if need be*, alike with your physical and your spiritual eyes, and will pray in true purity. *Yet you should gaze upwards only occasionally* because of the enemies that lie in ambush in the air."[28] The one who truly reaches this state of course does not need this qualification, since he is "free"; the degree of his freedom would correspond to his liberty to raise physical and spiritual eye alike to heaven—imaginative and intellectual methods of prayer are and have only ever been an extension of the prayer of the heart, for they are motivated by the one, defining creaturely desire for communion with the Uncreated.

These three methods, now revealed to be moments or facets of the one way of prayer, integrated together out of the foundation of the last-become-first, the prayer of the heart, lays the foundation for the path of spiritual progress in prayer of union with God through the invocation of the Name of Jesus. The affections of the heart for God alone, aroused and deepened into an all-consuming fire of love, through a hatred of one's alienation from God through sin tied

28. Ibid., emphasis added.

to felt recognition of the holiness of God, an awareness through sorrow and love that progressively extinguishes one's will for anything but God to the point of a pure "detachment" of availability for God and attentiveness to the divine Presence in the inward depths of the self: this is the path of the Jesus Prayer, the prayer at the site of the Uncreated Light that takes up its abode in the heart, at the crossroad of body and soul. Seen separately, the three methods are incommensurate: the monk must reject the first method, that of images, in order to pass through the critical fire of the intellect, which purportedly purifies the mind's attachment to creaturely things, which the first way always crudely identifies with the God who ever transcends them. And the second way must be rejected on its own because it is in effect a self-blinding, a mutilation, a rejection of physical sight and a blackening of mental sight; it ignores the heart, the affections, and cannot see the creaturely form of its own greatest conceptual productions, its own *masked anthropomorphisms*, and also ignores the most important question of one's (affective) attachments to whatever is not God. The intellect itself needs a guardian, which happens to be the desire of the heart, even as, through its critical work of *apophasis*, it guards the heart from attaching itself to anything but God. Seen from the proper starting point, the last or final method, the other two ways are made fruitful. In fact, the first way is proper, true prayer, but one must be prepared by means of the intellectual vigilance of the heart in order to pray, properly, with the images given by God, symbols which cannot ultimately be discarded or surpassed, but are rather sites of encounter, theophany, presence. Prayer, normatively speaking, is the chanting of the psalms, for St. Symeon the New Theologian, but one is liberated to pray them properly only through an intellectual vigilance within the heart that rests on a cardiac vigilance over the intellect.

This threefold integration in prayer corresponds, in my view, to the much commented upon but less understood "ways" of theological knowledge, ways of "hymning the divine" (if we are to understand theology most properly, since God is only properly known through being loved, in praise): the cataphatic, the apophatic, and the way of excess or redundance, wherein what is affirmed originally, accepted as given by God—the world, the self, the entire cosmos of images of God contained within the Image that is the Son—is rightly seen and felt, rightly considered through one's personal union with the God who so infinitely surpasses them that he precedes them as the condition for their being and their being known, which is finally only the prior medium through which one has ever already passed in order to receive them as anything distinct from God. This personal union with the God who stands *there*, beyond one's highest intellectual reach and deepest interior descent, is the site of excess or redundance because it is the site of a humble encounter, of an unknowing immediacy with the Beginning and End of all things who is always beyond, and has addressed one from that beyond in one's deepest self, stripped of every creaturely support: "come, follow me."

Myth, with its symbolic nodes of presence, and its narrative ordering that surrounds and makes possible a total human understanding that can never be plumbed, corresponds to the first method; wisdom, with its intellectual purification and interrogation of myth, its refusal of a simple identification of the given words with the hidden things themselves, corresponds to the second method; apocalypse, with its in-breaking, its shattering descent into the realm of nature, corresponds to the third. To accept this threefold classification is to acknowledge that intellectual work is given from within and is inseparable from the horizon of narrative understanding, and that a wisdom from above leads one into the deepest path, which, through walking on its way, leads one to the greatest or most meaningful encounters with the questions that matter most and are always inseparably tied together: God, ourselves, the destiny of our world, goodness, evil, freedom, love, truth, justice, and beauty. On the way of prayer, one lives these questionings first as a questioning of oneself by another, to which one responds, and to which one desires to consummate one's entire life as nothing but a response, a faithful response. But this pathway, this transfer of one's depths through the extinguishment of the will in the will of another, a descent and transfer that is the hallmark of the practical domain of a Philosophy of the Word, the domain of religion—and here in the locale of its heart, the practice of prayer—bears a crucial analogy with the theoretical dimension of a Philosophy in Word and Name, an intellectual practice of Christianity. Prayer, prayer that is "pure, and makes progress," is found, for St. Symeon the New Theologian, through the integration of the three methods by their proper sequencing, a sequencing that carries (so to speak) the foundation of the house up through the walls and into the roof—a building is only as strong as its foundation, and the foundation, as the basis, runs through every part of the structure.

If such is the case for speech "to" God, the present sketchbook has sought something similar for speech "about" God in its inquiry into the three key "methods" of religious thinking. I have made sketches for the integration of (1) the affirmation of the symbols of revelation—the *mythic* given, with (2) their necessary negation, the recognition that the divine reality presencing through them is not identified, *sensu stricto*, with them, as creatures—the arrival of theoretical culture, of *wisdom*, together, finally, established on the foundation of (3) the redundance of the affirmation that breaks through the negation as its basis, the dawning or deepening recognition that the mythic given itself already pre-contains every possible intellectual negation as a transcendent and living presence standing higher than every intellectual reach and deeper than one's innermost descent—*apocalypsis*.

# Last Word: *Gnōsis*

THERE IS A STANDARD UNDERSTANDING of revelation
that conceives it as an unanticipatable cannon blast shot over
the wall of our finitude from the unknown beyond. This view
conceives wisdom, likewise, as a purely immanent analysis of our
natural experience by human intelligence taken on terms that it
immediately gives. Revelation and wisdom are therefore wholly separate intelligible orders. Theology, on this view, is an impossible
mash-up created by revelation, a wholly foreign or alien element,
colliding with a tradition or traditions of human experience and
reflection, whereas philosophy is the self-sufficient enterprise independent of any higher intelligibility, sealed off from the in-form-
ation of revelation in an *a priori* way.[1] I have found in the preceding
sketches and their accompanying studies, however, that revelation—
the communication of God, as Word—first and primarily, speaks
the language of Myth, just as Wisdom does. Wisdom is understood
to be intrinsic to the encounter between Myth and Word, the Call,
the intervention that forges a straight path *through* Myth, never
transcending it but hallowing and transforming its symbols in light
of what is "eschatologically" revealed as the direction and God-given
goal, as the Passover of God. This Passover is ritualized; the community of the baptized "remembers" it by re-enacting it. We make
the sacrifice and keep the feast. The traditions of human critical
reflection never surpass their mythic milieu, although they do suffer
complications, revisions, and even replacements of one by another.
If narrative understanding is constant, and its justification is in fact
its explanatory power of experience, namely, its capacity to give

---

1. In the preceding summary lines I appeal to some insightful pages in Louis
Bouyer, *Gnosis, la connaissance de Dieu dans l'Ecriture* (Paris: Cerf, 1988).

understanding of this world in reference to Origin and End that exceed theoretical understanding, then the good of ritual is found in the *enaction* of contact with that transcendence of beginning and end which myth gives. No theoretical account of the world that depends on an *a priori* bracketing of the field of intelligence which excludes the relevance of the higher realities that pertain to mythic intelligence may eclipse its possible (or actualized) value.

A last word, even if unfinished or whispered—and therefore not yet complete, not yet made known to all—is the *apocalypsis tou theou* to humanity in Christ. In human terms this word is weak: it takes the form of an offer, a proposal: it may be stomped on, ignored; like the true prophets of old its messengers may be abused, hated, killed. Yet again, this word, the word of God, defies every attempt to domesticate it, precisely through this weakness. It is not empty. This word is a word of God *to humanity*, and is therefore a word of *knowledge*: it is, again, a "wisdom from above," coming from the Source of all wisdom, to which it will return, fulfilling its intended purpose. It is a wisdom that in its apparent weakness claims a divine power, the peculiar power to "demolish fortresses" of "every pretension raising itself *kata tēs* gnōseōs *tou theou*, against the *knowledge* of God."[2] This knowledge therefore, this *gnōsis*—to use, as we have seen, the biblical term found in the LXX and distilled to a high conceptual status in St. Paul—is correlated to a Word, which is always the Word of a Presence. The God who speaks *to* humanity is a God who journeys *with* humanity: God reveals himself as the God who passes by, and who passes through the human journey itself. He calls humanity to follow; in following on the path he carves out for the human community in Christ, the "straight path of justice," God reveals his final wisdom, and indicates the last word that only God can give. The primary form of God's Word is therefore a Call. This Call requires a Response.

The Call is a Passover; the Response is an Exodus. Every human

2. 2 Cor 10:4–5.

word is predicated on a prior Word of God: both the word *about* God and the word *to* God. Wisdom is given by God; it takes the first and perpetual form of Myth, an overarching, authorized narrative, a sacred story, which I reduce here to its logical form: a Call of enactment of God's passage by, and a Response of human following in the Exodus. The Call unveils, *reveals* the End of the Response: the eschatological Land of Promise, a "New Heavens and New Earth": a last transfiguration of the world that will bring about his purposes, hidden since the Beginning, but revealed in "the latter days" of the Hebrew prophets, the days since the advent of the Son of Man.

The word *to* God, Prayer, is the condition for every valid word *about* God. The primary form of Response is the word addressed to God, the only properly valid "theological" word. Every properly valid theological word receives the entirety of its validity from the Call of God: the word about God receives all of its validity from the word of response to God's prior Call. This call founds human religious experience and provides the implicit content of its various cultural forms. The cultural forms of human life—primarily and principally religion, comprised of Word and Presence, Myth and Rite, and everything that depends on it, philosophy, art, science—are therefore patterns of response to the one divine word. These forms of life are *sacred* to the degree that they are *human*. They are symbolic "redistributions" of the given order of the world, symbolic cultural forms intended to signify the discerned ultimate meaning of the human order as it responds to the disclosures of the divine that the world continually gives. These disclosures of the divine in the given order of the world ultimately expose a radical break between the divine order and the human order: the divine becomes hidden in the face of Evil. The Origin and End is perceived not merely as Absence-in-Presence, an Absolute transcending the order of distinctions that comprise the intelligibility of the human world, but also, more radically, as an impenetrable hieroglyph tied up with that enigma of the destiny of the human world. Does the Good enjoy a finality and self-sufficiency that would allow the meanings of human experience, tied to freedom, to love, to sin, to evil, a final triumph?

The Word was made Flesh within the history of the People Israel, as its single *telos*: a disclosure of the mystery which the Creator of the World and the Covenant Lord of Israel had in mind from the beginning. This, at least, is the Christian confession, born from an apocalyptic sect of this people who discerned the definitive historical unveiling of their God in the Death and Resurrection of Jesus, the prophet from Nazareth. In this enfleshment of the Divine Word, the Call and Response assume an identification that is unprovable and even illegitimate according to the standards of judgment provided by the present form of the world within which it is nevertheless spoken: Myth may not "become" historical fragment. But it is this identification nonetheless that forms the entire wager of Christian faith. Its logic takes the form of an antinomy that manifests obscurely the higher truth only through accepting both sides of the contradiction with equal assent. This is the logic of the symbol, the symbol understood as embodying the higher truth in the given, human form. This identification, in history, does not take the form of human possession of an absolute truth, which one is justified in making present through violence; as such it would ossify, and the present life of faith be drained of all its power. The charismatic joining of the resurrected life of the world to come to the life lived now becomes "quenched."[3] Fidelity to the story of Jesus as the final word of God: there is no *proof* for this category mistake but only the invasion of standards, conditions, and realities from the other world, the higher world that is the enigmatic source at the foundation of Myth, the world that we meet through Death, and here and now only in symbolic, enigmatic modes of presence. This fidelity takes the form of divine *Promise* and human trust, *Entrustment* to the final validity of the apocalyptic Word, and the Invisible Presence to which it testifies and which it claims.

"Yet for us,

There is one God, the Father,
From whom all things are and toward whom we return,[4]

---

3. 1 Thess 5:19.
4. Inferring the action of this second part of the line wholly from the preposition: "kai hēmeis *eis* auton."

and one Lord Jesus Christ,
through whom all things are and through whom we exist.

But not all have this knowledge (*gnōsis*)."[5]

This *gnōsis* is a peculiar mode of knowledge. The knowledge of *recognition* is the knowledge of the personal identity of the One Origin and End manifest as the Background or Precondition unifying every Mythic expression of the human totality, each uniquely throwing its two anchors of stability into the boundless dark depths beyond the veil of Birth, on the one hand, and Death on the other, the veil that enshrouds every human gaze on the world like the theophany of the unfilled, Blue Expanse that covers all. This recognition of an identity, this knowledge, is contained within the whole apocalyptic manifestation of the One, the Uncreated God, in the Human Face and Heart of Jesus.

This great disclosure of divine Wisdom, of the End of the one human pilgrimage in the Passover of Jesus Christ, and the state of recognition that forms its reception, this *gnōsis*, will have to be pursued in a subsequent investigation. I would take as my starting point *The Three Methods of Prayer* that served as the analogate for a final classification of the three keys of this Philosophy in Word and Name. The question to be clarified and negotiated there—successful only if I am capable of persisting in the question as it deepens to the point of an obscure illumination—is how a necessarily anthropomorphic form for the human idea of God may be anything more than just that.[6] The answer, if already contained in this ring, the band of the heart that holds together the three keys, is named for the clasp that closes the ring, the word I lastly introduced in order to bring the present book to a close.

5. 1 Cor 8:6–7.
6. The text is entitled *Essay on the Apophatics of the Sensible*, referenced in the first words of this book.

# Postscript

## Exegetical Fragments A & B:
## On Myth and Logic *and*
## On Plato's Cave and Christ's

### FRAGMENT A
### On Myth and Logic (Between S. L. Frank and
### Edmund Husserl)

"That we could all bear being immortal—that would be the highest thing."

—Nietzsche

IT WOULD NOT BE AN EXAGGERATION to say that the fundamental concern of philosophy is death. The philosopher is self-consciously being-before-death for he knows himself and thinks as one who is, in fact, being-*towards*-death. Death (on this view) is the end of philosophy, for philosophy is the practice of attempting to know the truth of things that is hidden to us before death. Philosophy is practiced in hope: hope that one will die a good death, and through death be prepared for what one will face on the other side. Philosophy has classically understood itself in this way as the practice of death, for philosophy believes that death will give with *certainty* the answers it seeks *before* death—this "certainty" is only the recognition that philosophy can give the *good life* that one seeks in seeking that which philosophy gives, the life lived for truth and goodness; the truth of the goodness "beyond being" is a living-before-death. "Beyond being": that the conditions of human experience that lock humanity in tragedy by iron necessities in excess of the radically limited scope of my freedom, of humanity determined by these necessities that name "being," are themselves relative to that which transcends them, which I can live *for* and, hence, *from.*

This seeking of answers, seeking the truth that only death will give (one may hope), which is the truth regarding this life, philosophy believes it has found in itself, in the *practice* of philosophy. Philosophy, according to Socrates, who for Plato died the good death and therefore was the true philosopher, *lives* by believing in ultimate reality: Justice, Truth, Goodness. Philosophy also believes that these realities are unknowable in themselves but are nevertheless the measure by which humanity is finally measured. This measure is what must come on the other side of death, since there, through death, one meets final reality, what really is the case, about which I can only conjecture and hope and believe at present.

Philosophy's new and higher certainty regarding the conditioned character of the necessities that claim to rule human life is only a matter of what is commonly called faith, the "proof" of which is manifest firstly in and through the life lived: this is a fundamental truth contained in Socrates's teaching that the highest knowledge is to know that one does not know. This knowledge is the basis of philosophy. The final judgment of the truth, which exceeds death, is immortal and therefore divine, is why the highest knowledge is to know that one does not know—and through this highest knowledge, one can *begin to live* according to the highest, hidden realities, the realities to come (through death). One *can* live philosophically. It is worth being just, therefore, even if, for justice, one might lose one's life. This eschatological orientation is the philosophical attitude *par excellence* embodied by Plato's teacher.

## Mythologicality

It is well known that Plato presents an eschatological myth at the conclusion of three dialogues, the *Gorgias,* the *Phaedo,* and the *Republic.* What is debated is precisely the philosophical significance of these narratives. On the one hand there are those who quite cleanly separate the "philosophy" of Plato from the myths, reducing the latter to a pre-theoretical infection for which he can, perhaps, be forgiven. And there are others who would see the myth as a pre-philosophical mode of expression that contains, in a shadowy way, philosophical truths—that is, truths about the world in which I am living that should be grasped in an explicitly "rational" way, a way to which the myth must be reduced in order to remain or become philosophical.

On the other hand, there are those who see the necessity of myth, that is, who see myth as expressing in the only possible manner certain truths that transcend philosophical speech, which also is a language before death, and therefore circumscribed by myth. There are those, further (an even smaller group), who understand the myth as an integral and irreplaceable component to philosophy as such, not only as a mode of speaking about certain irreplaceable things at the margins of philosophy, but actually as fully philosophical as is the dialectical inquiry into concepts. For them the mythic form expresses precisely the most important human truths. The dialectical work of reason sifts through the mythic material but never exhausts it.

This extreme position is the natural conclusion to the second general position, since if myth is the highest expression of certain truths, then the mythic representation is itself the most philosophical manner of expression in their case. It is only arbitrary, and perhaps reductive, to conceive philosophy as a delimited inquiry outside of myth—whether one has a positive or negative view of myth, the position would be the same—for it is precisely there that I lose focus on the most fundamental human questions by which philosophy stands or falls.

Hence there are really only two positions: the extreme view that rejects myth as unphilosophical, based on a certain view of philosophy; and the other extreme view, that embraces myth as, in certain fundamental cases, the highest manner of philosophizing possible—a way that from out of the midst of mortal limits, somehow, strangely, exceeds them, albeit in a mortal fashion. Inasmuch, in other words, as these cases where intelligence reaches its excess in myth are the most important for humanity (inasmuch as there my humanity is more fully or dramatically encountered, confronted, revealed…), and hence for philosophy itself—the task of which, I recall, is to discern, seek, and live according to precisely the most important things for my humanity—then myth itself is *in these cases* most philosophical. Here of course I touch a paradox, one that pervades the thinking of Plato, and which touches the problematic essence of the philosophical itself. For philosophy concerns reason, and reason is (evidently) discovered through philosophy as the radical reaching of the truth of things that mythic consciousness could only reach in a shadowy manner, albeit with a deep intimacy that philosophy loses, whatever its specific and irreplaceable gains. The point is that what philosophy reaches through concepts is what is already known, and lived, within the mythical horizon. The ontic stands in excess, ever in brute, dense excess of the ontological. The "distinction" is an abstraction that may mislead. Myth is necessary for philosophy and to philosophy and it is therefore necessary within philosophy, exposing, at the center of philosophy, its limits. It depends on myth to reach the most substantial things, which are necessarily the most pressing things, the most philosophical things.

The most important things, the definitively human things, belong therefore to that domain *from which* and *to which* I *am* and therefore *through which* I *am*. These things are inaccessible in themselves; I am alienated from these things, at best, whatever my theory about these ultimate matters happens to be: whether, for example, that from which I am alienated is nothing at all, or the God that is infinitely good, supreme, closed in on itself as an idea, or even the *living God* who is such precisely because he *acts*. By being, I am alienated from nothing, in the first case, but death will reconcile me to the truth. In the second case, God is hidden from me, being both too close and too far for me to grasp, and this condition may or may not be tragically radicalized by what is mythically expressed as an original and all-pervading disobedience, as a disenfranchisement from the Garden, my home, and as the enduring of a curse, the bitter fruit of such an original embrace of evil, which somehow, terrifyingly, released it to run havoc in the world over which to be human means to be granted responsibility. For me, it is not clear or sure whether God is or is not; I can doubt for a number of reasons, the least important of which—that is, the most un-philosophical of which—is because I cannot grasp God, for whenever I would, it would not be God. What is clear, however, is that God is the most important philosophical question, for if there is God, then God matters the most. Even as a question. For it is also clear that God is the most challenging and difficult of philosophical questions, for if God is *God*—and by God I mean, finally, not merely the highest and most supreme principle in the world, but beyond the world with such a radical finality that the world plus God adds nothing to God—then to think God requires thinking, that is, the manner of making basic distinctions, to be extended to its farthest reaches and to stretch beyond its capacity, to break on the shoal of the Absolute. God is "beyond being" in this sense at least.[1]

This second clarity means that *God* is first given to me through myth, and it means that I *myself* am first given to myself through myth, and that the same goes for the *world* as well: I can only conceive of the idea of the world, an idea that I cannot fully conceive, because I have stories that give me the totality through narrating its beginning and end, its source and its goal. I would expect then that a philosophy involved with God must trade in myths, even if one's myth is implicit, presupposed, and *reasoned from*, perhaps even forgotten, veiled, hidden, lost. I can venture a thesis: All philosophy is an argument for some myth or another. A myth (my own) is simple: "In the beginning, God created the heavens and the earth . . . the Spirit and the Bride say 'Come.'" There is a beginning and there is an end. In the middle I am thinking, and I think from beginning to end, as passing through, as given to myself in a mystery, viz., my historical existence between birth and death, of which I cannot know the full meaning, but which is there in excess of my understanding.

## Definiteness

Like the Christian myth, Plato's is expressed in ways that, seen from the rules of conceptuality, contradict one another. This is most uninteresting. Myth is not bound by the rules of conceptuality.

1. See Robert Sokolowski, *The God of Faith and Reason*.

# Postscript

Truth exceeds these rules if myth is true. And I hope it is, since myth is necessary, and since myth expresses dimensions of my humanity that the laws of conceptuality, however necessary on their own plane, do not allow me to touch and to experience. These rules allow me to have fixed content, definiteness, and through these rules I make distinctions, forge concepts, abstractions that give me truths marked by clarity and distinctness, or individuality that stands by itself, asserts itself as compelling on its own terms (even if these are of course interlocked with every other concept, and implicitly sprout within the mythic horizon).

This definiteness depends on logical laws, of which there are classically three: identity, contradiction, and the excluded middle. (1) Identity: A is A, something is itself, is identical precisely to itself. (2) Contradiction: A is not not-A, something is not something else, is distinct by its own right from everything else. (3) Excluded Middle: This distinctness or separateness gives me the univocal character of A, that which I sought, and received initially, in the first law. Whatever is not not-A is A (when considering "what is A?"); whatever is is either A or not-A, there is no other possibility. Through this process I am making distinctions, which involves an affirmation (of identity) and then negation regarding what A is not, then a further negation, which is in fact a deepening of the negation. Nowhere are these absolute except within the strictures of reasoning, in its pathos to take hold of its own most basic distinctions. The threefold process is a process of clarification about the object of inquiry, and reflection on it gives me what is necessarily required to reach the definiteness that I seek in such knowledge, which takes the form of these principles themselves.

These principles can be understood from the vantage of the concept of being, for which they are, as it were, first principles. *Identity*: a thing is that which *is* (being as existence) and a thing is *what* it is (being as essence); *non-contradiction*: a thing cannot be and not be at one and the same time in the same way; *excluded middle*: a thing is or it is not. From this vantage we would also have to add the principle of *causality* (for contingent, or non-necessary beings, that is): every being that does not have to be, has a cause of its being. And if we add this principle for contingent beings, we would also have to add the "modern" principle, *sufficient reason*: being is in itself intelligible (although not necessarily for man, who can only grasp such in a partial way).[2]

S. L. Frank, whom I am mostly following here in this presentation of these laws, has shown that they are indivisible expressions of a simple principle, which he calls the "principle of definiteness"— that is, the process of *differentiation* that yields abstract knowledge. Reason moves by making distinctions, and distinctions are modes of comparison and contrast, which yield judgments, affirmation, and negation. To know something involves contrasting it with what it is not, to show its likeness and difference with other things in order to name its identity. Reason emerges for me with clarity when the irrational can be contrasted with it; male when it is contrasted with female; without darkness there would be no such thing for me as "light"; God is understood rationally when I come to realize that God is other than every other, and more fundamentally, beyond the very process of distinctions through which my reason can even think about him (at least according to the present order of intelligibility that determines all my thinking, that is, the "world").[3]

Further, as expressions, or as I have made explicit, steps, in the process of the intensification of definiteness, the fundamental logical laws also necessarily, says Frank, point to a final principle, "the principle of analysis," without which they would be, in fact, "meaningless, incomprehensible, contradictory, and impossible."[4] The principle of analysis Frank defines as "the separation of a continuous whole into a series of separate determinations," which he elucidates further as "the generation of an aggregate of determinations A, B, C . . . from the undivided unity of being." That which is—being as such, the inaccessible, the unknowable—is presupposed in its pri-

---

2. For this perspective see Louis Bouyer's discussion in *Dictionary of Theology,* "Being," 58–59.

3. I explore these limits, which I can now call apocalyptic limits, in *Eclipse of World.*

4. See Frank, *The Unknowable,* trans. Boris Jakim (Athens, OH: Ohio University Press, 1983), 25–26, for a summary (and the quotations selected here), and the sixth chapter of his *The Object of Knowledge,* for an extensive elaboration.

mordial unity and in its transcendence to reason by the pursuit of definiteness, the accomplishment of which is abstract knowledge in the domain of objects. This principle of analysis therefore points to a reality that fundamentally transcends this domain elucidated by the three laws, "a more primordial layer of reality." This transcendent unity of being "is itself not subject to the logical principles" but enjoys a "metalogical unity" that I can feel on the underside of my rationality, through which I receive distinct determinations.

This unity is immediately experienced as an anticipatory possession, and my rational process of differentiation does not affect the horizon of this already given unity: it is coincident with what Husserl calls the "world," the unified wholeness of reality that is only given implicitly and cannot be brought to thematic consciousness, but which can only be grasped as "pregiven," as infinite, intuited, or felt through all my thinking. My temporality, spatiality, historicity, materiality—the basic features of my "worldliness"—give me access, as a whole, to this pre-definite world, which is full of meaning, meanings that are given to me as already structuring my awareness in the world. My world is primordially coordinated by my embodied sensibility of movement and rest, of force and resistance, the experience of myself as a living body that is given to myself in the "originary ark," my body and its earth, a primary stability by reference to which I am always already oriented, a primal experiencedness *from out of which* I *can* think, that is, make basic differentiations, then categorizations of likeness and unlikeness.[5]

## Instinctuality

In France, in 1939, Frank composed a little-known book, *The Unknowable*. It summarizes his intellectual preoccupations: for him the Unknowable is the highest "object" of knowledge, and it allows a certain kind of peculiar certainty in excess of anything objective. I want to use its opening chapter as a goad for some provisional

5. Edmund Husserl, "The Originary Ark: The Earth Does Not Move," *Husserl at the Limits of Phenomenology*, trans. Bettina Bergo (Evanston, IL: Northwestern University Press, 2001).

reflections.[6] Frank begins his meditation with the acknowledgment that the differentiations of likeness and unlikeness described above first serve the dual end of the preservation and intensification of my life. I am aided by instinct, the forging of my very nature through aeons of self-preservation by my human ancestors and pre-ancestors. It is through these primal differentiations at the base of survival that I inexorably find myself pushed in a specific orientation or a coherent set of orientations in the world.

The world is perpetually changing. I latch onto the constant that is immediately discerned through this ceaseless change. Instinct first gives me an intuition of the familiar, that which will serve my immediate end of self-preservation; and instinct is confirmed and reconfirmed a thousand times from the earliest moments of my life—if it is not, then I am quickly dead, and the conditions for the sustenance of my life were not available, or available enough, for *me*.

The two basic features of the familiar are likeness or similarity and repetition, which manifest the familiar in spatiality and temporality. There is *regularity* in the world and I habituate myself through affiliating my being to it with the various regularities of the world, the world where I live that I find myself discerning. I conform myself to the world that is given to me; I make myself (so to speak) more and more worldly and find myself already worldly through the orientation provided by instinct and the already developed habits I find framing my life that is given to me through my self-consciousness, as its first content and support: waking, sleeping, crying out in hunger, slaking at the breast of my mother, etc., etc., etc. In this way the world unfolds a familiarity to me that I allow to define the world itself inasmuch as this world gives me the means to satisfy and intensify the demand of life.

Finally, I find things named and ordered, and I name them too by repetition. I orient myself amidst these names, and the world takes on an ever richer shape that continues through my life. When I learn a new skill or language, the world is inevitably altered, and opened in new ways that I understand by reference to what I have

---

6. For the following, I am deeply indebted to Frank's *sui generis* introductory chapter to *The Unknowable*, xii–xxii.

already named and known. "All teaching and all intellectual knowledge," said Aristotle, "come about from already existing knowledge."[7] Basically, my movement through this richer differentiation proceeds, as Aristotle said, through understanding the foreign, the new, the different, in light of the familiar, the understood. My ability to perform this activity, and by it to inhabit an ever-differentiated world, is called maturity. I come to see that my basic understandings are only ever partial, are themselves affected by the effect of the unknown that I come to know through inference from what is already taken as known. I see the inexhaustibility of the world and come to understand something of my "place" within it. The world is the place where I survive. Yet I know that it is unmasterable, and that the process of familiarization is radically restricted to an original orientation, that the unknown in being known by reference only to what is already known thereby only becomes partially known, that I inhabit a perspective with native limitations before a vast unconquerable reality. Conceptual knowledge (mediated, of course, by narrative understanding) is based on this more basic orientation towards that which I need, biologically rooted in my original and ceaseless activity of self-preservation, marked by hunger and fulfillment, desire and release, activity and rest, waking and sleeping, an orientation that fits with the cycles of the cosmic world, day/night, seasons, years, and my own lifetime of a rushing sporadic sprint to maturity and a slow, inexorable decline: the rush of the dawn and the long twilight into darkness.

## Common Sense and Concept

All the regularities never cease to surprise me. Even so, my "common sense" tells me that the world that is presently unknown, the world that is ever spreading out before me and through which I am moving, is *like* the world that I know, the world that is mine, that I have successfully navigated. And through the countless repetitions of experience I have learned to master its regularities. The world to come that time is always giving me is taken as essentially continu-

---

7. The opening line of the *Posterior Analytics* I, 1 71a 1 (Barnes, 114).

ous with the world as I retain it in my memory. *Common sense* says that the world pervaded by intelligibility and order in which I have successfully oriented myself will continue into the unknown that I always encounter in the future.

Conceptual knowledge and then scientific knowledge are advancements on this orientation of common sense, of the principle of familiarity as an orientation in the world. Concepts are based on the discernment of similarities, of features that are the same within the diverse material of experience, of reducing the already coherent and unified manifold to the lowest number of repeating features. And scientific knowledge is only an extension of this conceptualization, which common sense allows me to posit as universal, even without absolute knowledge, which it at the same time affirms that I will never possess.

The fundamental insight that Husserl's concept of the "lifeworld" names is that scientific knowledge rests on the more originary knowledge of embodied experience. It is from the latter that the capacity for recognition of difference and sameness derives, however irreducibly scientific discovery into the universes of the vast and the minute alter my understanding of the world of originary orientation, spreading out from the primal experience of force and resistance in my living flesh.

For example, Husserl makes the following observation concerning the origin of the geometrical science of ideal, abstract forms, which lies at the origin of modern science as a whole: "The geometry of idealities was preceded by the practical art of surveying, which knew nothing of idealities."[8] That is to say, measurement of spaces for immediately practical ends, such as constructing buildings, laying out agricultural fields, ditches, pathways, etc., even in the most primitive manners, is the "intuitive" source of meaning for the science of geometry itself, the science that claimed the equation of its results with the basic intelligible contours of reality itself, a claim resting on science's irresistible successes. Husserl makes the striking observation as a result: "It was a fateful omission that Galileo did not inquire back into the original meaning-giving which, as

8. *Crisis*, 48–49.

idealization practiced on the original ground of all theoretical and practical life—the immediately intuited world (and here especially the immediately intuited world of bodies)—resulted in the geometrical ideal constructions" that Galileo equated with the ideal-real itself.[9] The revolution of Galileo, in Husserl's words, which in fact formed the foundation of the modern sciences, was the "surreptitious substitution of the mathematically substructured world of idealities for the only real world, the one that is actually given through perception, that is ever experienced and experienceable— our everyday lifeworld."[10]

The "lifeworld," the ground and source of all meaning: ignorance of this world led to the assertion of the irreality of the sphere of human culture, affect, ethics, and religion, and the resulting dualism of the world of nature, a self-enclosed totality of bodies, over against which lay the psychic domain, understood as self-enclosed. This domain ultimately came to be reductively understood by reference to the rationality of the mathematized physical world of "nature" itself, which served as its model, thereby making this domain, and its source-character of all possible meaning, completely invisible.[11]

## Metaphysical Knowledge

Practical knowledge and scientific knowledge are complemented by metaphysical knowledge, at least in theory. Metaphysical knowledge radicalizes the original practical knowledge orientation of "familiarization" through *metaphorization*. It wagers that the metaphorization of knowing the unfamiliar in light of the familiar, reading *that* in light of *this* (reading the world of physical cause and effect in light of the abstract forms of geometry, say), allows us real access to the unfamiliar, that is, to pass to it from the familiar. Our knowledge, then, is not restricted to the horizon that the merely familiar *immediately* gives us: "That" is like "this," though not identical to it;

9. Ibid., 49.
10. Ibid., 48–49.
11. See *Crisis*, Part II, §§ 8–27, and Michel Henry, *Barbarism* (London/NY: Continuum International Publishing Group, Ltd., 2012), especially chapters 2–3.

"that" is therefore different, but I understand it in the terms that I already possess, which "this" has given to me. Metaphorization is the expansion of the field of understanding that comes about through taking the unlike in terms of the like. If the poet says, "the rose is a tiger," he is making a statement that has no meaning on a "literal plane." The poet is seemingly invoking that horizon of meanings which the rose materially represents—love, purity, affection, attraction and fragility, ascent, etc., dimensions of erotic love—in order to call them into question based on the bitterness and disenchantment that the dark travails of longing, loss, and pain that eros can violently inflict on me like, in fact, a tiger could, the tiger that itself can represent to me that attraction and fear of springing swift violence that is beautiful and savage at once: "The rose is a tiger." Here I am told something in an irreplaceable way about erotic love, but also about roses and tigers as well, at least as meaning-bearing phenomena in my cultural experience, which they most fundamentally "are" phenomenologically speaking (the "tiger" of mere zoological categorizations is a kind of useful abstraction). None of these three things are left the same in their meaning for me after the metaphor has struck me and there has occurred a startling convergence of meaningfulness shared by these meaning-bearing things. Similarly metaphorization asserts and endeavors to expose the common likeness between unlike things and expands the field of likeness by holding together unlikeness, exposing what is shared by things or aspects or ideas that are initially perceived as holding no explicit commonality at all—or at least not the commonality that metaphorization is meant to bring to light. Metaphysics is predicated on a basic "analogicity" pervading all things; it is the practice of the intellectual discernment of the thread of likeness running through "that which is."

Metaphorization is therefore the basic movement of metaphysics. Metaphysics is an ecstatic leap of intellectual energy, a setting outside of oneself, an expansion through a paradoxical remaining in the familiar while standing outside of it in the new. In this case all knowledge, through concepts—is metaphysical. Metaphysics names therefore the activity in general of naming, itemizing, and bringing out further the convergence of meaningfulnesses that fill the world of experience. And "metaphysics" as an intellectual discipline or practice is an acute instantiation of metaphysics in this broader sense: it asserts the coincidence of the meaningful connections made intellectually with those that exist in the world as a whole, of which the mind is only a part, the part that can think the whole and discern its basic intelligibility.

The phenomenon of *catáchrēsis*, the name for the fact of linguistic experience according to which metaphors are *necessary* in order properly to name the state of affairs, or in other words an "unconventional" use of a word or phrase in order to articulate something adequately, exemplifies the basic necessity of metaphorization in general.[12] The "back" or "legs" of a chair is an example of catachresis. I have to use elements of the experience I already have in order to name that which is (or was once) new. The "back" of the chair is where my back is rested, as the "seat" is what I "sit" on, and the "legs" hold up the chair like my legs do for me. Both kinds of "legs," animal and chair-like, extend from the "seat" on which rests the "back." Catachresis exposes to me the demand the world of experience places on my linguistic capacities and the solutions I endeavor to make through familiarization. Jüngel observes, therefore: "The relation of language to the world cannot be separated from the relation of language to the 'I,' which can only be addressed as a 'we.'"[13] My "humanness" and the "worldliness" of the world are mutually implicated with one another and are together brought into clarity through my acts of understanding that necessarily know one in light of the other.

Going a step farther Jüngel notes that, collectively, a host of the most basic intellectual realities derive from the catachretical transfer of terms from the familiar to the less familiar. He observes that the very conventional nature of signs actually testifies to this. There is a history to words. Many metaphysical concepts, in a process that demonstrates their origins, emerge through catachresis in "bodily

---

12. See Eberhard Jüngel, "Metaphorical Truth," *Theological Essays* (London: Bloomsbury, 2014), 16–70.
13. Ibid., 48.

experience of the world":[14] he mentions Latin terms, *animus* (wind), *sapiens* (tasting), *spiritus* (breath). And so I have to ask myself the startling question: if I do not experience the phenomenon of taste, can I properly conceptualize "wisdom"; if I did not breathe, feeling the subtle movement of expansion and contraction of my chest, would I conceptualize the "spirit" as humans traditionally have; if I had never experienced the force of the wind, its ability to pass invisibly from here to there while I only feel its effects, what would my concept of "mind" actually be? Because these metaphorizations are clearly "dead" for me does not mean that the concepts themselves are independent of them, any more than I myself in my personality am independent of the home within which I was raised, however much I might have overcome it, or differentiated myself from it.

I apply to intellectual domains the terms used through spatial and temporal relations of my basic embodied experience. I know the intellectual by reference to and through the material. Scientific knowledge of the universe, for example, discovered in physics, and the orientation in the world of practical life, are related in an analogous way to modes of knowledge contained in the world of practical life itself. The distance in miles from Melbourne to Paris cannot be contained meaningfully by my mind, even when I cross the distance by airplane. Nor can a millisecond be cognitively registered in my awareness, although every second of my life has one thousand of them. Both spatial and temporal magnitudes, either relatively great or relatively small, already exceed my normal, practical life orientation in which I live and move.[15] Concerning this fact, Frank concludes: "However distant and elevated its final ends and results, in the final analysis all scientific knowledge is nothing else but the expansion and improvement of the cognitive structure employed by practical orientation in life or even by every curious infant from familiarization with the surrounding world."[16]

---

14. Ibid. See also Owen Barfield, *Poetic Diction* (Middletown, CT: Wesleyan University Press, 1984).

15. Frank gives the example of rail travel over even relatively long distances.

16. Frank, *The Unknowable*, 14.

## Conceptual Formation

In metaphysical knowledge this commonality or unity with the life-world is all the more plain: metaphysics is predicated on the *adequacy* of the mind to the basic aspects of reality that are not plain, and even the mutual fittingness between the mind and therefore its products and the basic intelligible contours of reality itself, to which it responds. Typically this adequacy or mutual fittingness is reached through the process of the formation of concepts, "certain conceptually fixed elements . . . having for us the significance of something 'intrinsically understandable,'" that in themselves and as the basic power of the mind "make the rest of reality . . . i.e., the concealed part [the object of metaphysics] . . . also 'understandable,' 'knowable,' 'familiar.'"[17]

This basic order of the real has traditionally been understood (from Aquinas to Kant, in fact, and dominating even Heidegger) to be arranged in an interlaced twofold order that was never itself quite brought to clarity in the history of philosophy: on the one hand there was the inquiry into being in itself, *metaphysica generalis* (later called *ontologia*), and on the other hand the three-part inquiry into *metaphysica specialis*, into the basic domains of being, viz., God (*theologia rationalis*), the human subject (*psychologia rationalis*), and the world (*cosmologia rationalis*): being, God, the soul, the world, the basic concepts of metaphysics traditionally conceived. It would not be hard to demonstrate that the task of forging these concepts is a process that springs from and remains tied to the domain of ordinary life-experience, and in fact can be articulated as a process that I have been terming metaphorization. Frank takes two examples, and I will add a few more.

The concept of "substance," so important to classical medieval and modern metaphysics, "borrows" its intellectual force precisely from the domain of ordinary life-experience, the lifeworld: that of "base, support, or foundation." In fact, the concept is unintelligible apart

---

17. Ibid., xiv.

from the analogous application into the metaphysical domain of fundamental ideational structures from material experience. I call the wide, flat, bottom of a slender vase the "base"; it holds up the entire vase, keeping it from falling over and spilling its contents, or worse, shattering into bits; it is also the place where the vase touches the ground, the immovable support of the whole, the ground that allows things to stand on it. The fact that among the meanings of the word "substance" in everyday language there are included (1) the "essential dimension of something, by contrast to the changing or accidental properties added to it," and the various "quality" dimensions of the term, the "quality of being *solidly based* in fact" (for example, "his case against his wife for custody of the children has absolutely no substance"); (2) "the quality of being significant or possessing *intrinsic value*" (for example, "the philosopher has thus far written nothing of substance"); and (3) the "quality of being *solidly dependable*" (for example: "the captain of the team was praised for his substance"), would seem to exemplify this perspective.

Similarly for "God," which is the central, explanatory concept in *metaphysica specialis* and the point of its peculiar convergence with *metaphysica generalis* (for which the inquiry into being itself is explained by the First Cause that has no prior cause, which is identified therefore with "being" in itself, the "supreme being"): "the concept of God as the Creator and Lord of the world, is based on the idea . . . of artisan and builder as well as the idea of all-powerful lord and autocrat" as in, e.g., the *Timaeus* and Pseudo-Aristotle's *De mundo* on the one hand, and the Book of Proverbs and The Wisdom of Solomon on the other. This double origin of the conceptualization of God, as artisan and king, is a crucial point of overlap between Greco-Roman and the ancient Near Eastern civilizations. And subsequently the Platonic tradition of the wise king is closely aligned with the Egyptian and Hebrew traditions of the same. The king is most eminently divine and the most eminently wise in his rule: his wisdom is a share in the divine wisdom, to whom in heaven he is the earthly correlate.

Other fundamental metaphysical concepts like "ground" and "root" and "foundation" serve basic explanatory *functions* in metaphysical modes of thinking and gain their specific force *and* func-

Postscript

tion from the lifeworld itself: the concept "ground" lends an organic and perhaps even chthonic "air" to one's thought, whereas "foundation" provides a feeling of sobriety and a necessary starting point for a well-ordered, substantial, and lasting intellectual "edifice."

Whether in metaphysics or theology, as well as in other philosophical-conceptualist modes, the embodied spatio-temporal orientation of lived experience furnishes nodes of intelligibility that can be utilized to understand and express fundamental relations in the intelligible sphere: I *turn* my mind toward an issue of concern; I think from *within* certain presuppositions; and I *draw* conclusions *out of* them. The metaphorization of basic features of practical experience, like *separation* (ideas are far from or near to one another), *motion* (I ascend toward or descend into the most important topics), and *place* (through an imagined topology of importance), furnish in turn the basic intelligible features of rational thinking.[18] My body philosophizes, as Nietzsche said.

## Initial Sketch of Results

Hence "practical" knowledge is primary, and both scientific and metaphysical-conceptualist modes of knowledge lie in continuity with it; so much so that I can say that the latter two, like the poetic attitude that precedes them, are merely kinds of a more general attitude expressed within or built upon the original practical-biological mode. The foregoing suggests that all three modes of knowledge, or more fundamentally, attitudes of life-orientation, are all metaphorizations of that primary practical knowledge: knowing normally, even normatively, appears to be at root a process of *familiarization* in which the lesser-known is known by reference to the better-known, or, more adequately, the familiar.

The process of metaphorization "explains" metaphysics as a discipline, and, adequately developed, would demonstrate its necessary origin in the lifeworld. In establishing this recognition, I do not

18. See the first chapter of Sokolowski's *The God of Faith and Reason* for a discussion of the importance precisely of these spatial metaphorizations in theology.

265

deny the truthfulness of metaphysics itself—that is neither here nor there. I, for one, am optimistic about reason's capacity to grasp *appropriately* deep layers of reality itself, and to speak, in an adequate if merely relative way, about the all that is, the world, the soul, and their relation to the Source and End of all, about the nature or character of "being" and of "nothing," which help me categorize and get a handle on this experience of my mortality on the earth before God. This process also explains the "metaphysicality" of concepts within other domains such as science.

Therefore this transposition of significant ideational structures from embodied lived experience into separated intellectual domains, the process I here call "metaphorization," is of the essence of metaphysics and its (necessary) kind of thinking. Metaphysics is, like physical science, only an extension—a powerful one—of the original practical orientation of coping with concrete, lived reality that Frank calls "familiarization." The lesser-known is known through the better-known, whether the *notior* is the abstractions of mathematics, as for Galileo through contemporary physics, or the immediate self-knowledge of the subject, as for modern metaphysics from Suárez to Kant, Husserl, and Michel Henry. The important point is that both these fundamental, powerful traditions of physics and metaphysics make the passage from better known to lesser known by an extension of the Aristotelian principle of likeness—the lesser-known is *like*, and *necessarily* like, the better-known. The unknowable, even expanded to infinity is *potentially* knowable (or irrational and non-existent). Metaphysics ancient and modern makes this a principle of its thinking: and it is less an *a priori* decision to accept only as true that which is possibly like what is already known, than it is an extension of the original pragmatic attitude of familiarization.

## Habit of Being

If Aristotle made the passage from better known to lesser known the principle of science, the kind of knowing proper to philosophy, the medievals made analogy, the principle of "causal likeness"—*omne agens agit sibi simile*—the condition for their own holistic intellectual inquiry, *scientia.*[19] Husserl considers this principle—which I can now call that of *ontological familiarity*—a necessary presupposition for all rational inquiry whatsoever. For him it was the essence of the Greek genius to discover this principle; and it lies at the heart of philosophy as such and its renewal from within the present "crisis" of the European sciences. "If," he says therefore, "we take the intuitable world as a whole, in the flowing present in which it is straightforwardly there for us, it has even as a whole its 'habit,' i.e., that of continuing habitually as it has up to now. . . . However we may change the world in our imagination or represent to ourselves the future course of the world, unknown to us, in terms of its possibilities, 'as it might be,' we necessarily represent it according to the style in which we have, and up to now have had, the world."[20] The possibilities native to that which is are determined in advance for me from out of my experience of the world up to now; they are determined by the lifeworld. Hence, in this way, he says, "we can make into a subject of investigation the invariant general style which this intuitive world, in the flow of total experience, persistently maintains." This is the very work of phenomenological inquiry. "Precisely in this way," he continues, "we see that, universally, things and their occurrences do not arbitrarily appear and run their course but are bound *a priori* by this style, by the invariant form of the intuitable world. . . . *This is self-evident* a priori, *no matter how little is actually experienced of the particular causal dependencies, no matter how little of this is known from past experience or is prefigured about future experience.*"[21] Philosophy makes a principle of the infinite *a priori* unity of the basic intelligibility of the world of experience as experienced. And experienced in this way it is experienced rationally. This *a priori* is likewise the ground of the sciences: "This universal causal style of the intuitively given surrounding world makes possible hypotheses, inductions, predictions about the

19. See Philipp Rosemann, Omne agens agit sibi simile: *A "Repetition" of Scholastic Metaphysics* (Louvain: Leuven University Press, 1998).

20. *Crisis*, 31.

21. Ibid., italics mine.

unknowns of its present, its past, and its future."[22] Philosophy is, explicitly, "scientific knowledge of the world" and demands that the world be infinitely open as rational in this way, in its very essence. It learns this from the lifeworld.

## Philosophy as Science

"Philosophy," said Husserl, "in its ancient origins wanted to be 'science,' universal knowledge of the universe of what is; it wanted to be not vague and relative everyday knowledge—*doxa*—but rational knowledge—*episteme*."[23]

The "founders of the modern age" understood this vision and sought it through an absolute qualification of mathematics and natural science. Though they misunderstood the ground of all knowledge, the lifeworld, they sought, according to Husserl, however problematically, precisely the right goal. "Is there anything," he observes, "in the history of the world more worthy of philosophical wonder than the discovery of infinite totalities of truth, realizable in infinite progress either purely (in pure mathematics) or in approximations (in inductive natural science)?"[24] One may sincerely hope so. Regardless (for the moment), what is striking is what I want to call Husserl's "legitimization" of the modern age through this myth of "infinite tasks" (a simple variation on the Enlightenment mythology) bearing the destiny of humankind: "What is the universal science of this new idea but ... omniscience?" he asks. "This then is for philosophy truly a realizable, though infinitely distant goal. ... The world is in itself a rational systematic unity—this is thought to be a matter of apodictic insight—in which each and every singular detail must be rationally determined." This unfolding and evermore clearly elaborating rational determination is the work of all the various sciences organized according to methods appropriate to their particular domain of inquiry. He concludes: "This is the

22. Ibid.
23. Ibid., 65.
24. Ibid., 66.

path—infinite to be sure—to *omniscience.* Thus one lives in the happy certainty of a path leading forth from the near to the distant, from the more or less known into the unknown, as an infallible method of broadening knowledge, through which all the totality of what is will be known as it is 'in itself'—in an infinite progression."[25]

Yet there is a problem. This description (in §12 of *Crisis*) of "omniscience" characterizes the modern rationalism that is the source of the *very problem* to which he is responding. But the whole point of Husserl's text is lost if it is not seen with all seriousness that the aim, as scientific, and indeed, philosophical *par excellence,* is precisely one that he lauds and that he claims for his own phenomenology. Phenomenology, according to him, succeeds where modern rationalism fails because of its central discovery and its comprehensive thematization of the great, hidden mystery of the history of philosophy, the "correlation" of subjective and objective domains, which is the very *telos* of the history of philosophy and which finally makes possible the dream of "universal objective science" as an infinitely unfolding but sure rational exploration of the world in all its dimensions, even towards God, the Absolute, whose traces, as the origin and end of all that is, can be more and more adequately discerned in the "marvelous teleologies" found everywhere and always.

Husserl exemplifies Frank's observations regarding the basic "tendency" of "familiarization" that I have been explicating. Frank, however, proposes that this tendency is based on the double assumption that I find perfectly expressed in this last quotation from Husserl: everything that is, however surprising or astonishing, can be explained, that is, everything possible possesses a reason for its existence that can be grasped; the unknown and unfamiliar can be properly reduced to the known and familiar. This is, as Husserl said above, an *a priori* condition for philosophy's very being and the very being of the thing itself. The second assumption radicalizes the first, but only expresses it more fundamentally: even if it will never

25. Ibid., 65.

be known, could never practically be reached (say, because of its distance, being located on the other side of the universe), nevertheless "we have the right to recognize it as knowable and familiar in principle...."[26]

## The Question

S. L. Frank concludes his own presentation with a distillation of the entire orientation of familiarization from embodied intuition to metaphysical abstraction into the double-principle just summarized with the help of Husserl. I have brought him into direct encounter with Husserl, and in doing so have elaborated on aspects of his basic notions, but only partially, and in basic fidelity to what Frank provided in a few introductory pages to a little-known book. Though Frank does not mention the lifeworld or Husserl (or in fact any other philosopher but Kant in this introduction), it seems clear that his description of the orientation of familiarization, rooted in the biological-practical tasks of the sustenance and flourishing of life, is close to Husserl's notion of the lifeworld. The universalization of familiarization as a principle is the totality of what matters for Husserl, and *only* insofar as the lifeworld is rationally discerned as "pregiven" source brought to rational clarity, a threat to the absolute aspirations of rationality that is neutralized by means of the thematization of the primal phenomenon of correlation as the source of meaning in experience, and *as the foundation* of scientific knowledge. In light of this, I want to ask myself: is this *a priori* extension of necessity itself necessary? Perhaps it is possible, but is it true to things? Is it right? Are all things framed, exhaustively, by this *a priori* schema of knowability, or do they exceed this schema, relativizing it or qualifying it, *even if* it is necessary for my knowing? Are there other, higher, paradoxical modes of knowing that may be reached through this schema? Is it a launching point into some unfathomable higher intelligibilities that do not take the principle of familiarity as starting point and omniscience as end?

26. Frank, *The Unknowable*, xv.

Postscript

# The Unknowable

From beginning to end Frank describes this entire intellectual edifice within which Husserl self-consciously falls with three adjectives: "prosaic, rationalized, secularized."[27] However necessary and normative for the habits of thought, however explicable, however successful in its presuppositions and movement, this conception of the world is all the same. "This world is banal and unsanctified . . . without holiness. . . ."[28] In more adequate terms, this viewing of reality as "*the objective world,* as a unity of graspable, essentially 'transparent' contents and data which stands open to the cognitive gaze and admits logical definitions . . . is frozen for us into the *familiar world.*"[29] This is in fact only *one possible orientation.* According to Frank it is a *habit* that, precisely in its universalizing tendency, comes with a massive cost: the veiling over of "everything that . . . makes up our genuine essence."

Here another orientation begins to tower into view, one that can never fully disappear for me, or would only do so, I feel, at the very cost of my humanity. This orientation, for anyone (as they say) with a pulse, emerges for me even through the hard shell of practical orientation and even sometimes in overwhelming flashes: the experience of beauty, in art, nature, or the human face; events of the entrance into and exit of life from this world (birth and death), the sublime and terrible power of the natural world before which humanity is sometimes reduced to powerlessness (tsunamis, earthquakes, hurricanes, outbreaks of devastating viruses), social cataclysms that rise up and unfold with a force that transcends the collection of its actors, seizing and changing this world (wars, terrorist attacks, unrest, overthrowing of governments, revolutions), erotic love—that strange union of rapture and agony (all the way from, Frank observes, the most materially obscene animal lust imaginable to the "cult of the Madonna"), one's selfless sacrifice for another, religious experience, even the brute experience of myself

27. Ibid.
28. Ibid.
29. Ibid.

as, simply, unwittingly *alive*, feeling myself as living—all these are, says Frank, "astonishing mysteries," revelations of "terrifying and blissful depths of being." What unites all these aspects of reality? What can I *affirm* about the source of the intrinsic meaningfulness to these realities, about their proper depth of meaningfulness?

Evil and goodness are equally profound and disturbing revelations of the sacred quality of life, that which I possess without having, and that is taken away despite my passing possession of it. Life is the terrible, "material" holiness (everywhere tangible but nowhere graspable) of which I myself am not the author but over which I have some relative authority (in the plant and animal domains) and yet to the law of which I am invariably and unquestionably bound. Its source, for religious believers, is divinity itself, the presence of which, affectively speaking, makes alive and sustains in life, and the removal from which destroys, kills. Life, in other words, is sacred.

From the site of this awareness, God is felt or understood as ontologically holy, because God *is* Life itself. God freely and sovereignly gives and takes away life, without consulting me, and whether I believe or not. Death, with its absolute rule over me, only shoves in my face the sacredness of life, and when I stop wearing clothes—a sign of the sacredness of our bodies as the flesh of our life—when I stop fearing death, when I stop being in awe of the innocence and power of my children, when I cease to shudder before the rapturous beauty of the natural world, then I would no longer feel my own humanity, I would kill others at will, eat my own children to sustain myself. I would be an animal. And sometimes this happens in the world.

In all these cases of the revelation of the holy sacredness (for lack of a better word) of Life, observes Frank, "it appears that we stand before something unknowable." And if I *name* this unknowable phenomenon as the disclosure of life to me, felt as overtaking me in the breakthrough of an alterity that exposes me to myself in the experience of it, this does not make it any more knowable—in the practical, scientific, or metaphysical senses of the word—knowable in the world of the familiar, which conceives of the unknown in the image of the known. This is why, in Scripture, the revelation of

God's name only reveals that it is unknowable. If I determine that the regime of ontological familiarity is the regime of all that possibly is, then I can make the revelation of holiness opaque to myself. Or through a daring habituation to it, through *religion*, this dimension of reality as the unknowable, wholly other than the familiarized and familiarizing world, irreducible to it without losing the very phenomenality of the unknown itself, can be known according to what it gives; it can be *un-known*. I can habituate myself to the undying shock of the unknowability of existence, ever there in its vast silence on the other side of my *familiarized* objectivities. From within the habituated objective world this "unknowable" seems irrational, the content merely of a subjective state, a psychological by-product; but as Frank says, the universalization of the objectively rational is itself an irrational or pre-rational determination and cannot prove itself. The admission of only one kind of reality, known and existing according to a rational order to which the human intellect is exhaustively calibrated, is a supposition that is not self-grounding. It is a strategy for dealing with the transcendence of existence to the existent.

Skepticism regarding the transcendent that objectively transcends our objective grasp, the unknowable, is only a species of rationalism here. Frank's question becomes, in light of this recognition, (1) whether (or not) the "objective presence of the unknowable," encountered in our experience precisely as that which matters the most, can be found in the composition of reality itself, thereby justifying or liberating the weight of significance I sense in moments of embrace of my humanity, or (2) whether in rapture or terror, or, in some dimensions (the erotic, the religious), the strange unification of both of these in an intensification of both sides at once is the truth of things, or (3) whether the *a priori* reduction of determination of the real to the proto-familiar is in fact the truth of things, or (4) whether this latter orientation, *at least when made absolute*, is not in actuality a convenient fiction that neuters my humanity at the same time as it deforms the world—free, terrifying, rapturous—into an ugly image, a flattened-out conception of ourselves.

At the end of his introduction to *The Unknowable* Frank will finally come to describe this basic alternative to reductive rationalism I just sketched, and his personal election of the transcendent freedom of that which is before and beyond the familiar (yet without negating the latter but properly fitting it into a broader picture of reality) as the supremely valid *philosophical* viewpoint. The justification of this thesis will be the task of his book, an exploration of the possibility of the paradoxical knowability of the unknowable as "found" in the domains of the external world and in our own subjective interiority; and finally, the transcendent unity of these two in God (the unknowability of the world, of ourselves, and God as our common Source and End: the three parts of the book). Frank describes the orientation toward the unknowable in the following way: "the orientation for which reality is something greater and other than the combination of familiar, understandable contents and connections; the orientation for which reality has not only the significance of the environment in which we must 'orient' ourselves but also its own inner significance, which *essentially illuminates our life.*"[30]

The alternative between the two orientations would seem absolute, but it is not. Even the most radical ascetic, vowing to live continually *coram Deo*, must orient himself practically: he must relieve himself, must sleep, must eat, must protect himself from the elements, must flee from those who want his attention or even desire to kill him (if he lives in certain regions of the world…), etc. Ideally the former orientation can serve as a condition for the latter, but there is a danger, a radicality, a warning: the attention that "the unknowable" demands can never be adequately fulfilled; it is only ever greater than my mastery of it and I can at best attend to it at the edge of the practical, normative world, a world that I can never eclipse. Nevertheless, this world itself can become—and in fact must become—a mode of perception for the unknowable, a symbolic structuring that manifests the unknowable through natural appearing and human symbolical dwelling.[31]

30. Ibid., xxii.
31. This task, as I see it, is the central one of Jean-Yves Lacoste's *Experience and the Absolute.*

# Postscript

This "dwelling" before the Unknowable archetypically happens in religious ritual and its myths, as basic, framing stories that according to their own transcendent logic, irreducible to conceptual-logical expression, irreplaceably express the origin, the end, the meaning of the totality of what is and our access to this source. I order the world of my experience in such a way as to anticipate, and even to communicate, with this other more basic order that ultimately furnishes me with the key to comprehending the meaning of the order of my practical-life orientation.

The sacred myth of the Book of Genesis in the Judeo-Christian Scripture describes precisely the predicament between the two orientations I have just outlined. The myth expresses a mythic constant in my experience, a *pre*-pragmatic structure to my human world. The pre-lapsarian existence of humanity precedes the *agón* of survival, proposing within a myth that of which myth as such is the proposition: the order of rest, of the surplus of meaning of the human world beyond what is taken up by survival, is not only the site for the generation of mythic accounting of the totality, wherein the question of the meaning of human existence is generated and narrated. It is also the site, consequently, wherein the meaningfulness question is generated as that which the *agón* problematizes. The myth says that the *agón* is original, but not *ab origine*. The Genesis myth is an account of the mythic as such, arguing, further, for its primacy. It proposes itself as the myth about all myths, the myth, therefore, of myths. The myth teaches me, in its own terms, how the orientation to the unknowable, toward that which "essentially illuminates one's life," is problematized from the beginning, as a permanent feature of my existence. It also teaches that which I feel as true, and which myth as such demands to be true: that this permanent feature of my existence is not an essential feature. My struggle for existence, my toil for the sustenance and protection of my fragile existence in a harsh world, is a first word, it structures the totality of my existence, and it even fundamentally determines it. But the fact that I can understand this totality through primordial mythic framing (a mythicality I find already framing and organizing my practical life orientations), that I can symbolize my being through myth, and through the myth that says this framing is not written into the being of the world as a product of an *agón* generative of being, but is rather an *agón* generated by a constitutive action set over against the fundamental order of being itself, means that the order of total meaningfulness that myths implicitly argue for by their existence is explicitly argued for within the myth itself.

Toil and fruitless labor depending on uncertainties, generating anxiety, as well as the absolute reign of death, the all-pervasiveness of its icy touch, resisted with such utter feebleness—all this in the myth of Genesis. It describes the "absolutism" of the world of survival as sourced in human freedom and responsibility, originating from an original, permanent, and constitutive turning from an original freedom and wonder and innocence that now is only associated with childhood and moments of the invasion of the unknowable into the sphere of the bio-practical (whether by human hand, in religion and culture, for example, or through events out of human control) toward this practical, habituated survival orientation pervaded by fear, ignorance, confusion, and frustration that living in the world demands. The "curse" of Genesis is that I am required to toil and to suffer the absolutism of a naked existence that I must enclose, protect; I am alienated from the primal conditions that were my protective womb and home, and yet I feel the absence of and interior searching for that very paradise lost where the practical world is one, conducive to, manifest of, the ontological world wherein *agón* comes second, and peace, security, and fruitfulness is primary. I always try to build this world of truth for myself, but of course it necessarily cannot be realized (hence Genesis 6, the tower of Babel), since the practical order of survival cannot generate out of itself that from which it is originally separated: the order of an ontological blessedness.

A critique of Husserl by recourse to Frank, and the return to an original, "religious," myth (other than that of "European Enlightenment destined to realize the telos of rational humanity," the true humanity, *through* a scientific approach to the world that denies the validity and necessity of myth), leads to a fundamental revision of the account of the philosophical itself: the truth of that which is in itself—the goal indeed of philosophy—is no longer "scientific" in the reductive, rationalist sense of Husserl, explicitly, in the reduction to *a priori* possibilities contained in the "familiar." Instead, if it is indeed scientific (by which here I mean pertaining to and habituated from the principles sourced in the highest knowledge, the first knowledge) it is so in a deeper sense, the unknowable known precisely, objectively, in itself, as unknown. The ontic myth is, in other words, greater than the ontological conceptual apparatus that wants to bracket it; the use of an ontological apparatus of abstraction is simply a *technē*, a tool for the manipulation of that which cannot be manipulated, only told, witnessed to, acknowledged. Ancient and modern skepticism, as Husserl discussed in *Crisis*, denies the philosophical *epistēmē*, proposing that all is and can only be merely *doxa*, opinion—and this is the state of human being: absolute knowledge as an extension of practical mastery of the world of survival is a mistake.

*Epistēmē*, Husserl defined, once again, as "scientific knowledge of what is in-itself," that "assumes a rational in-itself and believes itself capable of attaining it." Whereas skepticism denied (and denies) this, proclaiming instead that "the world is not rationally knowable." Husserl understood the way beyond this stalemate by means of Cartesian *epochē*: "pressing forward," he says, "through the hell of an unsurpassable quasi-skeptical *epochē* toward the gates of the heaven of an absolutely rational philosophy, and of constructing the latter philosophically."[32] By contrast Frank, in a particularly Russian manner of rigorous thinking (following Pavel Florensky), sees skepticism towards the supremacy of intellectual *technē* as the means toward a higher awareness of the peculiar "objectivity" of the unknowable.

The upshot is that Frank, in the way I have described, deconstructs the absolute validity of *epistēmē*, placing it on a lower level, absolute even in its own sphere, but denying it the universality of ground which Husserl sought for it by proposing the multiplicity of orientations. He refuses the decision between *epistēmē* and *doxa*. In recognizing the primacy of *doxa*—or more precisely a deeper *doxa*, the *doxa* of mythicality, living before and beyond the technological reductions of the real to our concepts—over *epistēmē*, he does not

32. Husserl, *Crisis*, 76–77.

at the same time remain skeptical, but conceives the paradox of the knowability of the unknowable as the most meaningful truth, that is, the basic truth that characterizes human existence. This *doxa*, which I should have to qualify by the suffix *hyper-*, is fundamentally greater than *epistēmē*, perhaps analogous to the way aesthetic images are more densely intelligible than concepts and more saturated with the truth of things than the latter, however necessary these are toward the end of better understanding.

For Husserl the lifeworld matters only as the foundation for scientific knowledge; it is the ground and one must return to it in order to discern the conditions of the higher modes of knowing in the horizon of meanings that it has already given—these, for Husserl, can be scientifically known themselves through phenomenological analysis. I believe Frank shows us that Husserl's approach is only an account of the lifeworld *related to* one possible orientation to reality—one that is neither fundamental nor absolute, except relatively. These latter characteristics he reserves precisely for the zones of reality that we find always "unfamiliar," the most humanly meaningful ones that are impossible to reduce to the strict limitations of the conceptual. If touched through *doxa*, this rich domain is also saturated with meaning, and it would allow me thereby to give philosophical science its own infinite significance, but would at the same time take away from such rationalism the very mythicality it requires in order to propose itself as universal and absolute ground of truth. Primordially conceiving itself as such, the technological-scientific approach rests on what it rejects, nothing but the original mythic assertion of its own truth, and the desire to make that which is *my own possession*, not only no longer threatening, but actually the ultimate truth of things, a *means* to my own sustenance, potentially or actually.

## True Myths?

Through this confrontation of Husserl with S. L. Frank on the lifeworld I discover, or rediscover, in a pressing way the absolute frame of myth for reason.

Could we now, in drawing to a close, attempt a definition of myth? A definition is perhaps impossible, but let me sketch at least a few basic indications. Myths are those narratives that tell the story of the whole—whether as historical or metahistorical events or not (it does not matter if "science," as materialism, determines the myth out of itself or if "religion" does, and science finds a free place within it). Myths thereby give meaning to that which is said and done in the name of the myth, whether that name is uttered or not (and all is said and done in the name of some myth or other).

Myths communicate the ultimate frame of significance for the practical orientation of survival and for the theoretical articulation that stems from it, that is, for any thought or action for those who do the thinking or acting. There are civilizational myths, national myths, political and personal myths, theoretical myths, "religious" myths, secular myths, myths of reason, myths of science (as such, and of the various sciences themselves), philosophical myths, myths of origins and ends, myths of the totality, myths of parts vis-à-vis the totality, myths that assume other myths, and myths that frame the whole horizon of myths. There are myths of myths, hidden myths and unspoken myths, living myths and dead myths, myths rehabilitated, partially or fully, myths that destroy and myths that give life. All myths are human. Nietzsche's myth was the eternal return; Schopenhauer's myth was the transmigration of souls; the Enlightenment's myth was the mythification of reason in its emergence from myth (understood as proto-*lógos*, which thereby "mythified" itself) and the progress it promised through the courageous shedding of all prejudice; the German Idealist myth was the myth of the ego that produces itself and the world as the means of its own realization; Hegel's myth was of the God who becomes himself through the human recognition of itself as the moment of divine self-realization through this moment of recognition that defines philosophy itself; Husserl's myth was a variation of the Enlightenment vision: for him the *telos* of European culture, itself the *telos* of the Greek essence of humanity, is realized in his own phenomenology, which captured, like Percival's grail, the core mystery of human meaning, the mystery of the source of our meaningful world, "correlation"; Heidegger's myth concerned the epochs of Being spoken by a nameless voice, and the role of the thinker calling for the coming of a last god, for which, like John the Baptist, he can at best prepare; Hans

Jonas's ("hypothetical") myth was that of God placing the responsibility for his own happiness into the hands of man; Blumenberg's myth, indebted to biological and social accounts of evolution, was that of the "absolutism of reality" that created the necessity of myth when humanity's ancestors erected themselves on two legs, leaving the protecting shade of the primeval forests for the open savannah, thus creating a new situation that required the creative leap toward myth as the necessary, perpetual foundation for our "humanity" itself; Bultmann's myth involved, among other features, the greatness of the (invisibly mythic) myth of the modern scientific "worldview" and the perennial "contemporaneity" of the primitive Gospel; Aristotle's myth was of the Big and Pure Philosopher with the cosmos as a Body; the Gnostic myth would take too long to tell, but involved the fallen spark of divinity searching in this dark world for its lost origin; the myth of Second Temple Judaism, or at least a significant myth told in that place in that era, involved the impending return of the God of Israel to Zion and the subsequent elevation of the Nation over all others through the iron, just rule of the Messiah, through whom God's "justification" would be accomplished, his fulfillment of the ancient promises; the myth of Paul of Tarsus, a variation of this last kind (given here with *some* of its peculiar, knotty detail) saw the Creator's (still unfolding) accomplishment of Israel's glorification by means of the Crucified Messiah (and the suffering of his *ekklesia*) through whom God returned to Zion in person and dealt in a final way with Israel's complicity with the rebellion of the nations, and simultaneously in his death and resurrection gives Israel ("first") and through her, the nations, a new and final orientation towards the Last Judgment when all will stand before this God-in-Person to give an account before the One whose purposes for the creation will finally, fully be accomplished, namely, a "new," or rather "renewed" creation destined for liberation from decay, from death and suffering and the primordial *agón*, and an eternal reign of the Just One through the accomplishment of perfect charity...[33]

---

33. See Hans Blumenberg, *Work on Myth*, especially II.4, on the "final myth," meant to accomplish the impossible end of myth itself, as well as for a discussion of a number of these myths itemized here.

## Postscript

I could not even attempt to give an account of the myths of modern and contemporary Rabbinic Judaisms, or those of the various and ever-multiplying kinds of Christianity on the globe—to say nothing of other religions, of Islam(s), of Hinduism(s), and so on and so on: all these are inflected again and again in extraordinarily rich ways by figures thinking within and across this kaleidoscope of traditions, cultures, civilizations. Myths do not sit still, and although, for example, I myself am utterly captivated by one—so much so that I feel myself physically straining with elation in the center of my chest at the moment of writing this sentence—it only means that I am a believer of one kind or another, and that it is for this myth that I live. It means that I recognize the myth, to the final truthfulness of which—a belief that seems constitutively previous to any intention on my part and a truth beyond any ultimate understanding of my own—I find myself committed, a commitment that I desire to embrace in a manner concomitant with what the myth says, a myth for which I burn within, and in which I hope. This burning and this hope means only, I think, that I am human and that I have here successfully reached a point where I see an essential aspect of my humanity with startling clarity.

"The beginning and end," said Blumenberg, "are symmetrical ... in that they [equally] escape demonstrable intelligibility."[34] Myth is the all-framing narrative that cannot be demonstrated but lends the feeling, the air, of definitive meaning to all thought and action within it. Myth is necessary, ubiquitous, and permanent, even if myths change. Rationality demands myth, and it always serves the justification of some myth or other. That is myth which "while not providing answers to questions, makes it seem as though there is nothing else (but it itself) to talk about."[35] And, let me add that all talk, consequently, is most fundamentally about nothing but myth, in the end. Myths may or may not be true; they may grasp greater or lesser dimensions of the truth of things; this or that myth (who knows) may or may not be the greatest path of encounter with

34. Ibid., 270.
35. Ibid., 288.

the truth of that which is; but in any case myths *are*, and they are the most intelligibly saturated modes of our knowing; we live and move and breath in myths. The myth gives us God and ourselves, gives us the world and our reason; myths give us each other. Myths give us, place our awareness in the presence of, the unknowable dimension.

## The End

Only the End will decide the truth for us, an End that we can only believe to be more than the end, an End which we all face individually, passing through death, and collectively at some unfathomable point of completeness, an End that determines all. Judgment, says myth, is God's (alone) and for those with whom he will share it in the End—"to sit at my right or left hand [in my kingdom]," said Jesus of Nazareth, "is not for me to grant. These places belong to those for whom they have been prepared by my Father." *Therefore do not*, he continued, exercise lordship "like the rulers of the Gentiles" but instead "serve" and "be a slave." In that way you will be "great" under my reign. Your self-abandonment to others will manifest on the Day of my reign as the true lordship it is. Serve, then, "just as the Son of Man did not come to be served, but to serve, and to give his life as a ransom for many."[36]

What can *I* say, debtor to the path that Jesus lived, the myth he gives me to live? The reign that is coming in excess of death and therefore in excess of world and even (lastly) of myth is the real and lasting reign, says a *doxa*, and *even now*, it places me in the presence of the truest truth, although muffled harshly by the forms of truth that order the world that I know, a world of survival, of success through *technē*, of domination and control. Nevertheless that myth is, in the form of this *doxa*, the measure of life, of thought and action, an apocalypse of wisdom for believers in the last judgment he proclaimed and served.

36. See Matt 20:28.

## FRAGMENT B
## On Plato's Cave and the Caves of Christ

"To this roofed cave we have come."
—Empedocles [B 120]

"Happy is he who has gained the wealth of divine thoughts,
wretched is he whose belief about the gods is dark."
—Empedocles [B 132]

## Introduction to an Exegetical Fragment

What is commonly called "Plato's allegory of the cave," I intend to
come to understand, or rather, come to an understanding not only
"about" it, but, more importantly "through" it: I intend to come to
understand something of what the "allegory of the cave" means for
me, a living human being—that is, what it means philosophically
and what it means as philosophy. "Philosophically" means: what
does the allegory teach? "As philosophy" means: what does it mean
to philosophize this way? And hence a subsequent question: what
does it mean for philosophy that philosophy, at one of its major
early moments, is, or was, practiced in *this* way?

## Image and Allegory

In the first place I must ask: what is this story? Is it indeed an "allegory"? And what do I mean by that term? Plato, of course, calls it an
"image," which appears to be something like a thought experiment,
a necessary means toward the grasping of something that cannot be
grasped except precisely through this image.[37] Plato says the same
thing about the "image" of the "dividing line" at the end of Book VI,
with which the present "image" of the cave is explicitly correlated.[38]

37. *Republic*, 517b.
38. Ibid., 509a.

By "allegory" is commonly meant a story that expresses something else, a properly conceptual truth, by other—lesser—means,
which, once grasped, exhaust the meaning of the story, which was,
all along, merely a shell. This common understanding of allegory
refers indeed back to the Greek term—*allēgoria*, speaking otherwise,
from *állos* ("other") and *agoria* ("speaking"). From this perspective
the parables of Jesus of Nazareth are allegories. But the stories Jesus
told about the kingdom, the last judgment, about himself, about
Rome, about the Temple, about the future..., these stories are not
merely allegories in the common sense. Once the message of Jesus is
understood, once the disciple comes to an understanding of what
Jesus is telling him in a veiled way, the disciple cannot disregard the
narrative itself, as if it were a useless husk. Jesus's parables refer to
aspects of a higher truth by reference to the things of ordinary experience: by higher truth I do not mean a mere spiritual lesson in garb
that helps uneducated people grasp it (in this case the parable *would*
be a mere allegory), but, rather as truths, words about realities that
are impinging on this world itself in and through the person of
Jesus: the "kingdom of God" is here, now, pressing into the world of
human experience (ruled by political, economic, and social powers
set explicitly against Jesus and his mission) and the parable itself
provides the hermeneutic for understanding how the kingdom is
here, what it means, and how to enter it. Further, the parable itself is
an event of the inbreaking of that very kingdom precisely in the very
peculiar, "hidden" manner in which it is "breaking in." It is worth
hoping that the "allegory of the cave," if not on par with the parables
of Jesus, is at least more than a mere allegory. Perhaps it is a matter
of truth, as far as Plato is an authority on the truth, on philosophical
truth (on the question of what matters most to my humanity), and
it therefore is a matter of an event of some truth or other, and
through it, the truth itself. The enterprise of philosophy, at least for
Plato, in fact depends on this possibility.

## Heidegger

In his opening lecture of *Vom Wesen der Wahrheit*, the first half of
which is a patient philosophical exegesis of this didactic story of the

Postscript

cave, Heidegger uses two terms to name this story under our examination, "allegory" and "sense-image" (*Sinn-Bild*), and he uses them interchangeably to express what Plato means (according to him; at least this is implied for it is not explicitly stated) by calling this story an image.[39] According to Heidegger what is crucial about this story in Book VII of Plato's *Politeia* is the specific function it enacts, namely, "to provide a hint or clue." This means, on the one hand, that the "image" is not meant simply to stand for itself, as if there is nothing to be understood through it. Like the parables of Jesus (at least in this way) the *Sinn-Bild* of Plato performs the work of "indication": it tells us "*that* something is to be *understood*," specifically by "providing a *clue* as to *what* this is." This activity of "hinting," of offering a "clue," Heidegger explicates further: "The image provides a hint—it leads into the intelligible, into the region of intelligibility . . . into a *sense*. . . ." The passage towards meaning, towards understanding that which is indicated, that to which one is directed by it requires—Heidegger is adamant—*the story itself*: one passes to understanding not from the story, but *in* and *through* it. The *Sinn* requires the *Sinn-Bild*, without which it is merely a story, something to entertain, a tool for passing the time.

Yet the *Sinn-Bild* is not merely a story but is *philosophical*; it is not told for its own sake, like entertainment. It is a meaning-bearing image *because* it is and *as* it is a sense-bearing image, an image as such. And as an *image* it concerns the intelligible, which it symbolizes, and is told for the sake of that something else that it "indicates" or suggests or invokes, namely, understanding. And as a *meaning-*bearing image, the work of understanding it means interpreting it philosophically. And already here, Heidegger provides the critical clarity by which any proper understanding of this story stands or falls: "*what* is to be understood is not a sense, but rather an *occurrence*." As philosophical, this story is an *event*; I must think what it gives to be thought on its own terms. What are these terms?

39. For the following I quote from the English edition, *The Essence of the Truth*, trans. Ted Sadler (London: Continuum, 2002), 13, unless otherwise noted.

## The Terms

If it is the case, says Heidegger, that the *Sinn-Bild* is simply the "pro-vision of a clue through something which is presented sensuously," then this simplicity is deceptive. I could be tempted to think that the "allegory of the cave" is in fact a *mere* allegory, and something which, therefore, I do not have to take seriously in itself, on the terms that it proposes to be understood. This understanding of the story would imply that the domain of intelligibility is itself reduc-ible to the abstractions of my mind, that the concepts I can forge through my own power are precisely adequate to that which is. Heidegger's entire exegesis of this story is intended to deconstruct precisely this conception of reason, of truth, and hence of human being and of being itself. And Heidegger understands Plato to be ambivalent on this very point. For him Plato is the critical point of an original obfuscation, the veiling-over of the original experience of the truth as "unhiddenness" and its transformation into mere "correctness." And Plato's ambivalence about the "image" that he himself presents, and, more broadly, about myths and poetry more generally that he employs in his philosophy and which he appropri-ates but always critically, respectively illustrate precisely this fact in the history of philosophy, which is, for Heidegger, the story of an unfolding inadequacy to an original "philosophical" experience: the truth as *a-lētheia*.

Heidegger says therefore at the beginning of his study: "Such a clue *leads* us to what simple description, be it ever so accurate and rigorous, can never grasp. There is thus an inner necessity to the fact that when Plato wants to say something fundamental and essential to his philosophy, he always speaks in an allegory and places us before a sensory image." Why does Plato do this? The answer is that *he has to*. His philosophical fidelity to the transcen-dent and unqualified truth *requires* him to make recourse to image and to story. Heidegger does not say this but I want to acknowledge here that precisely this is something like a sacred paradox and something that lives at the heart of Plato's philosophy.

The necessity, says Heidegger, is not a matter of incertitude on Plato's part. On the contrary, it is precisely a matter of a certitude, though of a specific kind: "On the contrary," he says, "[Plato] is *quite sure* that [what he is speaking of in the story] cannot be described or proved." And here I reach, unless I am mistaken—what I can call, following Jean-Luc Marion, a "negative certitude"— something basic to "all genuine philosophy" ("genuine philosophy," which is, I think, the central concern of Heidegger himself). Heidegger draws the unavoidable conclusion:

> In all genuine philosophy there is something in the face of which all description and proof, however brilliantly scientific, fails and sinks down into empty business. This fact alone, that Plato speaks of *aletheia* in an allegory, gives us the crucial clue as to where we must search, and where we must stand, if we want to come closer to the essence of the truth.

Philosophy must understand what it itself is in order to philosophize, but it cannot understand what it itself is through the medium of its primary language, conceptuality. In the case of the question of the "essence of the truth," which Heidegger finds to be the central matter indicated by the allegory of the cave, this self-understanding takes on a fundamental form of being serious about the radical limitations of one's knowing, limitations that, when embraced, are the means by which I would most deeply enter the truth itself. The allegory teaches this very truth about the essence of philosophy, namely, that the "indescribable and unprovable something" that philosophy seeks in no other way but through the allegory itself, is "what the whole effort of philosophy is about."

## Image of Philosophy

I have already found myself transcending (but not yet explicitly) Heidegger's main interpretation of the allegory—as a story giving access to the essence of the truth as *alētheia*. Rather I find that, before *that* (and whether that conception of the truth—for and against Plato—is what the *Sinn-Bild* hints at or not is not my concern, for it now appears secondary) the story is first about the meaning of the philosophical itself. A question immediately arises. Is the "allegory of the cave" a—for lack of a better term—*parable* about the meaning of philosophy, and, more specifically, about the relevance, even centrality, of allegory, image, story, and even myth to philosophy itself, a truth that can only be reached and articulated pre-conceptually?

This is the hint I would like to make, and I can only see how far I get through the interpretation of the "image" itself. What is called for, Heidegger will say later in his commentary, in any approach that aspires to be truly "touched by what is essential" and hence worthy of philosophy, is first "to give ourselves wholly over to the text," in order to be properly "moved by the power of Plato's presentation" itself, for the manner of presenting is, as far as philosophy is concerned, "not at all incidental, not at all an aesthetic addition," but the presentation of a philosophical truth, and through it, the saying of the "unsayable" truth of the matter itself.[40]

## Entering the Cave

Every philosopher is familiar with the "allegory of the cave." In order to enter into it in the way that Heidegger indicated I need to make it as unfamiliar as I can.

Before attempting an exegetical interpretation of the story, let me make my entrance by reflecting on Glaucon's reaction to Socrates's recounting of the allegory. His first reaction is "how strange!": *átopon . . . légeis eikóna*—"a strange image you are describing." The telling of this story is *átopon*; not only is its *lógos*, or intelligibility, peculiar or odd, but it, literally, has *á-topos*, "no place." The story does not fit in the ordinary state of things; it does not seem to tell me anything about the truth of things that I experience; it does not seem to speak to my human situation at all. Heidegger will rightly observe that Glaucon's first observation as the story gets underway is meant to express the reaction out of the midst of the "everyday" normal understanding of humanity, that the allegory is itself "something extraordinary . . . peculiar and removed from anything everyday and normal."[41] And yet, Socrates's response is crushing: "They

40. Ibid., 17.
41. Ibid., 28.

[the prisoners of the cave] are like us." Socrates asserts nothing less than that the image is a real description of my "normal" human state, that it is a presentation of the truth about me and my situation in the world. It is not strange or foreign at all, except insofar as my everyday situation is precisely strange and foreign. "Socrates assures us," concludes Heidegger, "that the allegory depicts precisely the everyday situation of man, who, insofar as he does not possess any standard other than this everydayness, cannot see its strangeness."[42] Glaucon says the story does not seem to be about anything relevant; Socrates says it speaks the very truth about us.

Here I have, with Glaucon's first interpretation as the story unfolds, a crucial paradox about the nature of the "image" in general. For Glaucon sees the "strangeness" of the story vis-à-vis the everyday, from out of an unreflective self-conception of humanity, wholly secure in his experience. But precisely because he looks from out of his ordinary everydayness, Glaucon does not see the strangeness of what the story is saying, namely, that the ordinary world of human experience, normally presupposed and passed over without reflection, *is itself the strange world* spoken of by the story. The paradox is deepened when I see that the narrative itself—far removed from ordinary description of the world that is seen, felt, remembered, anticipated, etc.—is the clearest, truest description of the world as it really is in itself. The world is strange; the "image," in its strangeness, gives me what can be given in no other way.

## Image

What is an "image" for Plato? The answer is everything of human experience: the world of experience in its totality and in all of its features that contribute to its wholeness is an image. There are "correspondences" between this world here and that world there, the world of the forms, between earth and heaven, the world of bodies, which changes and moves, and the world of ideas, which is eternal. The soul belongs to that world and the body belongs to this world, for the soul is divine, has kinship with the gods, and the body is at

42. Ibid.

best, and at root, an image of the soul. A beautiful myth, recounting the origin and end. Philosophy is the practice of death, that is, separation of the soul from the body, the ascetical intellectual work of passing from the real to the more real, from image to reality, from existence to its source.

Philosophy is the practice of what is essential to humanity, in order to habituate oneself to it, to be more fully conformed to what is true about me. The metaphysical fact of "correspondence" means that the one who knows the truth about the gods, about the other world, that it is dominated by goodness, the source of justice, truth—in other words that *that* world ought not to be conceived in the image of this world, as the traditional poets Homer and Hesiod have proposed, but rather that *this* world is the image or shadow of that world of realities: what is best in this world, relative perfection, beauty, autonomy, mathematical precision, approximates best to that world above—the person perceiving this, committed to it, can properly understand and live rightly, most divinely, here below, living here as if already, ahead of death, a citizen of that world, and hence appearing strange.

The basic metaphysical fact of correspondence that is a manner of exposing the intelligible structure of the "philosophical" myth of origin and end (which for Plato, recall, is simply the truth behind the core myths of Greece, cleansed of all the merely human accretions collected over time) means, strangely, that I have to tell myths in order to understand that which is, namely, the higher world and my relation to it from within the domain of shadows that owns nothing of itself and that is nothing in itself. Philosophy is simply an explication of *the myth*. My highest reasoning works from and remains ever within the broader grasp of the mythic pre-understanding. The meaning-bearing image awakens my understanding of the mythic ground of philosophical reason. This I consider to be the "indication" of the philosophical teaching of the cave-image, which itself cannot be grasped in propositional understanding and cannot be approached out of a desire to reduce it to such. The story is a "showing" of the truth of myth and an enactment of the passage from philosophy back into the new, or rather, renewed, mythography with which Plato wants to replace the old mythography of the poets.

The center of the story, and my interpretation, is the "sun of the Good." Plato only gives a "negative" definition of the Good itself, the source and goal of philosophy—the only "object" worthy of philosophical reflection, that which all philosophy is always about. The "Good" is unseeable, like the sun itself for physical eyes, and yet the goal of philosophy is precisely to look at the Good itself and to see it "clearly." But one cannot see directly that *by which* one sees: the sun is sight itself, and the Good is intellectual vision itself. One does not see the eye by which one sees. The fundamental impossibility of realizing the goal of philosophy is precisely the point where philosophy turns over into myth. This point is philosophy's perpetual center.

## Image of Philosophy's Myth

The story of the cave is not a myth *per se*—nowhere does Plato say this. It is an image, a story about the practice of philosophy, about the necessity of eschatological myth at the center of philosophy, which the philosopher enacts through the practice of philosophy ahead of death. Plato's is in other words akin to what is called an "inaugurated eschatology" in Christian theology: it is an enactment of that which is to come, ahead of the end that is coming, viz., death and the meting out of justice. It is the philosopher, whose knowledge and practice loosens the cords of desire that attach the soul to the body and its world, who may escape the cycle of reincarnation ruled by death.

Though not a myth in itself, the story of the cave is, as Blumenberg says, "grounded in the mythic tradition and authorized by that tradition."[43] Blumenberg goes so far as to name the story a "myth," a denotation that is true enough in his own philosophical lexicon: myth is the first and primordial response to the brute fact of reality, an original arranging of the basic furniture of experience into a livable, meaningful world. In the case of the cave story of Plato this "arranging" is a matter of authoritatively summarizing and tran-

---

43. Hans Blumenberg, *Paradigms for a Metaphorology*, trans. Robert Savage (Ithaca, NY: Cornell University Press, 2016), 79.

scending the traditional authorities of culture in a time of intellectual crisis brought on by the new mysticism of the philosophers (to speak like Eric Voegelin),[44] a turning point from which there was no return, once introduced. Myth therefore "explicates a particular feeling about the world" that can be communicated in no other way.[45] For Blumenberg, faithful to the modern self-conception that he is committed to legitimating, the "myth of the cave" is situated in the "twilight zone" between *mûthos* and *lógos*. As he puts it: "The formal ground plan of the cave myth, upon which an escape route of human self-fulfillment, indeed self-transcendence, has been overlaid, is thus rooted in the primeval mythic vision while at the same time having the function of an absolute metaphor."[46] Myth is not a "preliminary form" of *lógos*, but in actuality, for Blumenberg, the necessary background for every *lógos* as it springs from metaphors rooted in ordinary experience and hardens into concepts, becoming "metaphysics" when these concepts are conceived as naming the real in itself. Myth is "absolute metaphor" in Blumenberg's terminology because it is the first springing forth of human intellectual prowess in its attempt to manage the absolute character of existence. Myth, as a primary "symbolic form," lives in every culture and is that primary order which makes truth "true"—that is, functionally believable—in that world.

Much can be gained from listening to Blumenberg regarding the permanence and perenniality of myth, the irreducibility of myth to reason, even the grounding of the story in the primordial mythic vision of Greece (wherein the world was imagined, as in the Ancient Near East, as a giant cave, with the dome of the sky set on pillars planted into the earth), and therefore philosophy's new, critical reception of this tradition. Like Heidegger, Blumenberg understands the cave story as the communication of a "primordial event." It is the setting for the defining passage for humanity from subterranean darkness to elemental light, of—expressed in "religious" terms—salvation, the realization of the meaning of humanity. Like Heidegger,

---

44. See "Plato's Egyptian Myth," *Journal of Politics* 9.3 (1947), 307–24.
45. Blumenberg, *Paradigms*, 80.
46. Ibid., 79.

Blumenberg recognizes the primordiality and irreducibility of myth; for him likewise the cave-image cannot be called an allegory in the modern sense of the word, for the truth that it communicates cannot be grasped if the image is discarded. And further, the mythic "background" makes possible the "foregrounding" activity, when it appears for humanity, of theoretical intelligence and its culture.

## Primordiality

A few observations are finally necessary about the primordial mythic vision, determinative of Greek culture, into which Plato enters and wants to think anew in the story. Plotinus, and Porphyry following him (*De antro nympharum* 8), refers to the caves of Plato and of Empedocles in the same breath. Plotinus: "In the Cavern of Plato and the Cave of Empedocles, I discern the universe, where the breaking of the fetters and the ascent from the depths are figures of the wayfaring toward the Intellectual realm." Plotinus sees all previous philosophy as greater or lesser expressions of the mystical experience of the soul, escape from the body, and concert with the divinity, which is the sole task of philosophical practice. Heraclitus, Empedocles, and especially Plato have expressed this very task that is humanly experienced "many times" (IV,8,1): "lifted out of the body into myself . . . beholding a marvelous beauty . . . enacting the noblest life, acquiring identity with the divine. . . ." But this is not all they have expressed, for there is the return: "yet there comes the moment of descent from intellection to reasoning." Ascent and descent are the two moments of the philosophical experience. And philosophical experience enacts *in nuce* the metaphysical experience of the soul in its arising and falling back into matter that determines the repeating lifecycle of the soul in its many "lives." Philosophical practice repeats over and over again therefore the very over and over again of the soul's rising and falling within the cosmic cycles, of which it is a part. Enacting this, philosophy becomes the path of escape from this cycle of reincarnation toward permanent return to the divinity that is the soul's own truest nature in a union that transcends the intra-cosmic order of difference. Philosophy practices death, and sees the paradox that the "cave of the world" in which one lives and to which one is bound is the real death, and that physical death is the path of liberation, if the soul can free itself, through philosophical *ascēsis*, from the strong ties that bind it to the material domain. "Everywhere," he continues, Plato teaches therefore that the "commerce of the soul with the body" is an "enchainment, an entombment." In other words Plato "upholds the teachings of the Mysteries that the soul is here a prisoner" (IV,8,1). The mystery religions and Plato teach the same universal truth. Likewise the Cave of Empedocles and Plato name the same universe as a death tomb in which we can awake, by, as it were, dying to this world of material attraction and living in the midst of this tomb with eyes already awoken to the invisible world of the one divine life. The mystery religions indeed teach this truth, but it is philosophy that can accomplish this escape from death they themselves promise.

Regardless of the validity of Porphyry's Neoplatonic "allegorical" interpretation of Empedocles' cave,[47] drawing it together with Plato's cave story has determined our understanding of it until today. For Empedocles himself, it seems, the cave is the site of a passage through a new womb into which one can descend and be reborn, after passing through it into the underworld. The philosopher-magus descends into the cave, the womb of the earth, and comes back enlightened. Evidently, Empedocles performed this, quite literally, by physically entering a cave and "incubating," experiencing the sleep of death and passage into the other world at the depths of the earth and then experiencing the rebirth of a return, entering the light of day with new magic powers.[48] The innovation of Plato is to make the cave myth that he inherited as an heir to the Pythagorean-Empedoclean tradition(s) itself a metaphor for our present circumstances, as the cosmological myth of the *Phaedo* demonstrates with its elaborate geography of the underworld of rivers dominated by a central fire.[49] The "cave" of Hades into which

---

47. See Peter Kingsley's contesting of this traditional reading in *Ancient Philosophy, Mystery, Magic* (Oxford: Oxford University Press, 1995).

48. See, for a starting point, Kingsley's discussion of the controversial Diels fragment 111 in ch. 15, 217–32.

49. Ibid., 71–132 and Blumenberg, *Paradigms*, 79.

our souls descend at death is a symbol of this world in which we presently live.

The concern of the Phaedo myth is "eschatological," as I noted above: it is about the fate of the soul, the salvation of which can be accomplished through philosophy. Here as everywhere Plato recasts the mythic landscape. The philosopher tells *new* myths, or better, he *renews* the mythic inheritance through philosophical insight, insight into the truth of the myth, which is insight about what it means to live—what better word is there—truly "religiously." To understand the cave story I must allow myself to put behind me the fruitless and banal and wholly obfuscatory "debate" about *mûthos* versus *lógos* in Plato. The fact is that *mûthos* and *lógos* are equally "philosophical" precisely *for the one who is truly a philosopher* in Plato's sense. They are different modes of access to the truth, and *mûthos* precedes and remains transcendent to the reach of dialectical clarity (although at the far end of dialectical clarity, Plato thinks, one can penetrate properly into the mythic truth, truly experiencing those realities of which the myths speak). Philosophical "perception" allows the vision of myth more scope. As I ready myself to study the cave of Plato, I give the last word to Kingsley, since he summarizes what seems to me to be the sanest point of view in a few words: "Certainly [Plato] was interested at a theoretical level in distinguishing between *mythos* and *logos*; between 'myth' as the conveyer of ideas that are beyond logical demonstration, and the positive certainty arrived at by reasoned argument. Even here, however, the matter is complicated by Plato's refusal to draw a clear line between *mythos* and *logos*, and by his repeated insistence that what to a superficial person is just a 'myth' may have all the decisive attributes of a *logos* for someone whose perception runs deeper."[50] If the task of philosophy requires fidelity to the human experience,

---

50. Ibid., 80. For (stage 1) the theoretical distinction between *mûthos* and *lógos*, see *Protagoras* 324d; for (stage 2) the basic complication of the distinction resulting from the fact that myth reaches truth beyond dialectic, see *Gorgias* 523a, *Timaeus* 40d; for (stage 3) the programmatic ambiguity of *mûthoi* as *lógoi*, see *Republic* 376d, 501e, *Phaedrus* 237a, 245c.

including the peculiar vaguenesses that are essential to it, then the traditional consensus about Plato is indeed quite correct. He is a remarkable philosopher.

## An Exegetical Fragment for The Cave, *Politeia* VII

I will proceed in exegetical style with the text, commenting on the story in English translation, not with the end of giving a complete ("exhaustive") or even adequate commentary on the text, but rather with my question in mind: What does the story indicate? What is it that the story, precisely in its explicit form, says that cannot be said in any other way? Commentary is therefore an exploration of the indication of the image—it is philosophical because it understands precisely where it stands in relation to the text, in a secondary place. We are attempting to understand the given on its own terms. Commentary is also, however, thought thinking the best it can *through* the text, toward that which the story, as an intellectual correspondence, displays—the best Plato could himself perform under the conditions given to him. And these are conditions that I fundamentally share with him as a worldly being.

First, let me frame the image in its immediate context. Book VII begins with the reason for the presentation of the image: "Next, I said, compare the effect of education and of the lack of it on our nature to an experience like this: Imagine. . . ." It follows directly from what Socrates said above it and is contained within the same speech. It is the presentation of an "experience" entered into by the imagination, made for the sake of a comparison. The story "corresponds" in other words with the "effect of education and the lack of it" on the soul. Education, affiliation with a teacher, a school, a manner of life, a tradition, is my initiation into the truth. What is this truth?

Following the presentation of the image there is an explanation, much like Christ's explanation for his disciples of the paradigmatic parable of the thrower of the seed. "This whole image," Socrates explains to Glaucon, "must be fitted together with what we said before." And this explanation is concluded again with a reference to "the image described before" the present one. The image of the cave is therefore a corollary explanation of the previous image, and it accomplishes its task only "if indeed things fit the image I described before." In answer to the question just posed, then, the truth of the cave-image is also that which is presented in the previous image, that of the dividing line. Before returning there, let me provide Socrates's explanation of the story, which is the enactment of "fitting it together" with the previous image and its explanation. For by this enactment, Socrates says, is the proposed "fitting together" of that image with the way things are itself enacted! Hence the supplementary character of the second image is disclosed to be in actuality a deepening of the first image, a passage into and through that which it initially gives. The layering of image on top of image enacts therefore the most essential activity of philosophy: one passes from image to explanation, and the explanation only refers to the image, which already contains that which the explanation simply repeats in a more abstract mode, aiding the understanding of *that which the image gives*. The image makes perceptible that which rational explanation only further explores: although the image is the lowest form of truth, corresponding to the bottommost state of the soul and the emptiest form of reality, it is only through it that the higher modes of truth can be reached; it corresponds to the truth in its entirety as a repetition of it. The first image attempts to present the basic conditions of the soul and their correspondence with the fourfold ordered truth of reality. The second presents the activity of educating the soul—philosophical *paideia*—within this reality made perceivable by the first image, the "turning a soul from a day that is a kind of night to the true day—the ascent to what is, which we say is true philosophy," as Socrates will say later (521c). What is the first image?

Before answering that question I still have to give Socrates's explanation of the second image. "The visible realm," he says "should be likened to the prison dwelling, and the light of the fire inside it to the power of the sun. And if you interpret the upward journey and the study of things above [of the liberated cave dweller] as the upward journey of the soul to the intelligible realm, you will grasp what I hope to convey." The entire story of the cave is an image of reality itself, like that of the first image, only a deeper entering into it (as I discovered above). Here I can add that education makes that first image meaningful and is the means to the discovery of it itself and of its significance, namely, the experience of how it corresponds to reality. It ascends through reality like a ladder, which is simultaneously a descending into the depths of the soul.

The cave image has two basic features, corresponding to the visible and invisible realms, namely the cave and the world outside, illumined by the sun. The visible world is a shadow of the invisible world—the fire within the self, the soul, corresponds to the sun of the world's day, as the sun in the visible world corresponds back to the Good that rules the invisible world. The cave to the outside is like the body to the soul. "Whether it is true or not," Socrates continues, "only the god knows. But this is how I see it." With this remark Socrates acknowledges the impossibility of certainty regarding that which matters the most, and the corresponding necessity of presenting an image about it that is not less than the reality. This gives what I can call, echoing Blumenberg, the mythical character of the image. In fact, this is the way Plato talks about the myths he often presents.[51]

Regarding the most basic and most important things, Socrates must present stories that convey the truth that humans, unlike the god(s), are powerless to see in the truth that truth enjoys as it enjoys it in itself. These stories taste and feel the truth from within, communicating in an irreplaceable way that to which the world of my experience corresponds, a truth that is invisible to me in itself by virtue of its blinding light. *How* does Socrates see it? He explains: "In the knowable realm, the form of the Good is the last thing to be seen, and it is reached only with difficulty. Once one has seen it, however, one must conclude that it is the cause of all that is correct and beautiful in anything, that it produces both light and its source in the visible realm, and that in the intelligible realm it controls and provides truth and understanding, so that anyone who is to act sensibly in private or public must see it." If the goal of philosophy is the vision of the good, then its outcome is sensible action in the totality

51. See for example *Gorgias* 523a.

of one's life. The basic fact of a calibrated correspondence between the two worlds, with the higher world "grounding" the totality, means, paradoxically, that the highest truth of the higher and lower worlds is communicated with through the image, and more broadly the mythic: the lower is the richest path into the higher. This hidden highest truth is the "cause of all that is correct and beautiful," "produces light and its source" in the visible world, including the sun and even sight itself. It "controls and provides truth" and my relation to it, giving "understanding." My vision of it makes possible right action, a relation much like orienting myself in the world by the sun. *Paideia*, education, begins with this understanding, which can be all but directly stated.

The Cave of Christ: can it be interpreted philosophically as a cave of emergence, of illumination? There are, traditionally, two caves in Christ's life, the cave of his birth, and the cave of his death, the tomb. The cave Christ emerged from on Easter morning represents the mouth of hell, into which, on Holy Saturday, he descended in his death. Yet Christ's cave is not only the mouth of hell but the womb of the world, of the created order, the cosmos, which includes the earthly and subearthly regions. It is the cave, the cosmic vault ruled by elemental powers, the *stoicheia*, out of which humanity is born into a heavenly vavasourship. The transformation of death happens *within* the cave, *in* the sleep of death. One could almost say that the first cave of Christ, which is the womb of his birth in the Virgin, symbolized by the maternal cave of the nativity, is itself a symbol of that to which it is first and primarily ordered, the cosmic cave of his death and resurrection, which is a birth into a transfigured, liberated existence, the New Creation. The teaching of the Cave of Christ, serving as the mythic backdrop of the *vera philosophia* of the Christians, is that the whole cosmos is a womb of germination; at death (prefigured, shared in, through baptism) one is born into the real world, the new world beyond every possibility of conceiving from within the womb, but which is nevertheless the real world toward which we are ordered (and the kingdom by which we are ordered), into which we—and the entire cosmos that we know—are finally thrust in the end, with violence through the pangs of birth. Who *knows* what lies on the other side of this thick but nourishing physical membrane of our present existence? Only the dead really know, those who have been reborn, who have passed through into that world. From within the womb of our present life we only have some sketches, disparate indications, muffled sounds, rumors, dull lights, always grossly condensed and simplified when pressed through the thick order of our leaden world, a world that for now only vaguely reverberates the real world within itself like a fading echo.

# Acknowledgements

With *Eclipse of World* and *Essay on the Apophatics of the Sensible*, this book was mainly composed during a yearlong appointment as Visiting Scholar at the Center for the Study of World Religions at Harvard Divinity School and a concomitant appointment at the Department of Philosophy at Boston College. I owe an unpayable debt to Francis X. Clooney, S.J. at Harvard and Jeffrey Bloechl at Boston College; I speak first of the debt of friendship. I also thank Australian Catholic University for supporting a sabbatical year in Boston. I especially thank my colleagues in the Faculty of Theology and Philosophy for sponsoring a second semester abroad. If begun in such places, this book was brought to maturity in others: during a three-year period of academic expatriation earning my daily bread as a pizza delivery driver and then "inventory specialist" in a warehouse. I could recommend such an experience for reasons relatively similar to Descartes' in the first part of *Discourse on Method*, but not lightly.

Two studies from the present book had former lives: Study IV was based on a text I presented in 2014 at the "Overcoming Dualisms" conference in Melbourne hosted by my friends at the John Paul II Institute for Marriage and the Family. Study V is based on my contribution to *Phenomenology for the Twenty-First Century*, ed. J. Aaron Simmons and J. Edward Hackett (Palgrave Macmillan, 2016), entitled "The Philosophy and Phenomenology of Revelation: A Primer on the Question."

All quotations of Holy Scripture in this book are from the New Revised Standard Version unless otherwise noted.

# Index

# Index

# About the Author

William C. Hackett is Assistant Professor of Philosophy at St. Meinrad Seminary and School of Theology. He is the author of *Essay on Apophatics of the Sensible* (Notre Dame) and (with Tarek Dika) *Quiet Powers of the Possible* (Fordham), as well as translator of works from French to English, including Emmanuel Falque, *God, the Flesh and the Other* (Northwestern), Jean-Yves Lacoste, *From Theology to Theological Thinking* (University of Virginia), and Miklos Veto, *The Expansion of Metaphysics* (Cascade).

Made in the USA
Monee, IL
03 February 2020

21268681R00185